PUBLIC
PROSECUTOR

The memoirs of
SIR NORMAN SKELHORN

PUBLIC
PROSECUTOR

Director of
Public Prosecutions
1964-1977

Harrap  London

First published in Great Britain 1981
by HARRAP LIMITED
19–23 Ludgate Hill, London EC4M 7PD

© *Sir Norman Skelhorn* 1981

ISBN 0 245-53763-5

Designed by Michael R. Carter

Filmset by GRP Typesetters, Leicester
Printed and bound in Great Britain
by Robert Hartnoll Ltd, Bodmin

Contents

PART ONE

1 An early start   3
2 Murders and other matters   19
3 Differing defences   32
4 Silk and its consequences   41

PART TWO

5 Director of Public Prosecutions   63
6 The terrorists   84
7 Under attack   100
8 Matters of security   122
9 What is obscene?   138
10 Murder most foul   151
11 The rule of fear   166
12 Nothing but the truth   187
13 After fifty years   197
Index   203

ACKNOWLEDGMENTS

IT IS NOT practicable to mention individually all those who have helped me in the preparation of this book, especially my old friends at the Bar—whether they are still practising there or whether they have now been promoted to the Bench—to all of whom I am most grateful. I must, however, express my sincere gratitude to Jeffrey Simmons, who has throughout so unfailingly helped and advised me, and to the department of the Director of Public Prosecutions, both to the Director personally and to members of his staff, for the great assistance they have given by affording me access to a number of relevant papers. Finally, I wish to express to my publishers and to Mr Roy Minton on their staff my appreciation of all their kindness and forbearance, beyond that normally required in the difficult task of writing a legal autobiography.

Illustrations

(*between* pp 52 *and* 53)

The young barrister

Dingle Foot, Malcolm Wright and the author, on being granted silk

HRH the Duke of Edinburgh on a visit to Plymouth, with the author, Recorder there at that time

John and Janet Armstrong, with their daughter (*Syndication International*)

John Poulson (*Popperfoto*)

The Tavern in the Town, Birmingham, after the IRA bombing (*Keystone Press*)

An Angry Brigade 'arsenal' found at Stoke Newington (*Keystone Press*)

Andrew Newton (*Syndication International*)

Norman Scott (*Syndication International*)

Scott's dog Rinka (*Syndication International*)

Peter Hain reading a statement to the Press after his acquittal (*Keystone Press*)

Sir Gerald Nabarro with his wife and Mrs Margaret Mason (*Keystone Press*)

Sir Gerald and Lady Nabarro (*Keystone Press*)

Leila Khaled arriving in Amman (*Popperfoto*)

(*between* pp 180 *and* 181)

Outside the Spaghetti House restaurant during the siege (*Popperfoto*)

David and Maureen Bingham (*Keystone Press*)

Myra Hindley (*Keystone Press*)

Ian Brady (*Keystone Press*)

PUBLIC PROSECUTOR

Mrs Gerald Richardson *(Syndication International)*

Joseph Sewell *(Popperfoto)*

Nizamodeen Hosein *(Syndication International)*

Arthur Hosein *(Syndication International)*

Rooks Farm *(Syndication International)*

The Kray brothers *(Popperfoto)*

The author in his office

Lady Skelhorn, with the family dogs

The author at the date of his appointment as Director of Public Prosecutions

PART ONE

CHAPTER 1

An early start

IT IS A GREAT advantage to start a career young. By the time I was called to the Bar in January 1931, not yet five months beyond my twenty-first birthday, I had already had three years' practical experience. It was usual to read for the Bar and to serve twelve months' pupillage after being called, but in those days it was still possible to be a pupil while actually studying, and I was fortunately able to do this by being taken into chambers in Bristol, the head of which was F. A. Wilshire—not to be confused with a barrister of similar name, Myddelton Wilshere; there was no love lost between the two!

I benefited enormously from the experienced advice I received, and while most of my contemporaries were academically involved in studying Law I was finding my way round chambers, accompanying barristers to court, drafting pleadings and even on occasion helping to write opinions. Most important, at a time when other young men were unknown quantities, from the day I started in practice I was known to—and fortunately liked by—a number of the big West Country solicitors.

I had had a firm desire to become a lawyer from about the age of nine or ten. I cannot explain this. I knew no lawyers, and had no legal background, although I do remember that my father used to discuss with me interesting legal cases that were reported in the newspapers.

My father was in fact a Congregational minister. Or to be exact, he was at the time I was born: in Glossop, Derbyshire, on 10 September 1909. Thereafter he led a somewhat chequered career, moving around the country and taking my mother and me—I was their only child—in his wake. Not long after my birth he left the ministry and moved to London. Early in the First World War, when I was about five or six, we went to Seaford in Sussex, where he served as curate, having in the meantime been ordained in the Church of England. We moved just after the war to Bristol, where he became curate of two

3

churches—one very High, the other very Low. If that caused him any problems, I was unaware of them. He was renowned as a good preacher, and was once invited to preach in the Cathedral. He was next appointed Vicar of Great Wollaston and Middletown. The vicarage was on the borders of Shropshire and Montgomeryshire, Great Wollaston being in England and Middletown in Wales. Still later he returned to Bristol as minister in a non-denominational church, but again embraced the Church of England, and later—following the death of my mother and his subsequent remarriage—went to livings in Lincolnshire, in Lancashire, and to a parish on the outskirts of London. But I had left home long before then.

I always had a very good relationship with my parents. My mother's father was a naturalized British subject of German origin. I remember her as a very accomplished pianist, but most dearly as a wonderful stand-by for my father, whom she helped devotedly in his work. She died after a long illness in June 1931, and it was a great joy to me that she lived long enough to know that I had been called to the Bar.

It will be readily recognized that my father's changes of situation and our consequent changes of address did not exactly help my education, which suffered from more than the average disruption, but he always sent me, even if briefly, to good preparatory schools such as the XIV at Clifton, Bristol, and when he became Vicar of Great Wollaston and Middletown, to Kingsland Grange at Shrewsbury, where I passed the Common Entrance for Shrewsbury School. Unfortunately (though quite understandably), my father decided that he could not afford the fees, and proposed instead that I should educate myself with the aid of correspondence courses. Like most self-respecting boys of school age, I did precisely nothing that I was not forced to do, and after little more than a year my father realized the error of his—or my—ways and sent me to Shrewsbury after all. It is an interesting comment on the failure of his educational ideas that I passed into a lower form than I had done when I sat for the Common Entrance!

Whatever the shortcomings of my education, they do not seem to have hindered my career, and I have always been grateful to my father for the financial sacrifices he made to enable me to read for the Bar and to make my early career in the Law. As I have said, I had the advantages of starting young, of gaining practical training while still in my teens, and of being elected to the Western Circuit and practising on it. In those days there were positive drawbacks to operating from chambers outside London, particularly for an ambitious barrister. Very few appointments were made from the local Bars, and there was little prospect of advancement. Indeed, it was not then even possible to take silk unless one was a member of chambers in London, and practising from there. I well remember over twenty years later receiving a letter from the Lord Chancellor's office (when I had applied for silk) indicating that I would have to remove my name from the Bristol chambers if I wanted to become a Queen's Counsel! I had in any case by then set up my own chambers in London.

The Western Circuit—which covered an area from Hampshire to Cornwall—was, however, a great place for a barrister content to make a good living in that part of the world. For a young barrister it was a truly wonderful place in which to function, and the years during which I practised there were among the happiest of my career.

I practised in Bristol for seven years, and by the fifth year I was doing very well indeed. In my first year I earned about £250; in my second, £500; in my third, £750; and in my fourth—a princely sum at that time for a young man of twenty-five—£1,200. This was one of the advantages of joining a local Bar. I could have waited years to achieve such results in London.

The local Bar in Bristol was quite small in those days. We were no more than a dozen or so barristers, which is why, once I got going, there was always a reasonable amount of work for me. I learnt more from Cyril Williams—senior member of our chambers, next to Wilshire—than from anyone else. He never took silk, probably never wanted to, but had he done so and gone to London he would doubtless have attained the top of his profession. I had the greatest admiration and respect for his ability, and he was, I think, generally recognized over many years as being one of the foremost members of the circuit.

Wilshire was kind enough to recommend me to Mr Justice Swift, and within weeks of being called I went as his marshal to Leeds. When Geoffrey Lawrence, K.C., went in Swift's place to Stafford as Commissioner of Assize (he was made a High Court judge the following year) I went as his marshal too. This was marvellous experience. It gave me the opportunity to see the law in operation from another angle. I heard, for example, the comments and discussions between judges about the various advocates appearing before them, and learnt some of the ways to impress judges, and—more important—some of the pitfalls to avoid.

A marshal to a judge is not unlike an aide-de-camp to a general. He is required to assist in whatever way he may be needed, from dealing with seating arrangements in lodgings when guests are invited, to looking up cases and checking points of law that have arisen or are likely to arise. In those days a judge on circuit never went anywhere without his marshal.

Of course, the disadvantage of marshalling is that if it continues too long it interferes with a barrister's practice, but I will always regard my time as well spent, if only for the opportunity it afforded me to get to know Rigby Swift. I once sought his advice over an incident that had occurred shortly after I started at the Bar. I was instructed to draft a divorce petition. I was struck by the prolonged delay in commencing proceedings following the alleged conduct providing the ground for divorce. At that time delay unless satis-factorily explained could be a bar to a petition being granted, so I sent for the managing clerk of the instructing solicitors, telling him that I needed an explanation. Instead this gentleman—greatly older than myself—picked up my draft petition, perused it, and informed me that he found it satisfactory. I told him angrily, with all the outraged assurance of a 21-year-old, that I had asked him to come to explain the delay, not to teach me how to draft a petition—and I showed him out!

The distinguished judge listened to me and nodded his head. 'Quite right, my dear boy, you should keep these fellers in their place—but don't kick them out with your right foot until you're sure you can stand on your left.' It is advice that I have never forgotten.

One of his foibles was that when an accused was acquitted he always insisted on counsel applying for his client to be discharged. There was one occasion when counsel made no move to do so. 'Do you have any application to make to me?' the judge inquired. 'No, m'lud,' counsel replied deliberately. 'Are you sure?' 'No, m'lud, none at all. Perhaps your lordship is not aware that my client is already serving a sentence of imprisonment.'

Rigby Swift was never short on repartee, and always managed to give as good as he took. 'Oh, yes,' he said, 'I know that, but I didn't think you would want him to serve it in the dock.'

There is a very good story about him and Herbert du Parcq. Swift was invited to the Bar mess at Exeter when he was on circuit. Du Parcq, as senior silk that night, presided, and had the duty of saying the two-word grace: 'Benedictus benedicat' before dinner, 'Bene-dicto benedicatur' after.

'My dear du Parcq,' said the judge, 'do you think the Almighty will be very angry with me if I don't stand up while you say grace?'

'Oh no, Judge, I don't think so,' was the reply. 'He'll just think you don't understand Latin.'

There was a sequel the next day. Rigby Swift was trying a claim for damages for personal injury. Such cases were always heard by juries in those days. A doctor had been in the witness-box for some time, itemizing the plaintiff's various injuries. There was suddenly heard the sharp tap, tap of the judge's pencil. This was his characteristic way of controlling his court, and he had developed the technique over many years. 'Doctor,' said Mr Justice Swift, 'before you leave the box, will you please translate for myself and the jury all the Latin words you have used?'

The doctor duly obliged. Tap, tap. . . .'Doctor,' complained the judge, 'I asked you to translate *all* the Latin words. Sepsis. That's a Latin word, isn't it?'

The few people in court lucky enough to be near du Parcq heard him say, sotto voce, 'Well, it may be Latin to your Lordship, but it's always been Greek to me.'

Marshalling was an interesting interlude for me, which I took in my stride, as I did my first case with a jury in Bristol. Two labourers were accused of entering a shop in Barton Hill with intent to commit a felony on 4 March 1931—less than two months after I had been called to the Bar. One of them was additionally charged with assaulting a policeman. The case was tried at the City Quarter Sessions, and it was a happy moment for me to read my name in the local press: 'Mr K. C. Bennett prosecuted, while Mr N. Skelhorn appeared for the defendants', who incidentally were both three years older than myself. I was, of course, proud when the Recorder, in his summing-up, commented that the argument for the defence had been put by me 'with great ability', and prouder still when both my clients were acquitted on the main charge, although I was unsuccessful with the assault charge and that particular client was sent to prison for a month. What perhaps is interesting is that this was the first of many cases in which I argued that a client had acted under the influence of drink, a form of defence familiar to every lawyer.

The early cases of a young barrister are rarely worthy of particular notice, but one case remains firmly in my mind, perhaps because I was opposed by F. J. Tucker, K.C. It was his elevation to the High Court Bench four years later that created the vacancy that enabled me to be taken into London chambers.

I represented a street vendor who was appealing against a conviction by the Salisbury City Justices for obstructing the highway with her fruit barrow. The case involved consideration of rights granted by royal charters dating back to the thirteenth century, and at one point the town clerk produced the Charter of Henry III. The Recorder upheld my submission that there was an ancient right to sell fruit on market days, and that the highway in question was within the traditional market area. The conviction was quashed, and the costs of the appeal were borne by the Salisbury Corporation.

In retrospect, I think it was remarkable that a barrister of only two years' experience should have been briefed in such a difficult case, especially in view of the eminence of counsel for the respondents. It says a great deal for the fairness of British justice that equal weight was given to my arguments. Of course, there are obvious advantages in briefing experienced counsel, but I have never detected any deliberate failure on the part of judges to consider arguments advanced by young advocates.

An interesting comment in support of this statement arises from a case in which I was involved in February 1936. I had been asked to apply at Axbridge Brewster Sessions for a full justice's licence for the Caveman Restaurant near the entrance to the famous Cheddar caves. A similar application had been rejected two years earlier before the restaurant had been built, and since around a quarter of a million visitors were expected to come to the area within the year it was suggested that I appear with a leader, and then the almost incredible idea was advanced to brief Sir Henry Curtis-Bennett, K.C., the great man himself. I was delighted with these developments, since my fee kept rising with each new proposal, and it was this happy occurrence that enabled me to afford an engagement ring for my future wife.

The highly unusual circumstance of one of the great advocates of the day appearing before local justices to obtain a liquor licence attracted much attention, particularly in the area. A full Bench sat to hear the first King's Counsel to address them in over fifty years.

'I wonder', he said, 'if any application is being made anywhere this year for a licence where such an enormous number of customers can be proved to have visited a restaurant which is at the moment unlicensed.'

Unfortunately, perverse as it may seem, he failed to persuade the justices, who gave more weight to the arguments of the Bristol Waterworks Company, owners of the local Cliff Hotel, the Licensed Victuallers' Association and the Methodist and Baptist ministers, all of whom opposed the application.

I understand that the following year the restaurant's solicitor made a similar application on his own. This time he did not even brief me. Instead of a full Bench, only a bare quorum sat, and this time he succeeded. So much for Sir Henry Curtis-Bennett, K.C., and Mr Norman Skelhorn!

Goddard was of course a great name on the Western Circuit, where he was affectionately known as 'Doggy'! He was considered by many to be a formidable judge long before he became Lord Chief Justice of England, but I was always aware of a twinkle in his eye. I only knew him by reputation, however, when I first appeared before him. I was twenty-three years old, and he had not long been a High Court judge, but he was on his old circuit and it was an intimidating experience to appear before him. I was defending a young man accused of rape. I thought it was common ground that he and the girl had gone out together by arrangement, and that the only serious question was whether what then happened was with her consent, so I did not ask the girl anything about a telephone conversation that the accused said he had had with her when they had arranged to meet.

When Goddard came to sum up he looked down at the jury in his characteristic fashion. 'In a case of this sort', he addressed them, 'as I have already explained to you, you need to have corroboration before you can properly convict. You remember that telephone conversation? Well, this accused is represented by able and experienced counsel. Not a word of that conversation was put to the girl. Not a word. Now, if that's the sort of thing you think this young man was making up as he stood in the witness-box, that's the sort of thing you can look at to see whether there is corroboration.'

The able and experienced counsel in question, who had not yet been called three years, rose with a deal of trepidation to interrupt this august judge at this crucial stage of the proceedings.

'Well', Goddard said severely, 'what is it you want?'

'M'lud', I managed to get out, 'I must tell your Lordship I had instructions about the telephone conversation. I did not put it to the girl because I did not then think—and with great respect, I still do not—that it was material. But he did not make it up as he stood in the witness-box. I had instructions, and if there is any fault to be found, it must be with me.'

'Very well.' That was the first time I saw the twinkle. 'Well, members of the jury, I said this young man was represented here by able and experienced counsel. Forget all I've been saying to you.'

My client was acquitted.

I came to know Goddard much better over the years. It was, I believe, partly on his recommendation that in due course I became Recorder of Plymouth. I appeared before him on many occasions, and always found him to be a strong but fair judge. He had no rival in his knowledge of the Common Law, and was possessed too of a very agile mind. It was often said of him by critics that he was inclined to form a view too early, but I believe his strength as a judge lay in his capacity to be persuaded after he had formed a provisional opinion. It was said of him that on one occasion counsel in putting his case referred to a particular authority with the words, 'That is an authority with which your Lordship will be familiar, because you decided it.' 'Do you say that that was what I decided?' Goddard asked. 'Yes, my lord.' 'Well, then, I was wrong.'

This attitude was in sharp contrast to that of some judges of his day who made up their minds at an early stage and were reluctant to change them. Goddard would always listen attentively to intelligent advocacy, although he never took kindly to a time-waster, and one had to get round him in the right way. Once, during a judgment, he said jokingly, 'Mr Skelhorn made some plausible arguments. Most of them are, until you come to look into them.' He kept one on one's toes. As far as I am concerned, he drew from me the best I had to offer.

It had been something of a lesson for me to appear so early in my career before Goddard, but I had a lesson of a different sort a couple of years later in a less serious case in a County Court. A woman who had injured her finger in the course of her work sued her employers, who denied liability. I was just arguing that such a trivial mishap could not seriously affect her earning capacity when my own finger started to bleed profusely, following a minor operation, forcing me to rush from court, and leaving my opponent to explain that I was unable to earn my own living that day!

Talking of fingers reminds me of a more interesting case in which I defended a labourer accused of assaulting a woman of sixty while armed with an offensive weapon. It was alleged that the victim bit her assailant on the finger, which still bore the scar. The case was tried at Bristol Assizes before Mr Justice Charles. J. D. Casswell, who prosecuted, called evidence that a man wearing a cap, and with a pistol in his left hand, came into the woman's house and demanded to know where she kept her money. In the course of a struggle the brave lady bit him hard on the second finger of his left hand, at the moment when he must temporarily have put down the weapon. The prisoner claimed to know nothing of the affair and to have been elsewhere at the time. He did, however, have a scar on the second finger of his left hand which was consistent with the woman's bite, but he said that it had been caused by a screwdriver. Evidence was also given that he had bought a toy pistol on the morning of the assault, and he admitted throwing it into a pond after he heard of the case, fearing that he would be suspected. The judge made a great point about the coincidence of there being what could be a bite-mark on the man's finger, but the jury did not even retire, and after discussing the case in court for only ten minutes found my client not guilty. Although the judge had commented on the difficulty for the woman in identifying her attacker, the jury must have given weight to the fact that at an identity parade she not merely failed to identify the accused but had picked out another man who of course had nothing to do with the matter.

It was about the same time in 1936 that I was involved in what I suppose may be called a local *cause célèbre*. The charges were very unusual. A Bath woman aged thirty-one was accused of improperly assaulting a boy aged thirteen. Her ordeal was a terrible one; doubly so because at her first trial, three weeks earlier, the jury had failed to agree.

The case was retried at Bath Quarter Sessions before the Recorder, Reginald Croom-Johnson, K.C., later Mr Justice Croom-Johnson and father of the present judge. He could be difficult at times, but personally when appearing before him I usually found him sympathetic. However, I had quite a problem with him on a different occasion when I was appearing for the defence in a personal injuries case at Exeter Assizes, following a car crash. Every time I obtained a favourable response from a witness he intervened to restore the balance. He interrupted frequently while I was making my final speech to the jury, and at one point said, 'Mr Skelhorn, I know you very well'—which indeed he did; I had known him before he was a judge, and we had once appeared on opposite sides in the same case, so that I can attest to his kindness—'I know you so well that I can tell you just what is passing through my mind.' 'My lord, I appreciate that,' I commented, 'but I also appreciate that most unhappily I am not in the same position.' He joined heartily in the general laughter, but I still lost the case!

In the case at Bath there were three women on the jury and the court was cleared while children gave evidence. The young lad was a close friend of one of the woman's six children, and it was alleged that he had been shown unsuitable books, and had been seduced into committing improper acts.

The handling of such a case, where children are called as witnesses, puts a heavy responsibility on counsel for the defence. My client denied the charges most emphatically. The boy claimed that on a number of occasions when he said he was in bed with the woman a friend of his was under the bed. He admitted that he had a girl friend, and that he had once thrown a knife at my client. Fortunately for her, the jury must apparently have accepted that this story was too fantastic to be credible. Unfortunately for her, nothing could bring back her husband, who had committed suicide five days after she was arrested.

As every lawyer knows, one has to exercise extreme caution before accepting the evidence of children. With this in mind, if I may jump

11

ahead in time for the moment, this could be a good opportunity for me to deal with one of the most extraordinary episodes of my legal career. It started at Winchester Assizes in 1960, and ended nearly nine years later. A boy aged eleven was accused of murdering a girl aged nine. Mr Justice Pilcher presided, Peter Rawlinson, Q.C., M.P. (now Lord Rawlinson) led for the prosecution, and I led for the defence.

Iris Dawkins went out to play in Mayfield Park, Southampton, just before two o'clock on a Saturday afternoon in February 1960. There were six other children in her group that day, three boys and three girls, much about the same age, although they included her older brother and one boy aged fourteen. They were playing Cowboys and Indians, and all had toy guns. At about three o'clock Iris slipped, fell on her knee and splashed mud over herself, so she left to return home to clean up. This meant her going up the path that would take her near a landmark known as Fox's Monument. When she had not reached home by 6.30 p.m. police help was sought to find her, and an organized search was made, with the assistance of dogs, all over the 58-acre park, about half of which was wooded and contained thick scrub. At eleven o'clock she was found dead, lying in the thicket and undergrowth less than seventy yards inside the wooded area.

The details of her attire were to be an important feature: she was dressed in a turquoise woollen cardigan, blue jeans and black plimsolls. Her right plimsoll lay near her, as did her yellow woollen hat.

The poor girl had been stabbed thirty-nine times. The fatal wound, according to the pathologist who examined the body, was administered from the front while she was standing or sitting. The cuts on her right hand and forearm were clearly defensive wounds, and would almost certainly have caused her to shriek out in pain. Many of the wounds to the chest were apparently inflicted after death.

This terrible crime attracted national attention. Immense publicity was given in the Press and on radio and television. In particular photographs were published two days after the girl's death, taken at a time when she was wearing a striped T-shirt.

Well over three thousand people were questioned by the police, and statements taken from over five hundred. A lady whose house backed on to the wooded portion of the park said she had seen what appeared to be two teenagers, a boy and a girl, from her kitchen window at around three o'clock. The girl was wearing a 'powder blue' cardigan or woolly. The boy was wearing a black waterproof jerkin that glinted in the sun, but she was unable to be precise about the children's age or size because they were some distance away from her.

The extensive police inquiries were mainly directed to children who might have been in the park, but the officers soon realized that they dared not place too great reliance on the children's evidence because of the tendency that they had to romance. Indeed, there were eight instances in which children gave to the police stories that proved on investigation to be completely unfounded. An example is that of a boy who alleged that a week before a large ginger-haired youth, with a scar on his face, had attacked Iris Dawkins in this very park. He had gone to her defence, jumping on the youth's back. The youth got free and threw a knife at him, which fortunately landed between his legs. He later admitted inventing the story.

On the Friday following the tragedy the police called at the house of the young boy who was to become the accused in this case. They were looking for a boy with a black windcheater. He was asked whether he had such a garment, and readily produced one. It was observed that it had been washed, though by no means thoroughly. He was asked to account for his movements on the day of the murder between 3.30 p.m. and six o'clock. In a written statement he admitted wearing a black windcheater at the time, and said: 'About 3.30 p.m. I was standing near the monument when I saw a little girl playing with some other children near the bridge over the stream. I think the little girl was Iris Dawkins. She was dressed in a blue and white T-shirt and dark, tight-fitting slacks.'

She was not at the time she was murdered wearing such a shirt at all, and the one described by the boy was what she had been shown wearing in the Press and on television.

The boy also said that he had seen another youth, aged about twelve or thirteen, watching football at the time. He described him as about 4 feet 9 inches tall and of medium build, adding that he wore black jeans and a black windcheater 'like mine'.

Three days later he was taken to the park and asked to point out the various places mentioned in his statement. According to the police, it was impossible for him to have seen the girl he thought was Iris from his position near the monument (if indeed she had been near the bridge over the stream). They then questioned him at the police-station about a knife, and it transpired that he owned a penknife with a black handle that had some white specks on it, and which he said he had taken with him to the park on the day of the murder.

It was then that he made certain very damaging admissions. He described meeting Iris near the monument, and now said that they had played a chasing game, and that both had fallen in the mud. In reply to the question 'Were you playing with your knife at the time?' the boy said, 'Well, I may have been. I may have had it in my hand

13

when she fell over and I fell on top of her. I think the knife went into her shoulder; only a little way, though.' He also said, 'It accidentally went into her shoulder just here'—pointing to the right shoulder near the collar-bone—'I might have stuck it into her more than once. I cannot remember now.'

Later still he added the following words, which made headlines at his trial: 'I feel better now I have told Mum. I do not get to sleep very quick at night, but it was worse last week. I got excited and stuck it in her. Then I got frightened. I have seen stabbing on television, and next week you see them in another part. I watch all the murders. I like the way they track them down and question them.' Then he asked, 'Will I go to Borstal? I cannot go to prison because I am not twenty-one.'

He then made a statement which in effect set out what he had been saying, and which for the purpose of the trial was alleged to be his confession, although he subsequently made other contradictory statements, and the police officer who had been questioning him was not entirely satisfied as to the whole truth of the confession. In it he referred to having seen the boy whose clothes were like his own. Part of the statement read: 'After my knife went into her I saw her laying on the ground, but she was breathing normally, and she had her eyes open. I saw a little blood. I thought she was playing. I said, "Cheerio, I am going home now." She did not answer. I made my way along the path towards my home. I then saw the boy that was dressed like me was gone.'

The confession was, to say the least, unreliable, particularly when one of the doctors called for the prosecution indicated that in his opinion the time of death might well have been as late as eight or nine o'clock (although as to this there was an acute difference among the various doctors). More conclusive was the laboratory evidence that there was no sign of blood on any of the boy's clothing; the expert agreed that, even where clothes had been thoroughly washed, he not infrequently found minute traces of blood. Most important, it was established without doubt that the girl's wounds could not have been caused by the penknife that had been produced.

It will not in the circumstances surprise anyone that at the end of the prosecution's case I made a submission that the confession was worthless. The boy had purported to have seen the girl at a place where he could not have seen her. He described her dress wrongly. He claimed to have stabbed her with a weapon which was not the weapon that was used, and that he had stabbed her at a place which was not the place where she was discovered. Not even a trace of blood was found on his clothing. The medical evidence indicated

14

that death could have been somewhere near eight and nine o'clock, when it was common ground that he was at home.

After a certain amount of argument to the contrary on behalf of the prosecution, Mr Justice Pilcher accepted my submission that it was unsafe to leave the case to the jury, and he withdrew it from them.

There was a sequel to this extraordinary case. Eight years and nine months later, on Monday, 18 November 1968, a police officer was off duty, exercising his dog in the same Mayfield Park. When crossing the stream by that notorious plank bridge he saw a man come out from the bushes. He saw the man again, loitering in another part of the park, near some children's swings, although there were no children there. The officer went to his own home near by, and at three o'clock in the afternoon he left home in his car, when he saw again the same man, who this time appeared to be looking into the windows of each house as he passed. This made him suspicious, so he got out and spoke to the man, whose name was Ridley. Ridley was wearing black rubber gloves, and when he was questioned about his movements he was also searched. There was found on him a large sheath-knife. When he was asked about his behaviour, and what he was doing with the sheath-knife, he said, 'Well, the gloves are to keep me warm, and the knife—well, I just carry it.'

He was taken to the police-station, where he was found also to have on him a roll of adhesive tape and a length of cord, 6 feet 4 inches, knotted at each end. Eventually, after questioning, he agreed that he had been intending to steal. The officer said to him, 'When I saw you in the park you obviously had the knife in your pocket then. What were you intending to steal in the park?' The man replied, 'I was going to wait until I saw someone. Then I was going to threaten someone to give me their wallet, but I never got around to it.' The officer said, 'Are you sure about this?' and the man replied, 'No, I had better tell you the truth. I get the urge to kill every so often. I want to kill. I bought this knife, and came out with the intention of killing someone. I will tell you now. I killed a girl in Mayfield Park about twelve years ago. Her name was Iris Dawkins.' When asked how old he was at the time he did this, he said he was about twelve to fourteen—and fourteen would have been his age in 1960, since he was twenty-two at the time of his arrest.

The officer said, 'Sometimes people admit murders when they have not committed them. I cannot be certain from what you say that you have committed this murder. What is your reason for admitting it now?' He replied, 'Every so often I get an urge to kill someone, but now that you have got me I thought it best to tell you about it, and then I can't kill anybody else.'

Later in answer to questions by the police as to details concerning his stabbing of the girl, he said he had stabbed her in the back and in the neck. He also said that blood was coming from her mouth, and this, as it turned out, accorded with the pathologist's evidence in regard to her injuries.

Ridley then made a statement, the relevant part of which was: 'I caught up with her about half-way'—that is, when she was going up a bank towards the football pitches. 'I threatened her with a knife to do what I told her to do. I forced her into the bushes at the point of the knife. We went into the bushes until we were out of the way of the paths, and then I stabbed her in the back with the knife. I don't know how many times I stabbed her. I know it was quite a lot. I thought she was dead, and then she started screaming again, and I returned and stabbed her some more. After that I went home. My parents were out at the time. I was fairly upset about this at the time, but I was able to control myself within limits by the time they came home.'

The police very properly asked him a number of searching questions in order to try to see whether this indeed was yet another false confession. Suffice it to say that at the end of the day there were a number of details which were inaccurate, but the inaccuracy of which one felt could well be accounted for by the lapse of time. There were a number of details which were accurate, and which could only have been known to him had he not been the murderer if he had read and remembered what had been printed in the newspapers eight and a half years before. There were certain other details that could not have been known to him—at any rate, in the view of the prosecution —unless he was the murderer.

In those circumstances, and having defended the one boy eight and a half years before, I had the unique experience as Director of Public Prosecutions of having to consider this report and these papers, in order to decide whether this man Ridley should be prosecuted on his confession. Bearing in mind the extent to which I had been involved in the earlier case, I naturally sought independent advice. In the end there was a prosecution. Ridley was not called to give evidence. He was defended by leading and junior counsel, and all the issues were canvassed in detail, including those that had been raised at the earlier trial. He was found guilty, and he was sentenced —because of his age at the time of the offence—to be detained during what has by statute to be described as Her Majesty's pleasure. I always feel that this is an inappropriate expression.

I have been involved in many murder trials—and surprisingly was never given a leader when defending an alleged murderer—but few murders have caused me to reflect more than the one just described,

which underlines how careful one must be in considering confessions, particularly when they are made by children. I shall have
more to say later about a number of cases in which I took part, but in
the meantime I should like to return for a moment to 1936, because
that was the year I became engaged to Rosamund, the daughter of a
very eminent West Country consultant surgeon, James Swain,
C.B.E., M.S. We married the following year, and I am happy to say,
are still married. We met at a tennis party. She was an excellent
county hockey-player. She had been teaching in a school in
Switzerland, mainly for the purpose, she tells me, of getting a year's
skiing and mountaineering. Later we again met when she was doing
welfare work at Mardon Son & Hall, a branch of W. D. & H. O. Wills,
where she arranged sports and games and various evening classes.

We were married the following April, 1937, by my father, and we
spent our honeymoon in Switzerland. It was my first visit, and my
French, then as now, was basic to say the least. Needing some
change, I went up to a porter at Basle railway station, clutching some
English money in my hand and almost shouting in the way one does
when endeavouring to make oneself understood in a foreign
language. 'Changez, monsieur', I managed to say, whereupon he
looked at me with pity and, without much trace of accent, replied in
English, 'Tell me what it is you want.' On another occasion I went to a
tobacconist and asked the lady assistant, 'Avez-vous Players?'
'Certainly, sir,' she said in English. 'Would you like them plain or
cork-tipped?' After these episodes I decided that English would do
for me, and that my wife could deal with French. I am happy to say
that the rest of our honeymoon—the first, incidentally, of many visits
abroad I was to make with Rosamund—proved less complicated.

She helped me make the all-important decision about moving to
London the following year. I was doing really well in Bristol, and was
loth to put my success at risk by making a move to the capital,
although there was nothing to prevent me from concentrating on my
old home ground after I had chambers in London. It was a risk I
might have been willing to take for myself, but which I felt might not
be fair to my future wife. It was she, however, who persuaded me to
go when the opportunity arose. She was quite determined that I
should not suffer by marrying her. That was only my first experience
of her consideration for me. She has been a wonderful support
throughout my career; ours has been a marvellous alliance.

Before I left Bristol, I argued an interesting point. Although it was
only in the County Court, it was nevertheless an unusual case for a
young practitioner to be involved in, and I was opposed by
Myddelton Wilshere. The question was whether a son was under a

liability to maintain his mother, who was a patient in a local hospital. Bristol Corporation had already obtained judgment against the woman's husband and two other sons, and were now proceeding against the third son, whom I represented. I argued that at Common Law a husband was liable to maintain his wife, but that there was no obligation for a son to do so. Wilshere, however, called the Poor Law Act into aid, and the judge—who described the case as important— decided that under the Local Government Acts of 1929 and 1930 the Corporation could recover from my client also.

I was twenty-seven years old when I took the plunge matrimonially. The previous month I had made my first appearance in the Court of Criminal Appeal. I appeared for a Scoutmaster who had been convicted at Somerset Assizes on ten counts alleging offences against boys. He had been sentenced by Mr Justice Macnaghten to ten years' penal servitude, but I was able to persuade Justices Talbot, du Parcq and Atkinson to quash the conviction on the grounds of misdirection by the judge to the jury. Encouraged, as I have said, by my wife, I sought the opening at 2 Mitre Court Buildings left vacant when F. J. Tucker became a High Court judge. His place as head of chambers had been taken by J. D. Casswell, the Josh Casswell of course who had prosecuted in what I laughingly thought of as 'The Case of the Bitten Finger'. Both Tucker and Casswell had advised me against making the move. Tucker had in fact invited Josh and me to lunch, and they had both said in effect that while I was doing very well at Bristol, it was very risky to go to London where I was unknown, where I had no particular affiliations and where no one was particularly interested in me. Although I had made the decision against their advice, Casswell took me into his chambers, and I saw my name put up in The Temple in January 1938.

Those were heady days for me, and I was shortly to be involved in what was to become my first murder case—one that attracted great local and even national attention. Proceedings had in fact already been opened before the local magistrates while I was still in Bristol.

CHAPTER 2

Murders and other matters

OVER THE YEARS I appeared for the defence—and occasionally for the prosecution—in several notable murder trials, and gained something of a name in this field. I suppose that, until I became Director of Public Prosecutions, this was where I had my chief reputation. My record cannot compare with those of the great American advocate Clarence Darrow or the justly celebrated Marshall Hall, but only once was a man whom I defended on a murder charge actually hanged.

I will refer to that case later, but first let me deal with the trial that started it all. This was not long before the world was embarked on the second great war within my lifetime, and murder cases, however fascinating, took second place to the major events that were helping to settle the future of mankind. But for three nail-biting days in 1938 it was almost impossible not to be concerned with the fate of the young sailor accused of killing his father. The circumstances of the case, as outlined to the magistrates, had attracted widespread attention. Large crowds assembled each day outside the courts, and scores were turned away.

The accused was aged twenty-two. At the time of the trial he was serving aboard one of His Majesty's ships. He had been more or less continuously at sea for some time, away from his family and from his fiancée. His father was an unemployed man aged fifty. The prosecutor at the committal proceedings, E. G. Robey (son of the famous comedian with the bushy eyebrows), most properly and fairly painted almost as bad a picture of the dead man as I could have done myself. At one point during the preliminary hearing he stated that the man's wife and daughters 'went in fear of their lives'. 'Although one is reluctant', he said, 'to say anything against the character of a man who met such an end, there is very little to be said in the father's favour. To summarize his history, he was a violent man addicted to drinking, bad-tempered and somewhat violent. The female members of his family were afraid of him, and he was given to things grossly immoral.' In particular, Robey said that the father had been convicted and imprisoned for a serious offence against a girl aged six, and he listed other grave allegations that had been made, one no more than three months before his death.

Starting two months before her husband's death, the dead man's wife began to send a series of very troubled letters to her son. In one she wrote: 'Be sure to come home first chance. You are my eldest son and you are the one I want to talk to.' In a second she said, 'I have a lot to tell you when you come home. If anything happens to me at any time, I want you to protect your two sisters.' In yet a third: 'I am trying to be brave till I see you. . . . You are the only one I can talk to. . . . I am determined to start my life afresh when you come home. . . . Now do not worry. We can manage without you soiling your hands.'

A fourth and extremely important letter contained a horrifying allegation against the woman's husband, concerning a grave assault on his own daughter. 'I am as well', the mother said, 'as can be expected, but must tell you the news that is breaking my heart. . . . I told your father I knew of what had gone on. He said he had done no harm. . . . It is killing me with worry . . . we must get him out of the house once and for all . . . I am afraid of our lives.'

These allegations must surely have had a powerful influence on the mind of the young recipient. In a letter, obviously written before his mother's last letter had reached him, he announced his ship's imminent arrival in England. 'It has been a long three months, but it is all over now,' he wrote. 'You have got to tell me the truth about this matter, you have got to. This past week I have been trying to reason things out for myself. Either he has done it or he has not done it, and for myself I think he has. Looking back over his record, I cannot find one redeeming feature in his whole career. No wonder that I loathe and detest him.'

'This is the last straw,' he added. 'I have made up my mind that he has no right to live. I shall do it and take the consequences. If you tell or try to warn him I shall never forgive you. I shall kill him as sure as I am sat here.'

The accused arrived in England from Gibraltar and went first to his fiancée's home. Three days later he received a telegram from his mother: 'Come at once if possible. Urgent.' Apparently the father had made a suggestion to his elder daughter, and offered her money. Her brother arrived home the following day.

Within a short time his father was dead. He had thirty-four

wounds. His throat was cut, and his face was so badly smashed as to be almost unrecognizable. The son was found with a hatchet in one hand and a razor in the other. 'I have killed my father,' he announced. 'I will bring him down and put him in the gutter where he belongs.' Later he said, 'I did it and I am glad I have. I have been thinking about this for three months.'

The case looked very black against my client. However monstrous the behaviour of his father, the son had adopted extreme means of dealing with it, if indeed his own words were to be believed. It was clear to me that I had to present him in as sympathetic a light as possible, and one strong point in his favour was that he was a personable young man who might prove an excellent witness and make a good impression on the jury. I recall that he stood stiffly to attention when he entered the dock. His hair was brushed smartly back, and he wore a double-breasted blue suit and blue tie.

There was something of a surprise when I challenged two women jurors. Although women, particularly of the motherly sort, might have been kindly disposed towards the accused, I took the view that the facts of the case were too horrible to be expounded in front of them. I had particularly in mind the lurid photographs of the dead man's injuries. That, of course, was over forty years ago, and I doubt whether I would feel the same way today, when women no longer seek, and probably do not need, protection of this sort. I suppose that, after Belsen, we are all more immune than we were. Amazingly, the women were replaced by other women jurors, and it was some time before I had achieved an all-male jury. It soon became quite clear to the jury when the mother's letters to her son were read out in court that she was accusing her husband of serious offences against their elder daughter. 'She says these assaults have been going on for some time', she wrote on one occasion. Never, however, had she incited her son to do anything other than try to persuade the father to leave home. 'Do you think you can get him out of the house . . . but I do not want you to get hurt?' she had appealed to him. 'I am praying to God to help me because I cannot go on living in such a torment. You must try to think out the best way to get him to go peacefully.'

One of her last letters, written after her son's return to England, specifically warned him to be careful. 'I do think you should have a lawyer's advice', she wrote, 'as he is dangerous, and always carries a knife on him.'

All depended on the accused himself when eventually he went into the witness-box. Fortunately, he turned out to be the excellent witness I had hoped. His story was that he had killed his father with a hatchet in self-defence. Regarding the multiple wounds inflicted on the dead man, he admitted that he had lost his head.

I questioned him about his father's violent behaviour, and he spoke of an occasion when the father had threatened the mother with a knife. He said that he had taken the axe from the fireplace in the drawing-room before tackling his father about his conduct, because he knew that his father was a dangerous man liable to attack anyone on the slightest provocation. 'I took up the axe more with the idea of preventing him from attacking me than to attack him.'

'I said to Father, "Hey, you, I want to speak to you about the girls."' The father, he said, was in bed at the time, pushed aside the bedclothes, swore at him and leapt out of bed. 'He took hold of something from the dressing-table and walked towards the foot of the bed. I caught a glimpse of a black handle and it flashed through my mind that he had got a razor.'

'What', I asked my client, 'did you think he was going to do?'

'I did not *think*. I *knew* he was going to slash me with it. I put up the axe. I thought the only chance of saving myself was to stun him with it. I twisted it so that the back was towards him and aimed a blow at his temple, but I hit him on the cheek. He seemed to go mad and dropped the razor and sprang at me. He caught hold of the hatchet with one hand and my wrist with the other and tried to get it from me. I pushed him towards the dressing-table, but he seemed to gather himself and ran me back towards the window. My back smashed the window. I think he was trying to have me out of the window.'

'What do you think would have happened if he had got the axe?' I next asked, and awaited his reply with great interest. In a loud and clear voice he answered, 'I have no hesitation in saying I would have been killed, and any of the family who might have stood in his way.'

The jury acquitted him of murder after a retirement of only forty minutes. The judge had referred to the terrible provocation, saying that if the jury felt that it was such as to deprive a reasonable man of his self-control, this would justify the reduction of the charge from murder to manslaughter. The young man was found guilty of the lesser charge, but the jury added a strong recommendation to mercy. There was clapping in court, and prolonged cheers outside, when the sentence was pronounced: nine months in the second division. 'Nothing can justify the crime you committed', the judge told my client, 'but I have been able to feel that what you did . . . may be explained on grounds which do afford real mitigation. I am aware there were circumstances which must have tried you as a young man very greatly.'

The judge further expressed the hope that, because of the convicted man's positive good character in the past, he would in due course be permitted to continue with his career in the Navy. Five years later, during the war, I was appointed head of the Naval Law Branch, and I made it my business to inquire about what had happened. I was happy to discover that the judge's hope had become fact.

My first murder case had ended in reasonably satisfactory circumstances, particularly as the judge had been kind enough to comment that the defence had been conducted with 'admirable ability'. It is interesting to compare this case with one fourteen years later at Winchester Assizes where I defended another Serviceman, this time a soldier, also on a charge of murder. Haydon Wattam was only nineteen when he was accused of strangling a middle-aged woman in Southsea. Mrs Hands was known locally to some people as 'the dancing widow', and not surprisingly, the case attracted notoriety when it became known that someone had forced an entry into her house, had had sexual relations with her just before—or perhaps after—her death, and then stolen various articles.

This was an important trial for two reasons. Firstly, because it raised the whole question of the reliability of evidence of identification. From my first experience when a woman picked out someone other than the accused, resulting in his acquittal, to the time when as Director of Public Prosecutions I was strongly attacked over my handling of the Peter Hain affair, I have been aware of the fallible nature of such evidence. It is so easy for witnesses to be mistaken, and when evidence of identification goes wrong there is a serious danger of a wrong verdict.

In the case of Wattam the evidence of identification was highly unsatisfactory. Out of six witnesses, only two picked out the accused, and two picked out somebody else. A man in a passing car actually stated that he had seen that the accused's shoelace was undone! In normal circumstances I would have made mincemeat of this curious evidence.

Circumstances were not, however, normal, and this brings me to the second point. Unlike the young sailor I had defended, whose character was exemplary, Wattam was an ex-Borstal boy of low intelligence and a deserter from the Royal Inniskilling Fusiliers. Now, the jury were not entitled to know this. The law is that a person's previous bad character should not be disclosed except in cases where it is strictly relevant in order to prove the particular offence with which he is charged. Such was not the case here. Nor did the defence seek to attack the character of the prosecution's witnesses, which might have put the accused's character in issue. Unfortunately, however, I was compelled to introduce evidence from Borstal officers in order to refute a particular witness who said he had insisted that the man who had sold him the goods stolen from the dead woman should write out an authority for the transaction to be entered in his books. The surest way to prove that Wattam was not its author was to establish that he was incapable of writing it. The Borstal officers were able to attest that his mental age on leaving the institution was that of a child of six and a half, and that he was too illiterate to have written such a document.

I have no doubt that the jury were affected by knowing that Wattam had been in Borstal, and the way in which Mr Justice Pilcher dealt with the identification issue was no help to me. As in the sailor's case, the jury were out for only forty minutes. This time, however, the verdict was guilty, and Wattam was sentenced to death. Here was an instance where knowledge of bad character was perhaps allowed to outweigh the uncertainty about the murderer's identity.

I regarded the verdict as one that would not have been given but for the evidence that I had been forced to introduce. There were many unsatisfactory aspects to the case. On the amazing argument that, having provided evidence of Wattam's life in Borstal, I had put his character in issue, a revolver was produced in court and my client asked, 'Did you not buy this two days after the murder?' It was in fact a toy revolver, and I could not see what relevance its purchase had to this case, where there was no evidence of any revolver having been used, toy or otherwise. Prosecuting counsel had made a dramatic and sudden gesture, producing the gun from behind his back. The effect can only have been to create prejudice by suggesting that Wattam was the sort of person who would carry a gun to frighten people.

I had risen immediately to object to what I considered a highly irregular, prejudicial and inadmissible question. Mr Justice Pilcher, who at that time had presided over very few serious criminal trials, surprised me by his response. 'I do not know why you object,' he said, 'I would have thought that this assisted you. It is only an imitation revolver, and would indicate that he was not a person who was prepared to kill people.' 'I can only say,' I replied, 'that it is a type of assistance which I would prefer to do without.'

The judge's handling of the revolver incident was only one of several matters that made me think that we must succeed on appeal, but there had been no wholly successful appeal against a murder conviction in England for nearly eight years, as distinct from cases in which a verdict of manslaughter had been substituted. Additional information had also come to light which created doubt about the evidence given by the witness who had identified the accused as having sold him property stolen from the murdered woman.

I went before the Court of Appeal, therefore, with some confidence but not a little anxiety. I need not have worried. Mr Justice Oliver, who sat with Mr Justice Jones and Mr Justice Byrne, described the verdict as unreasonable and unsupportable having regard to the evidence as they now knew it. What to the popular newspapers was 'The Case of the Dancing Widow' was to me an object lesson on the danger of disclosing to a jury any evidence of bad character, although in this case I had no alternative.

Oliver had a way of regarding one with a withering look when he disagreed with some proposition. He had in fact a glass eye, and it was said of him on such occasions you could not be sure with which eye he was looking at you. But he was seldom misunderstood, and on this occasion it was plain that it was not the prosecution with whom he and his brother judges agreed.

Very shortly after the successful appeal, I was sitting beside Mr Justice Pilcher when he was a guest of the Bar mess in Winchester. 'I see that the Court of Appeal quashed the conviction in the case of Wattam,' he said, and added, 'I made an awful mess of that case, didn't I?' This, I confess, endeared him to me, and I came to like and respect him very much over the years, during which I appeared on a number of occasions before him.

However, one may respect a judge, but one may prefer that he should not preside in a particular case. I remember one such occasion. The circumstances were unusual, and I hope that I shall not be accused of breaching any confidentiality, having regard to the nature of the case and the many years that have passed since it arose.

I was appearing in a civil case for a plaintiff who was claiming damages from the farmer who had employed him for many years. In the course of his work he had been required to assist in the milking of a fractious cow. His job was to stand by its head, holding its nose. Unfortunately, the animal, in struggling to free itself from his grip, and with its rear legs tethered, fell sideways on top of him, breaking his thigh-bone. The case came on before Mr Justice Byrne, who called counsel into his room after the first day's hearing and told us that he had seen in court a vet whom he knew—indeed, who had treated his own dog—and asked whether this man was being called as an expert witness on behalf of the defendant, and if so whether there was any objection to his continuing to try the case. Defending counsel and I both intimated that we had no objection until the judge said, 'That's all right, then. I shall treat him like any other witness, and if he

25

persuades me, this will be solely by his evidence.' 'You did say if he persuades you?' defending counsel asked. 'Well,' said the judge, 'you can't avoid as the case proceeds forming a purely tentative view', indicating perhaps that at that point he had formed a provisional view favourable to the plaintiff, whereupon defending counsel became worried and after consulting his client asked for the case to be stood over to be tried by another judge.

'I only hope', I said to my clerk, 'that the other judge will not be'—and I named a particular judge—because he was a countryman who had a wide experience of dealing with animals. I had in mind that when a judge was by way of being an expert in some matter, there could be sometimes a tendency for him to decide a case upon his own expert knowledge rather than by using his expertise to assess the value of the evidence given by the experts called on behalf of the parties. 'No chance of that', my clerk assured me. 'He's out on circuit.'

Now, Mr Justice Byrne, once he had ceased to try the case, had recommended to defending counsel that he should settle the matter, and when asked what damages he considered appropriate had mentioned a substantial sum, having regard to the fact that the injury might have led to permanent disability, although pointing out that he had only heard the plaintiff's side. So I had some idea of what I might have got if I had succeeded before him. As luck would have it, however, my 'judicial expert' returned unexpectedly from circuit and I found myself before the very judge I had too lightly said I did not want. It was not long before he made his view clear. Indeed, even while I was opening my case, he indicated that he would not have thought that this was an accident that could reasonably have been foreseen, and I knew then and there that I was a probable loser. In the final result he found in favour of the defendant, so my client might perhaps have failed to win compensation because the original judge knew the vet!

It was always, of course, a great responsibility to defend a man on a charge of murder, but I have rarely felt a greater sense of responsibility—certainly not in my early years at the Bar—than when I was called upon to act for a police superintendent accused of fraudulent conversion of money he had received as a club treasurer. The trial took place in April 1939, which was period of nine months after my first murder defence.

My client was Deputy Chief Constable of Bath. It was thus a very grave matter for him that he found himself facing seven charges at Bristol Quarter Sessions. In his favour was his excellent record in the police force, and among those who gave evidence of his good character was the Mayor of Bath himself, the local police surgeon—who attested strongly to the accused's absolute integrity—and the Chief Constable, whose inquiries were the cause of his standing in the dock. It was also in his favour (or so it seemed to me) that the total sum involved in the charges was only £152, and that he had taken no steps (which he could easily have done) to ensure that other people did not know what sums of money were paid to him, and that he was surely too intelligent and experienced a police officer not to have covered his tracks if he had had any fraudulent intention.

There were, however, a number of difficulties. The sums mentioned in the charges had been handed to him on various occasions in his capacity as treasurer of the Bath City Police Athletic Club by the deputy treasurer, Detective Constable Evans. When the new Chief Constable examined the club's accounts he came to the conclusion that the Superintendent had not paid all the money into the club's bank, and my client offered no explanation for the apparent discrepancy when questioned by Constable Evans. It also transpired that he had been in debt at the time of the alleged offences, and that he had caused a delay in the audit of the club's accounts.

The accused did not deny that he had received the money, and he admitted that he had not paid it all into the club's bank. What he did deny was that he had any intention to defraud. There were reasonable explanations for all his behaviour, although strictly it was irregular.

The Superintendent spent several hours in the witness-box. In the course of his evidence he said that he had a cheque in his pocket to cover the whole amount of the deficiency. 'Have you ever been able until today to pay?' he was asked by the Recorder. 'I did not know the amount until today', he replied.

Here was a case where an accused was helped by his good character. The jury decided that there had been no intent to defraud, and there were emotional scenes inside the court and out when the Superintendent's ordeal was finally over.

In terms of the ordeal endured in facing a criminal charge, it must be easier if one is of bad character than if one is, say, a senior police officer or a clergyman. I remember defending a priest on charges of homosexual offences against boys. It was a very anxious time for him. The rural dean was present when we met at the magistrates' court for a conference before the hearing. The priest, dressed in his cassock and a biretta, wanted the matter dealt with as quickly as possible, but I advised him that he might stand a better chance with a jury, and recommended that we ask for the case to be sent for trial.

However, he was strongly opposed to this suggestion, partly because of the extra publicity that a trial would generate.

'At this moment', he said, 'I feel like St Paul. He too had to decide whether to be tried by Caesar.'

'Do not let us confuse the issue', I replied. 'So far as I am aware, St Paul was never charged with offences such as these.'

The priest stuck to his guns, and we asked the magistrates to deal with the case. He was right in his decision, for the magistrates acquitted him, and his awful burden was removed without further delay.

His was certainly not an easy ordeal, but never have I known an accused suffer more strongly than when I defended the daughter of the Bishop of Bath and Wells on a charge of manslaughter. The poor girl was so appallingly distressed by the death of a motor-cyclist with whom she collided while driving her father's car, that even twenty-eight years later I have hesitated to include a brief account of the affair in this book, particularly since to my knowledge the strain of the case severely affected her health.

She was only twenty-three at the time, but had been her father's official driver for six years, having covered over 120,000 miles in that time without once sustaining even the slightest accident. On the day in question she had driven her father to Weston-super-Mare for a confirmation service, and after supper in a local café with the vicar and his wife—during which she drank only water and coffee—she drove her father home at about ten o'clock. She pulled out to pass a small van travelling slowly—it was being run in—and while on her wrong side she hit the oncoming motor-cyclist with fatal results. Fortunately for her it was established that the motor-cycle was being ridden with its headlights switched only on to the pilot light, supporting her evidence that she thought the faint light was that of a distant bicycle.

A witness cycling on the same road said that he had been passed by a powerful car travelling at an excessive speed, which he estimated at between sixty and seventy miles per hour, but in cross-examination he admitted that it was very difficult to judge speeds at night, and that thirty-five to forty miles per hour might have been correct. In support of his daughter, the Bishop gave evidence that it had seemed to him to be perfectly safe for her to overtake the van.

I argued that the evidence fell far short of proving the high degree of negligence necessary to substantiate the charge of manslaughter. In the course of my speech I said to the jury, 'Here you have got this road, straight for an enormous distance, at night. She is going at a moderate speed. She draws out to overtake, sees what looks like a bicycle, but which turns out to be the oncoming vehicle. Has she done anything wrong yet?' 'No', said the jury out loud, or some members of it. It was the only instance in my experience of a jury answering a rhetorical question, and I wondered whether I should have sat down then and there!

The jury at Somerset Assizes were out only twenty minutes before acquitting her, but nothing could bring back the dead man, and I suspect that this, rather than the jury's verdict, was her most important concern. I was quite convinced that she was not guilty of any criminal offence, but I know for a fact she received many poisonous letters after the case was over. Even a long experience with the criminal law still leaves me disgusted by the astounding vindictiveness of the people who see fit in such circumstances to add to the misery of a person in trouble.

I will refer to one last case where a client of mine suffered an ordeal that I could have wished he had been spared. There have been very few cases where I have been totally convinced of my client's innocence, but this was one. (I do not, of course, by this mean to imply that I necessarily believe my other clients to have been mostly guilty as charged!) The case was a highly complicated one arising out of the crash of a well-known firm of West Country solicitors, Baker & Company of Weston-super-Mare. The local community was aghast at the failure in 1938 of a firm that had always been regarded as being as safe as the Bank of England. In subsequent bankruptcy proceedings involving the partners, it appeared that the firm had been in financial difficulties since 1932, and there were far-reaching allegations about the way in which clients' money had been handled.

A prolonged investigation was conducted over two years, and resulted in the two partners being jointly charged with fraudulent conversion of sums totalling £3,738 on dates between 1937 and 1938, and one partner—not my client—being separately charged with similar offences between 1933 and 1934. These were sample charges, because it became clear as the case progressed that nearly £75,000 had been lost by over two hundred and fifty of the firm's clients. Indeed, as Anthony Hawke (then number one Treasury Counsel, and later Recorder of London) said in the preliminary proceedings, 'A more disastrous state of affairs in bankruptcy of these two partners it would probably be difficult to find in the annals of the solicitors' profession.'

He prosecuted at Winchester Assizes. The judge was Mr Justice Lawrence, to whom I had been marshal nine years earlier—for this was early 1940. I represented Captain Picton Davies, who had been with the old and reputable firm since 1923. The second accused, who appeared on his own behalf, had joined as clerk as long ago as 1914. Since 1931, on the death of Ernest Baker, the two men had been sole partners, Captain Davies holding two-thirds of the shares.

In April 1938 Davies issued a writ for the dissolution of the partnership, as a result of which a receiver was appointed. Receiving orders were issued against both men in September of that year, and a joint statement of affairs was prepared, which revealed that money entrusted to the firm by clients for investment or safe-keeping was no longer available because of the bankruptcy.

Since 1 January 1935 it had been necessary under the terms of the Solicitors' Act for clients' money to be kept in a separate banking account. A new account was indeed opened on that day, at which time £116,935 was owing to clients, but the firm's banking accounts were overdrawn and there was no cash readily available to pay into the new account.

As witness after witness gave evidence it became clear that a horrifying state of affairs existed, of which we were only shown the tip of the iceberg, and Captain Davies's partner decided to plead guilty. Anthony Hawke naturally argued that, even if the junior partner had been primarily responsible for the disaster, the senior partner must surely be answerable for a series of events stretching over a number of years. There was, however, the very important question of my client's ill health. As the result of war service, he had frequently been away ill, including the whole of the time during which the offences were committed with which he was charged, and at the time of these proceedings his health was so bad that he had been attended in the police court by a uniformed nurse. He said that his partner had assured him that there was no need to worry about anything and that there was ample security. He had not the slightest doubt about what he was told, and felt he could rely implicitly on his partner's honesty and the representations made to him.

There was plenty of evidence that Davies was ignorant of the facts. It might have been argued that he could have made more inquiries, but when he asked questions he received what appeared to him to be genuine answers. He had no reason to doubt his partner. There was no charge of conspiracy between the two men, or any evidence of this. It could not be contended, therefore, that any acts done by the junior partner provided evidence against the senior, and in the absence of evidence that Davies knew and acquiesced in these acts, I believed that he must be acquitted. The prosecution, in my view, left it in the greatest doubt whether there was any conversion by Davies at all, but even if there had been, there was no proof that he had acted with intent to defraud.

On the contrary, there were numerous indications of his innocence. His wife was among the people defrauded, and surely he would not have been a party to that. It was he who insisted on calling in an independent auditor when he first heard adverse rumours about his partner's financial position. When a deficiency of £3,700 was reported to him he personally paid in £2,700 towards this sum. When later he heard that the deficiency was far greater he took the necessary steps to bring the matter into the open. He then assigned to the firm the whole of his private estate. He in fact did everything in his power to put matters right.

At the end of the case for the prosecution I made a very strong submission to the judge that there was no case for Captain Davies to answer. Mr Justice Lawrence agreed with me, and my client left the court, to use the proverbial phrase, without a stain on his character, but also without a penny in his pocket, for the tragic consequence of his firm's collapse was that the whole of his assets were lost, plus £9,000 belonging to his wife.

There was still time, in that period of 'phoney war', to contemplate the personal tragedy of one man. It was not long before we were all concerned with sterner stuff.

CHAPTER 3
Differing defences

GOOD HEALTH and a good constitution are recommended for anyone who plans a career in the Law, whether as barrister or as solicitor. A lawyer has a high duty of care to his client, and cannot afford to adopt half-measures or take short cuts. Long hours are often necessary to meet deadlines. It is almost impossible for a solicitor to take too much care in preparing a case, and a busy barrister can on occasions be run off his feet.

Fortunately, I have been blessed with good health. I decided that I could best serve my country during the last war in a way suggested to me early in 1940: that I join the Trading with the Enemy Department, which was set up by the Treasury and Board of Trade. I remained there for nearly three years until the opportunity arose of an appointment at the Admiralty, where in due course I became head of the Naval Law Branch, which naturally I found more suited to my experience.

I returned to the Bar at the end of 1945, and was almost immediately appointed Recorder of Bridgwater, a position I occupied until I became Recorder of Plymouth. My duties were to sit four times a year at Quarter Sessions. It was not, of course, a full-time occupation, and did not prevent me from functioning as I had before the war, except that our chambers had been badly damaged in the air-raids and we were temporarily housed in Essex Court.

I was very proud of the appointment as Recorder, particularly as the only recent holder of the office who had been at Bridgwater for any length of time was none other than my old pupil-master, F. A. Wilshire. He had been succeeded for short periods by two very distinguished silks, Roy Fox-Andrews and John Scott Henderson. My wife and I put up at the main local hotel for the swearing-in ceremony. Food and clothing were still rationed, and there was a shortage of goods in the shops. This dearth manifested itself in the complete absence of towels in our room.

I went downstairs to complain to the receptionist, who angered me by demanding a deposit before she would let me have any towels—a deposit of five shillings, if I remember rightly. I thought this a most impertinent requirement for a hotel to make of a guest. Were we not to be trusted to leave the towels behind us on our departure?

'Look here', I said, in as lofty a tone as I could assume—one appropriate, I thought, to my new status—'do you realize you are speaking to your new Recorder? I shall be coming here to try people who do things like taking or stealing towels.' And I refused point-blank to part with any money.

The young woman told me that she would have to see the manager, and made for the door of his office. As she was about to knock she turned round and looked at me suspiciously. 'You did say you were a reporter, didn't you?' she asked, effectively putting me in my place.

One of my earliest cases stands out vividly in my mind, for I discovered that I was due to try a man whom I had previously both prosecuted and defended, from which it will be realized that he was well known in the criminal courts of the West Country. I had prosecuted him at Winchester Assizes, when he was convicted. For some reason he was not, according to custom, asked whether he wanted an outstanding charge to be taken into consideration, and fresh proceedings were subsequently taken against him for that alleged offence. He was committed for trial, and I was allocated to defend him under the Poor Prisoners Defence Procedure, a precursor of Legal Aid. I asked his solicitors to find out if he wished me to act for him in the circumstances, and he said that it made no difference to him.

The offence involved was safe-breaking. There was strong evidence against him, but attention was focused on a glove of his on which were minute spots of green paint. The prosecution claimed that it was the same green paint as on the window-sill through which entry had been made to the room containing the safe. They called an expert witness to say this. I called another expert witness, regarded as perhaps the leading man in the field, who said the paint on the glove was different from that on the sill. The accused was acquitted. This is an example of a mistake that prosecutions can make in concentrating on one point when there is plenty of other evidence. The case then becomes a contest over this particular point.

A familiar prisoner came into the dock. 'I think that I know you', I said. 'We have met before,' and I told him if he preferred to be tried by another judge I would put the case back. But he said he was satisfied to be tried by me. The charge was one of breaking and entering and stealing. He was not represented by counsel and I offered him legal aid, although he was pleading guilty, but he refused this.

Now at that time it was possible in circumstances that applied in this instance to sentence persistent offenders to preventive detention for not less than five or more than fourteen years. This was a very severe sentence, not only because of the length of imprisonment—it was recommended by the Court of Criminal Appeal that seven years should ordinarily be regarded as the minimum—but because it did not qualify for as early a release, subject to good behaviour, as did an ordinary sentence of imprisonment. Years later, when I served on the Home Office Advisory Council on the Treatment of Offenders, we considered preventive detention and recommended its abolition, mainly because it was not being used for the sort of persistent criminal for whom it was intended. I was faced early in my career as a Recorder with a difficult decision.

I had before me a copy of the prison governor's report. 'The prison governor', I told the accused man, 'says you are both mentally and physically fit for preventive detention, and he can see no reason why you should not be sent there. Do you?'

He thought for a time. Then, 'No, I don't think I do really' came the unexpected reply.

Perhaps it was because of this indication of his honest recognition of his deserts that despite his shocking record I decided against preventive detention in favour of a substantial prison sentence.

Sentencing I have always regarded as one of the most difficult parts of a judge's duties. I remember a case in which I defended a soldier accused at Bristol Assizes of murdering his wife not long after the war. It was one of those tragic instances that are so often the result of enforced separation of a man from his wife under war conditions. The basic facts were not in dispute. While Reginald Burt was abroad in the Army, in Salonica, his wife gave birth in August 1945 to a child by another man. She wrote a pathetic letter to inform him in September, saying that 'loneliness is the hardest thing in the world to fight'. Nevertheless, when her husband obtained compassionate leave the following month she told him that she preferred the other man, and there was a violent quarrel. The husband was unable to return home again until May 1946, when the wife was stabbed in the throat, causing her death.

An eminent pathologist stated that if the wound had been half an inch either side it would not have been fatal. When interviewed by the police Burt said, 'What have I done? My wife, I love her so. Is she all right?' And later, 'I did not know I did that to her. I would not have done that for the world.' The police surgeon gave evidence that Burt, who was under the influence of drink, did not appear to know that his wife was dead.

In the witness-box Burt told a tragic story of how he had taken to drink after attempting unsuccessfully to get his wife to abandon her lover. He had been drinking heavily at all times of the day, and he could hardly remember anything during the week before his wife's death. He had only a hazy recollection of going to the house on the fatal night, and no recollection at all of anything that happened thereafter until he was charged at the police station.

This was a case, in my view, where there was a reasonable basis for a defence that the accused was so drunk as to be incapable of forming an intent either to kill or to cause grievous bodily harm, and where manslaughter—unlawful killing without intent—was the appropriate verdict. I addressed the jury for over an hour. When it came to the summing-up, Mr Justice Morris (later Lord Morris of Borth-y-Gest) said 'Drunkenness can never be an excuse for crime', but he added 'There may be drunkenness of so extreme a form that a drunken man may be wholly incapable of forming the intent to commit the crime.' The jury took only fifteen minutes to decide for manslaughter. It was what I believe is called a popular verdict.

I agree with the words of the judge: 'Whatever you may think about any of these who have figured in this unhappy and distressing tragedy, it is not, of course, suggested that in any circumstances was the accused justified in taking any action against his wife which could lead to her death.' I still thought the sentence rather stiff. Burt had been serving his country abroad for three years. Like many thousands of others, he must have had one thought uppermost in his mind, day after day—the time when he would be able to return home to the wife and young daughter he loved. Then, like a bombshell, came the letter that shattered his dreams from a wife who wrote that 'I have got no right to call you husband again.'

I wondered whether, if I had been a judge, I would have sentenced him to as much as five years' penal servitude.

At the luncheon interval before the jury's verdict I had been congratulated by a number of barristers and solicitors who were impressed by my conduct of the defence. I suppose it was because they felt it was no easy task to raise a defence of drunkenness in so serious a matter.

The case of Rex v. Sims, in which I prosecuted at Dorset Assizes in 1946, turned out to be of greater legal significance than I had at first anticipated. Sims was alleged to have committed homosexual offences with a number of different men who visited him in his house. Raymond Stock (now a circuit judge), for the defence, sought to have the individual counts in the indictment tried separately, but Mr Justice Wrottesley refused, and Sims was convicted on all charges. Sims thereupon went to the Court of Criminal Appeal, where he was now represented by J. D. Casswell, K.C., as well as by Stock. Although powerful arguments were advanced on his behalf, it seemed to me that they would be brushed aside, as being a matter for the judge's discretion, but I reckoned without old 'Doggy', something it was never safe to do. He announced that an important point of law had to be determined, and that he would adjourn the appeal to a full court of five.

It was in these circumstances that I found myself being led by Anthony Hawke, who in turn was led by Henry Willinck, K.C., who was perhaps a curious choice because, although a most erudite lawyer, he had done very little work in the criminal courts. The highly complicated legal arguments revolved around whether evidence on one count was admissible as evidence on another alleging a similar offence with a different person. The court reserved judgment.

Prior to the Sims case, the rule had been laid down that the prosecution might advance all proper evidence—and I stress proper —tending to prove a charge, notwithstanding that it might show that an accused had been guilty of criminal acts other than those covered by the indictment, without waiting for him to set up a specific defence calling for rebuttal. This is what is usually called evidence of system. The Sims judgment, which I understand was prepared by Mr Justice Denning (as he then was), but which was delivered by Lord Goddard, introduced a slightly different consideration—one that was developed in subsequent cases and that has come to be known as similar fact. In 'similar fact' cases, where alleged acts have a striking resemblance, evidence about them may be admissible.

One of the most interesting similar fact cases with which I have been involved was the famous Straffen murder trial. To be exact, I was directly involved with only his first murder trial. Straffen was originally charged at Taunton Assizes in 1951 with the murder by strangling of two little girls, to which he had confessed. As his counsel, I took the view that the only defence open to him was that he was mad within the definition of the MacNaghten Rules when he strangled the girls. To establish this defence we would have had to prove that he probably did not know what he was doing at the time, or that he did not know it was wrong, but the problem did not arise because at the trial the prison medical officer reported that he believed that Straffen was unfit to plead, and the jury so found in a case that lasted only a few minutes, Mr Justice Oliver actually interrupting another trial and having the same jury resworn to try this new issue!

Straffen was sent to Broadmoor, and his escape from that institution for the criminally insane attracted national attention, which turned into national outrage when he strangled another little girl, again for no apparent reason, there being no sexual assault. On this occasion I was not his counsel, and he made no confession. Indeed, he pleaded not guilty. This was six years after the Sims case, which of course was a very minor affair in comparison, but it had the result of permitting the introduction of evidence of Straffen's confession to the murder of the two other girls in similar circumstances. Straffen was sentenced to death but reprieved.

The case of Regina *v*. Kemp in 1956 was not a murder trial, but one of causing grievous bodily harm with intent. Its interest lay in the fact that our defence was one of automatism.

The Kemps were a happily married couple. One morning the husband got up and for no apparent reason attacked his wife with a hammer, seriously injuring her. The trial took place at Bristol Assizes before Mr Justice Devlin (later Lord Devlin). We claimed that the accused was unaware at the time what he had done, and I called a doctor who said that his condition was not due to a disease of the mind such as would fall within the MacNaghten Rules but to a physical condition—namely, hardening of the arteries.

We were seeking an acquittal on the grounds of automatism; we were not pleading insanity. I had always understood it to be a principle of law that the issue of insanity could only be raised by the defence, and that if they chose not to raise it it was not open to the prosecution to do so. The prosecution called rebutting evidence, however, and their doctor disagreed with ours. He gave his view that hardening of the arteries had caused a disease of the mind.

The judge broadly took the view of the prosecution. He said that it did not matter whether the cause was physical or mental. If it resulted in a person's brain being so affected that he did not know what he was doing, that was insanity. Kemp was found guilty but insane.

Devlin declined to follow a decision of Mr Justice Barry, where a man had recently thrown his son out of the window. Barry had agreed that automatism in the form of epilepsy or brain tumour did not constitute insanity and was a defence which if accepted entitled the father to an acquittal. I should have liked to have taken the Kemp case to a higher court, but paradoxically a verdict of 'guilty but insane' was in law an acquittal, so it was impossible to appeal although the court had to make an order that the accused be detained. Nowadays the verdict is more correctly described as 'not guilty by reason of insanity', and it is possible to appeal against it.

The question of automatism has been considered subsequently in the courts, notably by the House of Lords in 1961 and the Court of Appeal in 1973 and 1977. Devlin's ruling on the facts of the Kemp case has been generally approved, but certain behaviour—resulting, for example, from sleepwalking or concussion—has been held to raise a defence of automatism, in distinction to one of insanity arising from a disease of the mind.

It is perhaps interesting to compare the defence in Regina *v*. Pascoe and Whitty. The trial took place at Bodmin Assizes in 1963 before Mr Justice Thesiger. Norman Broderick, Q.C. (now a circuit judge) with Robert Hughes represented the prosecution. I appeared with J. H. Inskip (now himself a silk) on behalf of Whitty. J. P. Comyn, Q.C. (now Mr Justice Comyn) led for Pascoe. The facts of the case were plain. The two accused went to the farm owned by a Mr Rowe, with whom Pascoe had once worked, with the intention of stealing. Dennis Whitty carried a knife and a starting pistol, and one of the men—probably Pascoe—had an iron bar or jemmy. While one of the men was speaking to Rowe, the other struck Rowe from behind with the bar. The two men later ransacked the farmhouse and threw the bar and the knife into a reservoir. So much was admitted.

There was some dispute as to who had delivered the fatal blow, but this was not the real defence, since both men admitted assaulting Rowe, and it was clear that subject only to the question of duress, they were acting in concert, and each was responsible for the other's actions. The gist of Pascoe's statement to the police was: 'I did not kill him. That was my mate. He went mad, he did. I was afraid to stop him, or he would stick me. I had to walk away . . . I only knocked him over the head with the bar to just knock him out. When I did, I told Dennis that was enough, but he just went mad with the knife. Then he took the bar from me and kept thumping him over the head.' Whitty, on the other hand, said, 'Russell made me go. It was his idea. He made me knock at the door and told me what to say. When he was hitting the old farmer over the head, I cried. He made me stick him. . . . He [Pascoe] was going to hit me over the head with the bar, so I had to do it, honest he did.'

Whitty's defence was twofold. First, it was one of duress, but the judge invited the jury to answer two questions of fact, as a result of which it was clear they did not accept my client's view of events. The second defence was one of diminished responsibility. I called a psychiatrist, who said that Whitty was a hysteric with a history of fainting fits and blackouts, and that when in a state of hysteria he would very likely not have mental responsibility for his actions. He had once been found unconscious in the street, with self-inflicted scratches down his face. The Crown called their own psychiatrist in rebuttal, but he agreed that Whitty was a hysteric, and that his condition might be an abnormality of mind, at any rate during an attack; but he did not agree that the evidence showed that at the moment of Whitty's assault on Rowe he was likely to have been suffering from a degree of hysteria that would substantially impair his mental responsibility.

This was a defence that I failed to win before the jury or before the Court of Criminal Appeal. Both men were convicted of murder. Dennis John Whitty was the only man I ever defended who was hanged.

In the days when there was capital punishment, it was more difficult for a barrister to avoid an element of personal involvement in a murder case, but I am convinced that it is now, as it was then, unwise for an advocate to become emotionally involved, whether he appears for the prosecution or for the defence. It has often been said that prosecuting counsel should be a minister of justice rather than an advocate, thus ensuring that he retains a fair and impartial attitude at all times, and I have always felt when defending that one is more effective with a jury if one appears to be objective in one's own approach and to deal fairly and squarely with the evidence as a whole. A modern jury in particular react favourably if they believe that counsel is not trying to pull the wool over their eyes, and emotional involvement often leads to the opposite impression being conveyed. Whatever may be my personal view of a case, however grave the charge or however dreadful the ordeal of the accused, I have found that I served my clients best by being as detached as possible. An advocate as successful as Marshall Hall might well adopt a different technique if he were practising today, but in any case his apparent personal involvement in his clients' fate was all part of his advocacy, and he might have been less effective had this not been so. As far as Whitty was concerned, I had done my best for him, and I did not feel any particular regret about the law taking its course.

I shall have something to say elsewhere about hanging as a punishment for capital murder, but I should like here to refer to one particular murder trial where I prosecuted. This was the case of Michael George Tatum. The trial took place in March 1959 at Winchester Assizes before Mr Justice Cassels. I led Jeremy Hutchinson for the Crown, and Tatum was defended by Edgar Fay, Q.C., and Patrick Back. It was not a case of outstanding legal interest, but it had a peculiar significance for me. It was a sordid story. One night the previous January, Captain Barrett, a retired Army officer aged eighty-five, was brutally attacked by a left-handed man. His skull was fractured, and he died the following afternoon. His wallet was missing.

The accused man and his wife occupied a room in the same house where Captain Barrett lived, but he had left the house after quarrelling with his wife. He had retained his front-door key, and he was left-handed. He said at first that he had returned to the house to see his wife, but eventually admitted that one purpose of his visit was theft, and he also admitted stealing the Captain's wallet. He now said, however, that he had been accompanied by an acquaintance called Terry Thatcher, and it was Thatcher who struck the fatal blows. Thatcher, he claimed, had taken a knobkerry that had been hanging on a wall in the house, and this was the weapon that was used when Captain Barrett suddenly sat up on hearing, or seeing, the men enter the room. There had been no plan to use a weapon in the course of the theft, and its use had come as a complete surprise to Tatum—or so he said.

Unfortunately for him, no such person as his Terry Thatcher was ever traced, and the jury clearly disbelieved him, especially since, in alternatively pleading that he was suffering from diminished responsibility, he was forced, in trying to prove this, to admit that he was an atrocious liar. They were only out forty minutes, and although the case went to appeal, Tatum was convicted and sentenced to hang. Just as Whitty was the only man I defended who was hanged, so Tatum was the only man I prosecuted who suffered that fate.

It was in the middle of May, and I was staying in a hotel in Salisbury while engaged on a case there. I went down to an early breakfast and automatically looked at the clock on the wall. As I did so it struck the hour. It gave me quite a shock, as I realized that probably at that very minute Tatum was being executed. I had no doubt about his guilt, but I am not sure that I ate my cereal that morning with quite the usual relish.

CHAPTER 4

Silk and its consequences

I GAMBLED three times in my career, first by choosing to go to the Bar at all and second in coming up to London. Both moves worked out well. The third gamble was in applying for silk. Some barristers can be very good as juniors and then fail to make the grade when they take silk. There is also an obvious reluctance on the part of solicitors to employ silks in civil work, at considerable extra cost, when there are really good juniors available. With juniors like Cyril Williams and Humphrey Edmunds on the Western Circuit, the amount of work for silks was limited.

Having decided that I had reached the stage when I could shortly take the gamble—once again aided and abetted by my wife—I had opened new chambers in anticipation of my application being successful. It was unusual in those days to have three silks in one set of chambers, and we already had Josh Casswell and John Scott Henderson. There was also Joe Molony to think about. Though junior to me at the Bar, he was senior to me in the chambers. If I took silk and stayed there I would jump ahead of him, unless he too took silk, in which case we would be four. So I started my own chambers at 2 King's Bench Walk, where I was joined among others by Raymond Stock, Hampden Inskip and Nat Blaker. This was in 1952, the same year in which I became the first chairman of a new county Quarter Sessions created for the Isle of Wight. I served in that capacity, doubling up as a Recorder, until I was appointed Director of Public Prosecutions twelve years later.

I applied for silk in 1954, and found to my surprise that I was one of three applicants from the Western Circuit, and the junior one at that. The others were Dingle Foot and Malcolm Wright. Dingle's practice was far-flung—indeed, all over the world—and he specialized in Privy Council work. It seemed unlikely that we would all three be appointed, and I feared that I might be the one unsuccessful candidate. I had powerful sponsorship, however. Mr Justice Byrne, a delightful man whom I very much admired, Mr Justice Lynskey, another first-rate judge, Lord Justice Morris and Lord Oaksey supported my application.

I had written to Lord Oaksey, who had of course presided at the Nuremberg Trial of Nazi war criminals, and whom I had marshalled when he was Geoffrey Lawrence, K.C. He had responded to my letter most sympathetically, and after remarking that he remembered me not only as a marshal but as a fearless and competent advocate, added that he had never forgotten a case in which I had caused him grave doubts about admitting an accused's statement. He promised to speak personally to the Lord Chancellor on my behalf.

I had appeared before him on a number of occasions, including one when I was defending a woman accused of abortion. While the chief police witness was giving evidence I attacked an allegedly voluntary confession on the grounds that it had been induced, but Lawrence decided—after a trial within a trial—to admit it. When the officer returned to the box he claimed for the first time that my client had said, 'You know the trouble I have been in'—in fact she had previously been convicted as an abortionist—and I objected to this piece of damaging evidence that ought not to have been before the jury. Lawrence agreed, but to my surprise added, 'I shall direct the jury to acquit.' Perhaps in hindsight I can surmise that he may have been doubtful about ever admitting the confession in the first place.

His influence may—who knows?—have been a decisive factor. I am glad to say we all three got silk and my gamble paid off, for although I was still largely concerned with cases on my old circuit, my earnings rose fairly quickly. I was extremely fortunate in the people who joined me, who all combined to make our chambers a very happy and successful set. Further, I would like to pay a sincere tribute to the two clerks, Sydney Newland (later Mayor of Wembley and a Justice of the Peace), who looked after me at 2 Mitre Court Buildings, and John Walton, who moved with me to 2 King's Bench Walk. To both I am much indebted for the assistance they gave me.

It was also within this same year of 1954 that I was highly honoured by being made Recorder of Plymouth, in which capacity I made my first appearance in January 1955. This meant that I ceased to be Recorder of Bridgwater. I had been privileged to hold this ancient Recordership for nine happy years, during which I enjoyed a splendid relationship with the civic authorities, including the Town Clerk, Mr Clidero, who was also a most efficient and helpful Clerk of the Peace. The mayor and commonalty of Plymouth had been granted a charter by the monarch as far back as 1439 which gave them the right to elect a Recorder—whose stipend, incidentally, was fixed at the sum of £1 6s. 8d. Among my more recent and very distinguished predecessors were the man who was now Lord Chief Justice of England, Lord Goddard; Anthony Hawke, K.C., who later became a judge of the King's Bench Division; Lord Merrivale, later to become President of the Probate, Divorce and Admiralty Division; Dr Blake Odgers, whose contribution to legal literature will not have gone unnoticed; and, most interestingly, A. T. Denning, K.C., who never sat at Plymouth because he was appointed a judge of the King's Bench Division on his way to the very top of the legal ladder before he had the chance! G. R. King Anningson most generously said in welcoming me on behalf of the Bar that my appointment would doubtless turn out to be a stepping-stone to other things. 'But we should like to say', he added, 'we do sincerely hope you will be with us for a long time.' My appointment in fact lasted until 1961 when I became Recorder of Portsmouth, where I remained happily until I was appointed Director of Public Prosecutions.

In the meantime I had extra judicial duties as a Commissioner of Assize, trying civil work at Sheffield followed by criminal work at Leeds in 1959, and criminal cases in Birmingham in 1960. I was also made a member of the committee set up in 1959 under R. P. Morrison, Q.C., to inquire into the probation service, and we met over a two-year period before presenting our report. Shortly after this, in 1962, I was appointed to serve on the Advisory Council on the Treatment of Offenders. It further fell to my lot to be concerned as an Inspector, jointly in each case with a distinguished accountant, to inquire into the affairs of certain companies at the instigation of the Board of Trade. The inquiry of mine that attracted the most attention, however, called into question the conduct of the Metropolitan Police. This was the Woolf Inquiry which I was appointed to hold by the Home Secretary, to whom I reported in 1964.

Herman Woolf was a sixty-year-old artist who at the time of the following events was employed as a postal sorter. He lived alone in west London, being divorced from his wife, but they had remained on friendly terms, and indeed saw each other regularly about once a week. He was crossing Park Lane at 5.30 p.m. on 10 November 1962, when he was knocked down by a car. He fell on his back in the road, apparently unconscious. He was taken to the near-by St George's Hospital, where he was examined in the casualty department. He was then taken to the X-ray department, and while the photographs were being developed, was found sitting on the floor at the foot of the trolley on which he had been wheeled. The casualty officer, after inspecting the photographs, thought that the injuries were compara-

43

tively trivial. He certainly did not believe that the photographs disclosed any fracture of the skull.

It was admitted that Woolf had been in the habit of smoking marijuana cigarettes on occasion, and in fact he had two convictions for unlawful possession of Indian hemp. The police constable who had been sent to investigate the matter was handed what appeared to him to be a quantity of hemp which had been found by a nurse in the haversack that the injured man had been carrying at the time of the accident. When the doctor decided that his patient was fit to be handed to the police the officer arrested Woolf for being in unlawful possession of a dangerous drug, and Woolf was taken in a police van to West End Central police station, where he was examined at 8.20 p.m. by a police surgeon—who himself died before the Inquiry commenced—who concluded (in his Report Book) that Woolf was suffering from the effect of drugs but was fit to be detained. He was kept in a detention room and formally charged at 11.10 p.m.

He was visited and observed from time to time, and at about two o'clock the following afternoon was seen to be sitting on the floor, with his head slumped against a radiator. He could not be roused, and the police surgeon, summoned again, advised his removal back to the hospital, where he was taken by ambulance, arriving at about three o'clock. In view of his worsening condition, he was removed late that night to a hospital in Wimbledon, where he was found to have a fractured skull. Eleven days later, after two operations, he died. The cause of death was cerebral contusion and fracture of the skull, and at the subsequent inquest the verdict was that he had died from contusion of the brain following collision with a motor-car.

During all this time, up to his death, no one had informed Woolf's former wife that he was either in police custody or in hospital. This was despite a clear request to do so in the event of an accident, written on the first page of his diary, which was in his pocket at the time. Indeed, no one appears to have identified the unfortunate man with the Herman Woolf reported missing by different people on 15 and 16 November at Harrow Road police station.

Mrs Woolf came to suspect that her former husband might have suffered additional injury while in police custody. Moreover, she and two friends had asked the casualty officer at St George's Hospital whether the deceased's condition on his return there on 11 November was consistent with his having been involved in the accident the previous day. They claimed that he had replied, 'It would be tempting to assume that his condition was attributable to the accident.'

My principal task was to determine whether Woolf had been

subjected to violence or maltreatment while in police custody, and it was no part of my duty to judge the conduct of the hospital staff, although inevitably I had to satisfy myself about the medical facts. I came to the conclusion that Woolf did in fact suffer brain damage as a direct result of the accident, although it is fair to say that, according to the medical evidence, a competent doctor would not necessarily have been at fault in failing to interpret the X-ray photographs as so indicating. I was quite satisfied that his injuries were in no way caused by the police.

I was disturbed, however, by a number of matters revealed by the evidence in the course of the inquiry. Although the medical view was that the delay in returning Woolf to hospital was unlikely to have affected the eventual outcome, it was most unfortunate that his true condition was not recognized earlier. The police are not doctors, however, and they had reason to believe that Woolf was drugged or drunk. The most I felt able to say was that the experienced officer who acted as gaoler should at least have suspected that it was desirable for Woolf to be seen again much sooner by a doctor. I surmised that he might have been reluctant to enter the detention room frequently because of the stench—there was evidence of Woolf having fouled himself—and as a result of my recommendations, better cleansing facilities were later provided at the police station.

I was concerned too that Woolf's home had been searched without his consent, no warrant having been obtained. Indeed, the detective responsible admitted that in retrospect he doubted whether he had sufficient evidence that there was likely to be Indian hemp in the house to have enabled him to get a warrant. I suggested that new instructions should be given about searching prisoners' premises.

I was also dissatisfied with the circumstances in which Woolf had been charged. I formed the view that his condition was such that he was most unlikely to have been able to understand the nature of the charge, or the meaning of the customary caution, and I recommended that the practice of charging insensible or semi-insensible people should be discontinued.

Finally, I considered whether the missing-persons machinery, in the light of this case, was adequate. I was told that this was one of only three cases known at the time where a person reported missing had actually been in police custody and not been identified with the missing person. The failure in this case was due to error on the part of certain police officers at a time when they were under considerable pressure of work, but I am pleased to say that as a result of this serious mistake, new measures were, I understand, introduced to make a recurrence unlikely.

Doctors in the hectic conditions of a casualty department and policemen in a busy station in central London necessarily work under pressure, and one is entitled to have regard to this circumstance in forming judgments about their activities. I was pleased that the evidence in the Woolf case exonerated the police from any blame for the unfortunate man's death, but where the liberty of the subject is involved one cannot be too concerned for the individual, and it is only by pointing out failures in the system that one helps to prevent these failures becoming matters of everyday course.

The matter was of course of very considerable importance, since it called into question the conduct of the Metropolitan Police, and it attracted a great deal of publicity. I heard from seventy-eight witnesses over a period of three weeks, including all the police officers who were in any way concerned in the arrest and detention of Mr Woolf, the doctors and nurses who cared for him at the hospital, the pathologist who carried out the post-mortem examination, three of the witnesses of the road accident and a number of people who had known him well and were able to testify to his habits and mode of life. The only witness of importance whose evidence was not available was of course the police surgeon who had died, but even in his case I was able to inspect contemporary records made by him at the police station. Sixteen years later, I have no reason to differ from the conclusions I reached at the time.

To go back a little in time, one of the first cases I argued after taking silk created new law. It arose out of the legal work I did for the Royal Automobile Club, and concerned the extent of an employer's—in this case a company's—liability for the criminal acts of its servants. The timing was awkward from my point of view because I was due to sit as a Recorder, and wanted this somewhat complicated matter held over to a later date owing to my public duties. I therefore went to the Divisional Court to apply for a delay. I told the judges, Goddard, Hilbery and Jones, that an important matter of principle was involved, but Hilbery was rather scornful of the idea that there could be any questionable point of principle involved in this case, which was adjourned.

When I appeared again before the court, Mr Justice Slade had replaced Hilbery, but unfortunately not his attitude to my arguments. Slade had a habit of bobbing up and down in his chair and constantly adjusting his wig. 'Doggy' often appeared to be restless as he moved from side to side. It was obvious from their interventions that they differed in their views in this case. Suddenly, with all the authority of the Lord Chief Justice of England, Goddard barked: 'It's quite apparent that there is likely to be a disagreement in this court.

There's an important question of principle involved here. It must go to a full court of five.' He used almost the same form of words that I had first heard in the Sims case back in 1946, and I could have wished that Mr Justice Hilbery had been there to hear them.

The case was accordingly put over. Throughout I had been leading C. D. Brandreth, and the final hearing of James & Sons Ltd *v.* Smee was before Lord Goddard, Mr Justice Cassels, Mr Justice Lynskey, Mr Justice Slade and Mr Justice Parker (who eventually succeeded Goddard as Lord Chief Justice). Paul Wrightson appeared for the prosecution. A point of principle it certainly was, for this was an appeal by a company that had been fined only twenty shillings by justices for permitting a motor vehicle and trailer to be used with a defective braking system.

It was agreed that the driver and his assistant were at fault, and the company knew nothing about the matter. After lengthy argument the court reserved judgment. I felt confident that Lord Goddard supported me. 'I cannot see why', he had said on the first day, 'this prosecution was brought. The driver was convicted, and then the employer, who could not possibly have had anything to do with it, is charged. I can see justices in a case like this imposing a fine of sixpence.' I suspected that Slade would be against me.

Judgment was given nine days later. By a majority of four to one, Mr Justice Slade dissenting, the appeal was allowed. The outcome was that while the offence of using a defective motor vehicle is an absolute offence, that of permitting its use is not. For permitting an offence, there has to be knowledge of—or a deliberate closing of the eyes to—the circumstances. In the case of a company, someone for whom the company is criminally responsible must have permitted— as distinct from committed—the offence. The case is reported in the Law Reports and is cited to this day.

Another case that interested me very much took place in 1958 at Bristol Assizes before Mr Justice Gorman, for it raised an issue about which I feel strongly, and which came very much into focus during the recent trial of Jeremy Thorpe and others—namely, that an accused should not be obliged to give evidence. It is in my view rightly up to the prosecution to prove their case. Nevertheless, I believe also that it is wrong that counsel for the prosecution should not be able to comment on an accused's failure to give evidence. I had in fact been taught that even defence counsel may not explain why an accused has not done so, since if he were permitted to do so, he would himself be giving evidence. However, I am not sure to what extent that still applies in practice. In the famous Bodkin Adams trial Geoffrey Lawrence, K.C., was allowed by as meticulous a judge as Devlin to do so.

I recommend that prosecuting counsel should be entitled to comment on an accused's failure to go into the witness-box, that defence counsel should be entitled to offer as full an explanation as he may wish, and that the jury should be entitled, in arriving at their verdict, to take into consideration the fact that evidence has not been given. At the moment, although a judge undoubtedly has the right to comment, he necessarily does so in most circumspect terms. What he usually says is that the jury must consider only the evidence before them, and that they must not speculate on what an accused might have said had he given evidence. In the Thorpe case the judge actually told the jury—and perhaps correctly so—that they should treat the failure of all but one of the defendants to give evidence as neutral.

One of the problems, of course, is that when a man is being questioned by the police, as soon as the point arises when the officer has reasonable grounds to suspect that a person has committed an offence, he is bound to caution him. The man is then told that he need not say anything unless he wishes, but that anything he does say will be taken down in writing and may be given in evidence. Since the man has been told that he need say nothing, he cannot fairly be criticized for remaining silent. Personally, I would prefer the police to be confined to administering a caution at a later stage, as soon as a person is formally charged. It could then be permissible for comment to be made if he had refused to answer questions during the investigative stages.

I argued this issue in a paper I delivered at the third Commonwealth and Empire Law Conference in Sydney, Australia, in 1965, and I was a member of the Criminal Law Revision Committee whose eleventh report recommended something similar. But I am bound to say that this part of our report proved very controversial, and may in fact have been responsible for some of our non-contentious proposals not being implemented. The Criminal Bar as a whole were definitely not in sympathy with what we had in mind. I will only say that as a barrister who on the criminal (as distinct from the civil) side of his practice spent most of his working life defending people accused of crime, no one can have fought more strongly for the rights of these people, but I have come to think the balance too heavily weighted in favour of the suspect or accused.

The case before Gorman may be thought to argue against my recommendation that the prosecution should be entitled to comment on an accused's failure to give evidence, but in my experience examples of this kind are infrequent, and if they do arise a procedure could be formulated to ensure that any injustice could be avoided by application in the absence of the jury to the judge to rule that comment should not be permitted. On this particular occasion I had a client who refused to give evidence for very good reasons of his own that I could not explain to the jury. He was already serving several concurrent life sentences when he escaped while being transferred to Dartmoor from a prison in the North. While he was on the run a robbery occurred, and he was eventually accused, with others, of robbery with violence. The only evidence against him was that when he was found and arrested ten days after the robbery some scorched notes were in his possession. It was alleged that these notes had been scorched in the process of blowing the safe, and that they were part of the proceeds of the robbery.

He claimed to have been elsewhere at the time, but at the pre-trial conference he refused to tell me where in fact he had been. I pointed out to him that if he gave evidence he was bound to be asked that question, and that failure to reply would be virtually tantamount to admitting guilt. He told me that if he answered the question he would have to say who had been harbouring him, which he was not prepared to do. So he chose not to give evidence for what—if his story was true—would have been a reason that a jury might have accepted as being a satisfactory explanation of his failure to do so.

However, I could not tell the jury, not only because it would have meant revealing his dreadful criminal background, but because in practice, as I understood it, I was precluded from so doing. I did the next best thing. I gave examples of a number of hypothetical reasons —but not the real reason—that an innocent person might have for not giving evidence, but emphasizing that I was not suggesting that any of these was actually the real reason!

The case ended in a rather strange way. My client was convicted and sentenced to fourteen years' imprisonment consecutive to his concurrent life sentences. This was clearly an impossible punishment, because legally the sentence could never start, let alone end, for even if the man were released on licence, a life sentence never in fact expires during a man's lifetime. It took the Court of Criminal Appeal to rectify the matter when in upholding the conviction they altered the sentence to run concurrently.

I did not often appear at the Old Bailey, but two of my cases there attracted some interest. The first, in 1959, was the trial for murder of a young actor, Cavan John Malone, by Mr Justice Gorman.

I appeared for Cavan Malone, who when not out of town in a play, lived in his mother's flat in Chiswick. He was twenty-two at the time of these events. His widowed mother was a theatrical agent. Albert Mitchell, her secretary, also lived in the flat. She had a very good friend of over twenty years' acquaintance, a Mrs Momberg, who lived apart from her husband. 'We were like sisters', Mrs Malone said. On the afternoon in question the two women and the two men were watching television when the doorbell rang. Mitchell opened the door to Mrs Momberg's husband Jan, who appeared the worse for drink, and who burst in, presumably to see if his wife were there.

Jan Momberg was a large man, over six foot tall, who was described as 'big, tough and wiry'. There is no doubt that his sudden intrusion frightened the two women. There was considerable evidence that his wife had gone in fear of him, particularly when he was drunk, and that he had treated her badly, on occasions even violently. He would never treat her badly again, however, for within a very short time, before even he had removed his overcoat and gloves, he was lying dead on the floor with a number of stab wounds, including a savage injury to his throat. When the police arrived both the women were crying hysterically. A heavily blood-stained towel had been wrapped round the dead man's neck by Mrs Malone, and there was blood on his clothes and on the carpet. A neighbour had heard a crash followed by a woman's voice saying, 'You fool', and a man's voice saying, 'Shut up', and then a woman's scream.

The four people in the flat told much the same story, supporting Malone's statement to the police, in the course of which he said that the deceased had 'been a bastard for many years to his and my family and today he was very drunk and struck my mother'. Mrs Malone said that she had been hit across the left side of her face and with a clenched fist on the back of her head, and a doctor who examined her about an hour after the killing agreed that her injuries were consistent with that having happened. 'After being very abusive to my mother, myself and my friends', Malone's statement continued, 'he struck my mother and I grappled with him. He ran down the passage towards the bathroom and another bedroom. I grappled with him in the doorway of the bathroom and then ran back into the lounge, picked up a knife and then I ran back towards him. He was starting back towards the lounge. By grappling again, it forced him backwards because I was going so fast.

'It was one of those things, I suppose, where you face each other for a second or two, and then I made a pass at him with the knife because he was beginning to go for me. I, not fully realizing the extent to which I had hurt him, ran back into the lounge followed by him. We grappled again and I stabbed him. That's done it, but I want to tell the truth. He fell, and I asked—in between calming my mother down—my friend Al to call the police. . . . I didn't mean to do as much harm as

I did, but in the frenzy following seeing him hit my mother, I suppose I overdid things. I am very sorry.'

It was not difficult for a jury to feel sympathy for a pleasant and personable young man protecting his mother against assault from a violent, drunken bully, provided they believed his story and that of his witnesses, but he had to deal with the difficult evidence of the number of stab-wounds and their location. His statement implied that he had stabbed the dead man intentionally, although in self-defence, and I remember thinking perhaps he might be acquitted of murder but found guilty of manslaughter by reason of provocation. That was not what we were saying, however. Our defence was that, in trying to frighten away a stronger and bigger man, there had been an accident. The personality of Malone and the admirable way in which he gave his evidence clearly assisted him, for the jury accepted the defence and set him free.

The other case at the Bailey was what became known in certain sections of the popular Press as the 'Girl Guide Rape Case'. It thereby attracted more publicity than at first seemed warranted, but the instinct of the Press was fully justified, because the case had a dramatic sequel.

The trial began on 7 March 1961 before Mr Justice Hilbery, and the prosecution was in the hands of Mervyn Griffiths-Jones and John Mathew, the son of my predecessor as Director of Public Prosecutions, and incidentally senior Treasury Counsel while I held that office. My client, Arthur Albert Jones, was alleged to have raped an eleven-year-old girl to whom he had given a lift in his car. On 9 September 1960, dressed in her Guide uniform, the girl had gone by bicycle soon after seven o'clock in the evening to a meeting of the Girl Guides in Twickenham, and should have arrived home by ten. In fact she returned home in the early hours of the following morning, well over three hours late. She was in a dreadful condition. Her story was that after the meeting she had been stopped by a man who claimed to be a policeman, and who on the pretext of investigating the theft of bicycles persuaded her to leave her own machine by the roadside and to let him drive her home in his car. Instead he drove her some considerable distance into a lane where he attacked her sexually, almost strangling her in the process. He later dropped her not far from her home.

Jones had given his wife a very detailed account of where he was supposed to have been at the time of the rape. He subsequently admitted that this story was false, concocted to satisfy his wife, and he substituted a second alibi that was the basis of his defence. He had, he said, driven to Holland Park in London, where he had picked up a prostitute and gone back with her to her flat and later to a club. He had left her there and gone alone to a restaurant on the way home, arriving in the early hours of the morning because of trouble with his car.

The child in respect of whom the charge was brought was exceedingly fair to the accused. She was concerned to be very accurate, and she was one of the best witnesses I have ever come across. She described her attacker as having a scar down his right cheek. In fact, Jones had scars on both cheeks. I pointed out to her that, sitting as she had been in the front passenger seat, she would more readily have seen his left cheek. She agreed, but did not recall a scar there.

The judge was very much on the side of the prosecution. 'Let the accused come out of the dock', he ordered, 'so that the jury can see his right cheek.'

Somewhat abrasively, I requested that if my client was to be exhibited his left cheek also should be shown to the jury.

'Oh certainly', Hilbery said (somewhat reluctantly, I thought), 'but let his right cheek be shown to them first.'

He intervened again shortly afterwards. The witness had stated that her attacker had produced to her a wallet with a badge outside it that purported to show that he was a police constable. Such a wallet, with a badge inside, had been found in Jones's possession. I asked the girl to illustrate how the wallet had been shown to her, and she held it out, keeping it closed, so that the badge was not visible, giving at least the possibility that this was not the same wallet.

Hilbery called for the wallet. 'Are you sure', he asked, 'he did not show it to you like this?'—and he held it open with the badge in view.

'I'm sure', the girl replied.

Despite her fairness, Jones was convicted and sentenced to fourteen years' imprisonment, and had that been the end of the story it would not have been all that remarkable a case, horrible though it was. What the jury did not know, however, was that exactly seven weeks after the attack for which Jones was convicted another young girl, twelve-year-old Brenda Nash, had disappeared after attending a Girl Guide meeting in Heston, not very far from Twickenham. Two young friends had left her just after ten o'clock to walk the last quarter of a mile by herself to her house. She never reached home. It was not until 11 December that three boys found the girl's body at the edge of a common near Yateley in Hampshire. She was still in Guide uniform. Although she had not been raped, there were indications of attempted sexual assault. The poor child had been strangled.

The police had little doubt that the same person who had raped the

The author as a young barrister

Dingle Foot, Malcolm Wright and the author, on being granted silk (*Chapter 4*)

HRH the Duke of Edinburgh on a visit to Plymouth, with the author, Recorder there at that time (*Chapter 4*)

John and Janet Armstrong, with their daughter *(Chapter 4)*

John Poulson *(Chapter 5)*

The Tavern in the Town, Birmingham, after the IRA bombing *(Chapter 6)*

An Angry Brigade 'arsenal' found at Stoke Newington *(Chapter 6)*

Andrew Newton *(Chapter 7)*   Norman Scott *(Chapter 7)*   Scott's dog Rinka *(Chapter 7)*

Peter Hain reading a statement to the Press after his acquittal *(Chapter 7)*

Sir Gerald and Lady Nabarro after the former's retrial *(Chapter 7)*

Sir Gerald Nabarro after his first trial, together with his wife (centre) and Mrs Margaret Mason *(Chapter 7)*

Leila Khaled arriving in Amman *(Chapter 8)*

first girl had murdered the second. The girl who had survived her ordeal had led the police to believe that her assailant had almost certainly been driving a black Vauxhall, and two witnesses came forward who claimed to have seen such a car near Brenda's home on the night of her disappearance. It was in the course of interviewing over five thousand owners of such vehicles—for that was the number registered with Middlesex and Surrey County Councils alone—that the police came across Jones. They were still continuing their inquiries into the murder when it was decided on 30 December to arrest him for the first offence.

Jones was eventually charged in Wandsworth Prison with the murder of Brenda Nash, and thus it arose that only three months after his first trial he was back at the Old Bailey, this time before Mr Justice Sachs. Mervyn Griffiths-Jones again led for the Crown, but I had no part in the second trial. The case naturally attracted widespread publicity, but the point that most interested me was that Jones put forward almost the same alibi for the second occasion that he had advanced for the first. He had, he claimed, again driven to town, picked up a prostitute at Notting Hill Gate (down the road from Holland Park, for those who do not know London) and gone with her to a quiet road near by. He had been late in reaching home because his car had broken down.

Although, of course, no evidence about the earlier rape was introduced in the murder trial, it was essential for the prosecution to disprove almost the same alibi that had been rejected by a jury on a previous occasion, and for this purpose Jones was cross-examined in detail about another unspecified occasion when he had had to describe his whereabouts and had given an almost identical account of his movements to that which he had given in regard to the night of the alleged murder. The jury had taken nearly three hours to reach their decision in the first trial, but were out for only seven minutes on the second occasion before finding Jones guilty of murder. The admissibility of the cross-examination concerning the alibi evidence was tested in the Court of Criminal Appeal and the House of Lords, but the conviction was upheld by both courts.

Rape cases, of course, require the most careful handling, particularly in the cross-examination of the victim. The Jones trial brings to mind the time I defended a young man charged with raping a girl. They had been together in a public house, where they had been drinking, and then had sat down in a park by the side of a public footpath, where the alleged act had occurred. A policeman had come along and, to the young man's astonishment the girl had gone up to him and complained. I doubt whether anything further would have been heard of this had the youth not most foolishly given a false name and run away. He was caught and subsequently charged.

After the usual preliminary remarks, I asked the girl, 'Did you resist as hard as you could?'

'Yes', she replied.

'Did you scratch his face?'

'I tried to.'

'You could not manage that?'

'No.' It appeared that there were many other actions she could not manage.

'Did you kick him?'

'I tried to.'

'Did you do your best to keep your legs crossed?'

'Yes.'

'How long did this struggle go on?'

'About twenty minutes.'

'Then for about twenty minutes you were fighting as hard as you could?'

'Yes.'

'And at last he overcame your resistance?'

'Yes.'

'You sank back exhausted?'

'Yes.'

'He vented his lust on you?'

'Yes, that is quite right.'

They say that counsel should never ask a question if he does not know what the answer is likely to be, but I confess that the reply to my next question was entirely unexpected. Indeed, it was one of the most surprising answers I have ever elicited from a witness.

'What', I asked, 'was the first thing you remember saying to him after he finished raping you?'

'I said, "What's the time?" ' was her answer!

You will not be surprised to hear that there was an acquittal.

I suppose that one of the most famous murder cases in which I was involved was Regina v. John and Janet Armstrong, which was tried before Mr Justice Pilcher at Southampton Assizes (actually in Winchester Castle) for nine days in December 1956. It was in many ways a difficult and puzzling case. The accused were a young married couple, and the deceased was their 5½-month-old baby son. Although the possibility was briefly canvassed that their daughter Pamela—aged two years and nine months—might have given the baby the Seconal tablets that were proved to have caused his death, this really was too fantastic. It had to be that the parents had conspired to kill the child, or that one of them only was the guilty party. But which one? And whatever the truth, what could conceivably have been the motive? There was considerable evidence that they loved the baby, were even devoted to it. There was no evidence that they were in serious financial straits, and even if they were finding it difficult to make ends meet, surely that was not sufficient cause for one or both of them to take such extreme action? The wife alleged that while she was pregnant, the husband had said that he could not afford another child, but she also said that once the child was born he showed affection for it. Both denied that they had administered the Seconal accidentally, or for medicinal purposes—the father was a sick-bay attendant at Haslar Naval Hospital—or as an aid to sleep, and if this were correct there was no other conclusion possible but that the child was murdered.

A curious fact was that little Terence was not the first child of the Armstrongs who had died suddenly. Their second child, Phillip, had died unexpectedly of bronchial pneumonia when just over three months old, three weeks after they had taken a furnished house in Southsea. Terence died three weeks after they had moved into new accommodation in Gosport. It is absolutely necessary to emphasize, however, that there was never any suggestion at the trial that Phillip too had been murdered. It was expressly stated for the prosecution that this was not in any way alleged, and that the matter was only mentioned because it related to the parents' experience of dealing with sick children, and their knowledge of medical etiquette. I understand, in fact, that Phillip's body had been exhumed, and that no trace of poison was found.

As this was an alleged poisoning case, in accordance with the tradition obtaining at that time the Attorney-General led for the prosecution. Sir Reginald Manningham-Buller, Q.C., appeared with J. T. Molony, Q.C., and A. H. Bray. Malcolm Wright and Dudley Collard appeared for the husband. I appeared with J. H. Inskip for the wife.

The case could never have been set on its feet with any prospect of a conviction but for the statement made by the wife to the police over a year after the baby's death, when she had left the husband. She could hardly have expected that one consequence of this statement would be that she herself would have to answer to a charge of murder. On 24 July 1956, exactly a year and two days after the death of Terence, she applied unsuccessfully to the local magistrates for a legal separation from her husband on the grounds of his cruelty. She was granted custody of Pamela, and an order for maintenance. Following the proceedings, Inspector Gates—who had investigated the baby's death at the time—approached Janet Armstrong, as a result of which she made a statement that evening at Gosport police station. Although for purposes of the trial the statement was not evidence against her husband—the judge had incidentally refused separate trials for the two accused—it was of vital importance.

'I left my husband', she said in a long statement, 'because of his ill-treatment of me and his persistent accusations that if I had looked after Terry properly, he would still have been here. . . . Following the death of Terry I have been very upset and it has caused me a good deal of worry and concern. Every time I spoke to my husband, he said, "Let's forget it." '

The value to the police of her statement, however, lay in her admission that there was Seconal in the house, which she had previously denied on three earlier occasions. 'Shortly after my arrival . . . either on the first night or the day following, my husband told me there were some capsules and tablets in the cupboard of the dressing-table in the bedroom which he said he had brought from Haslar as he used them on night duty. They were contained in two bottles; the tablets were yellow and the capsules were pink in colour . . . I did not know what the pink ones were. They remained in the cupboard until some days after Terry's death, and when the police called at the house about Terry's death my husband told me to get rid of them as I would get the blame as well as him for Terry's death.

'I then took the capsules out of the bottle, I should say there were six or seven pink ones, and I threw them in the rubbish heap at the bottom of the garden. . . . I had thrown the capsules, tablets and bottles away before Inspector Gates called and made a search of the house. I asked my husband why I had to destroy them, and in addition to saying we would both be blamed for the death of Terence, he would get into trouble for bringing them out of the hospital. So on his advice I destroyed them.

'When Inspector Gates searched the house and asked me whether there were any tablets or capsules in the house, or if we had had any, I did not tell him about these as I did not want to get my husband into any trouble with the hospital and the baby's death. . . .

'The first time I learned that my baby had died from Seconal poisoning was when I was told by Detective-Superintendent Jones, and he described a Seconal capsule to me and asked if I had ever seen any in the house. I told him no at that interview because I did not know what Seconal capsules looked like, and although I knew about the pink capsules I had destroyed, I did not tell him because I wanted to help my husband. . . .

'After the Detective-Superintendent had left the house, my husband said words to the effect that it was a good job I had got rid of the capsules and tablets, because the baby had died of Seconal poisoning. The pink capsules I had destroyed were similar to those I saw produced at the inquest.'

A good part of the trial was taken up with medical and scientific evidence of the time at which the Seconal must have been given to the baby for it to have died when it did. At first it had been assumed that the drug had been in a gelatine casing, but it was eventually proved that the capsules were made of methyl cellulose. Because of the different time it would take for the drug to get into the system, according to whether there was a gelatine or a cellulose covering, the matter was of great importance.

The wife was in the house with the baby all the time, so she had ample opportunity to administer the drug. The husband, however, had been at work at his hospital during the morning, and returned for lunch at about 12.15 p.m., leaving for work again around 12.40 p.m. according to him, or just after one o'clock according to his wife. He was supposed to be back by one, and had to bicycle over four and a half miles, which would have taken him twenty minutes. He telephoned the doctor—presumably from his place of work—at 1.20, which would have been consistent with his leaving at about one o'clock.

Although I got an admission from Dr Keith Simpson that methyl cellulose capsules might vary in the time they took to operate, the consensus seemed to be that Seconal in a methyl cellulose capsule took maximum effect after forty to sixty minutes, and as the child died between 1.30 and 1.40 he was presumably given some Seconal between 12.30 and one o'clock, either just before the husband left for work or just after, according to whose evidence was believed. It was suggested that that might only have been the final dose, however, and that the baby might have been given a capsule as early as the night before.

Yet when, following a telephone call from the father shortly after midnight, Dr Buchanan had arrived the following morning to see Terence precisely five hours before the child's death—he was told it was unnecessary to come immediately—he found nothing wrong with the child. If he was right—and no one challenged his opinion—why had he been summoned? According to the father, the child had had a blue colour the night before, and had had such difficulty breathing that he had had to be given artificial respiration, yet neither parent reported this to the doctor, which the father at least might have been expected to have done. There had in any case been a remarkable recovery. Could this summons have been a deliberate ploy to prepare the doctor for the baby's death? The father was also criticized for waiting until he returned to the hospital after lunch before telephoning Dr Buchanan's partner, Dr Johnson, and again not mentioning, as he claimed, that he had had to give the child artificial respiration in the previous hour. One point that might have told against the wife was that she asked Dr Johnson, 'Will there be a post-mortem?' Why should she have asked this if she had no suspicion of murder? Yet it was conceded that she was genuinely distressed by the baby's death.

There were very real problems for the jury to resolve. John Armstrong did not appear to impress them favourably, but they seemed to sympathize with Janet. She was barely twenty, and I confess that I was somewhat apprehensive as to what sort of a witness she would make. However, she gave her evidence admirably, apart from one single outburst of temper after she had been hours in the witness-box. The prosecutor could not prove who had administered the final, fatal capsule, but it surely had to have been one of the accused. As I pointed out to the jury, however, they could not say, 'One or the other must have done it, and we cannot say which, so we had better say both.' I pleaded in Janet's favour that she was hardly likely to have made her damaging statement to the police a year after the murder if she had been guilty. Why on earth would she have wanted to reopen the matter?

There had been no suggestion either that her baby had been neglected. On the contrary, even eye-witnesses for the Crown had testified that Terence had been well cared for, and that she had produced the child to them with apparent love and pride. This was surely inconsistent with the attitude of a woman deliberately wanting to get rid of her child.

It will be recalled that Janet Armstrong had alleged in her statement to the police that she had been ill-treated by her husband, and the case, as far as she was concerned, may have turned on the admissions I was able to get from him when I questioned him. 'Your wife was frightened of you, wasn't she?' I asked rather sharply. 'What do you mean, sir?' he replied. 'Have you been violent to her?' 'I have struck her on occasions.' 'On how many occasions?' 'I think I have struck her about a dozen times.' He agreed that he had hit her on the first Christmas after their marriage. 'You take the view', I asked, 'that a man is entitled to strike his wife?' 'On certain occasions, yes', was the answer.

There was an almost noticeable change of atmosphere in the court. If husband and wife were jointly responsible, then it was surely the man of violence rather than his suffering spouse who was the guilty party. 'In July of this year', I pressed him, 'did you throw a knife at her?' 'I threw it into the fireplace.' 'Did the knife strike your wife?' 'It rebounded and hit her on the foot.'

My purpose in pursuing this line of questioning was to establish that my client had been frightened of her husband and had thrown away the tablets on his instructions because she was fearful of disobeying him, his case being that she had disposed of them of her own volition even before he had suggested she do so.

The jury retired at 3.15 p.m. to consider their verdict. They returned surprisingly after only forty-five minutes. They found John Armstrong guilty. They acquitted his wife. Armstrong was sentenced to death, but the sentence was commuted to one of life imprisonment.

PART TWO

CHAPTER 5

Director of Public Prosecutions

THE OFFER to me to become Director of Public Prosecutions was contained in a letter I received from the Home Secretary early in April 1964, in which he said how important it was that the office should be held by someone likely to enjoy the confidence of both the public and the police. I had served on two Home Office advisory councils and a Home Office committee, so I was not entirely a stranger to him. I assume, although I do not know for certain, that the Home Secretary would have consulted the Lord Chancellor and the Attorney-General before writing to me, for it is a curious fact that although the appointment of Director is made by the Home Secretary, the Director is actually responsible to the Attorney. Having been appointed by the Home Secretary, he is not responsible to him, nor paid by him, nor in any direct way concerned with him. He acts under what the relevant Act of Parliament refers to as 'the superintendence of the Attorney-General', and, under the Prosecution of Offences Regulations, is subject to the directions of the Attorney-General in all matters.

Whatever the circumstances of the offer—and, of course, I was flattered to receive it—it came right out of the blue. Not for one moment had it ever crossed my mind that I was in line for such an appointment. I admit that I had certain hopes about elevation to the Bench in due course. I had already been sent out twice as a Commissioner of Assize and was about to sit for the second time as Commissioner at the Central Criminal Court. While this did not necessarily presage a judgeship, either in the High Court or on the Bench at the Old Bailey, it was obviously a straw in the wind. I was probably in the running.

I was frankly very undecided at first as to how to respond to the offer. I did not wish to appear churlish or ungrateful, but no Director of Public Prosecutions had ever gone to the Bench, and in accepting the appointment I would almost certainly be sacrificing any chance of that. Acceptance of the post would also mean a substantial reduction in my income, for the salary of Director at that time was £6,185 per annum, considerably less than that of a High Court judge, and certainly less than I was earning currently. As in all important decisions of my life, I consulted my wife. I knew that all previous Directors had been knighted, and that was an honour I wanted for her more than myself, but that consideration did not weigh with us. She encouraged me to seize the opportunity. There were many judges, but only one Director of Public Prosecutions, but what finally convinced me to accept the challenge was that I felt that here was a job in which I could make some real impact. I had the advantage of practical experience in both civil and criminal work, as both prosecutor and defender. If my reputation at the Bar was more as a defender, that was no handicap in my eyes. Indeed, during my years as Director I found my experience as a defender a considerable advantage in carrying out my duties and making decisions. The office was one of national importance, and one in which I would have the opportunity to influence the standards of prosecution. If I exercised that influence rightly, I would be able to give substantial assistance to the administration of justice.

As Director of Public Prosecutions I would, of course, become a civil servant, with an entitlement to a pension on retirement, but since the pension would be calculated on years of service, it would in my case be very small. I was able, fortunately, to negotiate an arrangement whereby I would get the benefit of weighted years to the limit to which that could be done, and to be appointed for a fixed period. It was agreed that I could remain Director if I so wished until the age of seventy, provided I also remained physically and mentally fit. I was therefore entering into virtually a fifteen-year commitment. In fact, I retired after thirteen years in 1977, at my own choice, not, as one newspaper appeared to surmise, because the Attorney, Sam Silkin, was anxious for a complete reorganization of the Department, but because I felt I had done my stint, and because I was still at an age when I might again be appointed a Recorder if the Lord Chancellor saw fit. I never lost my zest for the courts, and I am never happier than when I sit now from time to time in that capacity.

I do not think in a book of this nature the reader will expect an exhaustive exposition of the history of the office of Director of Public Prosecutions, but I would refer anyone who may be interested in a fuller account to J. Ll. J. Edwards's admirable book *The Law Officers of the Crown* (Sweet and Maxwell). We have no Ministry of Justice in this country, where the legal machinery of government is divided between the Lord Chancellor's Department, the Law Officers'

Department and the Home Office. In broad terms, the Home Secretary has responsibility for the police forces of the country, and particularly for the Metropolitan Police in London, which is why Reginald Maudling resigned as Home Secretary when the police were inquiring into the part he might have played in the Poulson affair. The Home Secretary, of course, has political responsibilities, as have the two law officers, the Attorney-General and Solicitor-General. The specific function of the Attorney, as the Sovereign's first representative in the courts, is the control of prosecutions. As such, it is he if anyone who is the State's public prosecutor. The Director of Public Prosecutions has a non-political office, but the title is a misnomer. As my predecessor in the office stated, the Director 'can direct nobody and there are no public prosecutions in the ordinary sense of that term'.

Sir John Maule, Q.C., became the first Director in 1879 under the Prosecution of Offences Act of that year, and I was only the eighth holder of the position. At first the Director's duties were advisory, and the conduct of prosecutions was normally undertaken by the Treasury Solicitor, but in 1908 a new Prosecutions of Offences Act set up the Department as an entity, from which time it grew in size and importance.

Its establishment followed well over half a century of public controversy, and its functions are in the nature of a compromise of the type for which we in this country are noted, but which, like so many of our compromises, has the merit that on the whole, for some inexplicable reason, it works reasonably satisfactorily in practice.

In this connection I may perhaps be allowed to quote extracts from my Presidential address to the Medico-Legal Society in 1976, when I discussed the functions of the Department. It has always been a firmly entrenched principle in our Constitution that in England and Wales a private individual shall be entitled to institute criminal proceedings, and that in this sense the enforcement of law and order shall be in the hands of the ordinary citizen, and even today there are, strictly speaking, no public prosecutions. The police institute the great majority of prosecutions, but it may come as a surprise to the lay reader that in doing so a police officer, with one or two special exceptions, is not acting under any special powers, but is exercising the right of the private citizen. This right has been substantially curtailed by provisions that Parliament has made in various enactments, but subject to this, the private individual's right to institute criminal proceedings remains.

It may be noted that the Prosecution of Offences Act, under which I operated, expressly provides that nothing in it or in the earlier Acts shall preclude any person from instituting or carrying on any criminal proceedings, but the Director of Public Prosecutions may intervene and undertake at any stage the conduct of those proceedings.

In this respect England and Wales are unique, certainly as regards the United Kingdom. In Scotland all proceedings are instituted and conducted by Procurators Fiscal, Advocates Depute and the Crown Agent under the general supervision of the Lord Advocate, and in Northern Ireland there is a somewhat similar system of prosecution by the recently created Director of Public Prosecutions, and by Crown Solicitors and Crown Counsel responsible to the Attorney-General.

It was upon this subject of the enforcement of the criminal law being left to private individuals that prolonged controversy centred during the last century. The critics of this system and the advocates of a system of prosecuting by public prosecutors stressed that private individuals were often reluctant to assume the burden and incur the expense of a prosecution, and that there was danger of comparatively poor prosecutors being induced to compromise prosecutions and of being 'bought off' by wealthy defendants. These critics alleged also that prosecutions by private individuals led to proceedings being instituted in order to extort money, particularly in cases of alleged perjury, conspiracy and the keeping of gaming houses and brothels. It was also alleged that private prosecutions were often inadequately prepared and poorly presented. There was also a view expressed by the then Attorney-General, Sir Alexander Cockburn (later to be a Chief Justice), to a Select Committee as long ago as 1845, which in the light of recent public discussion and pronouncements on our current prosecuting procedures has a topical echo. He said 'I think it is of the last importance that policemen should be kept strictly to their function as policemen, as persons to apprehend and having custody of prisoners and not as persons who are to mix themselves up in the conduct of a prosecution whereby they acquire a bias infinitely stronger than that which must, under any circumstances, naturally attach itself to their evidence.' On the other hand, there was strong objection voiced to taking away the right of prosecution from private individuals on the ground that it would place inordinate power in the hands of the executive in respect of the enforcement of criminal law. It was further contended by the supporters that the retention of the right to private prosecution could be of value in stimulating a public prosecutor into action if and when he was failing in his duty. The controversy led to reports by commissioners on the criminal law and the appointment of a commission, of select committees and I think one departmental committee at various times between 1833 and 1884. Further, there were three privately sponsored Bills, in 1854, 1870 and 1871 respectively, none of which reached the statute book.

In 1884 controversy again arose because Sir Augustus Stephenson—who had succeeded Sir John Maule as Director the previous year—had declined to prosecute two alleged blackmailers who were subsequently prosecuted to conviction by a private prosecutor, and who received substantial sentences. This led to yet another committee, following which the duties of Director of Public Prosecutions and Treasury Solicitor were combined in the one person, Sir Augustus Stephenson, until 1894 and his successor Sir Hamilton Cuffe (later Lord Desart) until 1908, when the modern Department was created with Sir Charles Mathews as its Director. (For the record he served until 1920, when he was succeeded by Sir Archibald Bodkin, who in turn was replaced by Sir Edward Tindal Atkinson in 1930. He was followed by my immediate predecessor in office, Sir Theobald Mathew, in 1944.)

During the period 1884 to 1908 there was constant judicial and other criticism of the policies of the Director, and many criticisms were levelled—and continue to be levelled—at the Department, particularly in matters relating to the police. In those days the Director of Public Prosecutions habitually made an annual report, which was laid before Parliament, and while he had, it is true, often to wait some twelve months before he could retaliate to the criticisms made of him, at least he then had the opportunity of doing so—and he was able to do so in a robust and no uncertain fashion. Today the practice is no longer in use. No longer is there any report made to Parliament: the Director of today has to suffer any criticism in silence.

As I have explained, the Director of Public Prosecutions operates under the Prosecution of Offences Act of 1908, together with the earlier Acts cited with it, but also under the Regulations made thereunder, the current Regulations being the Prosecution of Offences Regulations, 1978. Under the Regulations he first of all has to institute, undertake and carry on certain categories of offences which are there specified. In addition, Chief Constables have to report to him certain categories of offences which broadly speaking cover the more serious of the indictable offences in order to give him the opportunity, first of deciding whether proceedings should be taken or continued, as the case may be, and secondly as to whether he should intervene and assume reponsibility for prosecution or whether he should leave it to the police together with their legal advisers to conduct the prosecution themselves.

The second of the Regulations makes a provision that I regard as one of the Director's most important functions. It gives him the statutory duty to give advice, 'whether on application or on his own initiative, to Government Departments, Clerks to Justices, Chief Officers of Police and to such other persons as he may think right in any criminal matter which appears to him to be of importance or difficulty', which means that he is in perhaps the fortunate position of being entitled to give gratuitous advice, although there is no provision for anyone having to follow this advice after it is given! This underlines the importance of this part of the Director's functions, for it is the quality of the advice given by the Department and the extent to which it merits respect and is followed that enables the Director of the day to affect the general standard of the enforcement of the criminal law throughout England and Wales.

There has arisen an increasing number of offences in which, by statute, prosecution requires the consent of the Director (or in other instances of the Attorney-General) before proceedings may be instituted. There were during my time fifty-nine Acts of Parliament making provision of this sort. Some provided for the Director's consent alone, and others required the Attorney-General's consent unless the proceedings were brought by or on behalf of the Director. Yet again, there were some, though fewer, other Acts requiring the consent of the Minister of some particular Department especially concerned with the enforcement of the Act unless the prosecution was by or on behalf of the Director.

The underlying basis of these provisions is, I think (in so far as it is ever safe to speculate as to the intentions of Parliament), that the offences are of such a nature that vexatious or oppressive prosecutions are thought to be more likely if prosecutions are left in the hands of private prosecutors. The Theft Act of 1968, for example, requires the Director's consent to criminal proceedings by one spouse against the other for the alleged damage to, or theft of property allegedly belonging to, the prosecuting spouse. In other instances the nature of the offence and the widely differing opinions with regard to its gravity may be thought to make it peculiarly likely to produce a lack of uniformity in prosecuting policy if prosecutions are left in the hands of individuals or prosecuting authorities throughout the country, and possibly also that this may lead on occasions to oppressive prosecutions. An example of this may be found in Section 8 of the Sexual Offences Act, 1967, which requires the Director's consent in prosecutions for homosexual offences when either of the parties is under twenty-one.

A difficult duty was further placed upon the Director by Section 49 of the Police Act, 1964, which was enacted within three months of my assuming office, in an attempt to satisfy the public that cases against police officers were independently and impartially considered and prosecuted where the evidence was adequate. Whenever a complaint is made by a member of the public against a police officer of any particular force, it is mandatory under that section for the Chief Constable of that force to cause an investigation to be made; and, upon getting a report, unless he is satisfied on the report that no criminal offence has been committed—and not just if he is satisfied that there is insufficient evidence, which is a matter for the Director—he is required to transmit the report to the Director of Public Prosecutions.

Many of the complaints do not allege any criminal offence but are entirely concerned with disciplinary matters that are entirely questions for the Chief Constable. Where, however, criminal offences are alleged, it is a matter which is to be referred to the Department.

The complaints received by my Department ranged from alleged traffic violations to grave offences, such as allegations of perjury, corruption, conspiracy to pervert the course of justice and assaults on suspects and prisoners. As to these grave types of offence, it is only fair to the police to say that in a substantial proportion we found that the complaint was completely unfounded. On the other hand, such offences did occur, and it was vitally important where there was adequate evidence that prosecutions should follow. The administration of the criminal law must depend on the integrity of the police, and if this is eroded, the whole basis of the enforcement of the criminal law is undermined and may crumble.

It is obvious that the intention of the legislature—and this is of prime importance—is that the public shall if possible be satisfied that complaints of this sort are independently and fairly investigated, and that prosecutions are instituted where the evidence warrants proceedings, notwithstanding that the person concerned is a police officer, just as they would be if he were a civilian. There must be no question of prosecution being avoided because it might prove embarrassing to the police, whether generally or in the particular Force concerned. It is also vitally important that police officers should be satisfied that the matter is independently and impartially investigated so far as they are concerned, and that they are not being prosecuted because they are police officers on evidence which in the case of a civilian would be regarded as insufficient, merely to avoid possible criticism or to placate some complainant. Nothing, I need hardly stress, could be worse than this in its effect on the morale of the police, who are naturally sensitive to what they consider to be unwarranted complaints.

A further difficulty in this case is that a large number—though by no means all—of the complaints that are referred to the Department are from crooks, often with bad criminal records. They are people upon whose word one would hesitate to rely, and coming from such a source the complaint must be approached with special caution; ordinarily action is not justified unless there is some corroboration in a material particular to be found in the evidence or circumstances. On the other hand, you cannot write off these complaints upon the basis that this is a crook whom no one will believe anyway, because invariably, if it happens in a particular case to be a 'true bill', it is just that type of person who is likely to be the victim of improper conduct by an evilly intentioned officer. If he is going to plant incriminating evidence on a suspect, or use violence in order to obtain a confession, he is likely to do this in relation to a person who has a bad record, and whom he thinks on this account is unlikely to be believed.

So it is that, judging the case as best one can upon paper, and bearing in mind that it is not the Director's province to endeavour to try it but merely to see whether there is sufficient evidence properly to put a man upon his trial—and a man should not be put upon his trial merely upon suspicion, or upon what I may call a 'paper' case— one has to see whether there is a sufficiently substantial case to merit the officer being put upon his trial, with all that that must inevitably entail for him. A police officer is entitled to the same protection against unwarranted prosecution on insufficient evidence, no more and no less, as any other person.

I always regarded myself as a sort of Criminal Ombudsman, whose job it was to try to ensure that all those who should be prosecuted upon adequate evidence were prosecuted without fear or favour, but equally that people should not be oppressively prosecuted in circum-stances and upon evidence that did not warrant criminal proceedings being taken. The public interest was paramount. There could be no circumstances, for example, in which a case of murder would not have been prosecuted on adequate evidence, and I would never have refused to prosecute someone simply because of the position he held. I am often asked whether it was my policy to take into consideration the circumstances of a defendant, and the effect of a prosecution on his family. The answer is yes in rare circumstances where the offence was not of a very grave nature; where medical evidence, for example, showed that a defendant would be unable to stand trial without risk to his life. Our acid test about launching proceedings was whether, on the evidence before us, if that evidence stood up in court and was not eroded, there was in our considered opinion a likelihood that a conviction would result.

In this context I recommend the words of the Attorney-General, Sir Hartley Shawcross (as he then was), in the House of Commons on 29 January 1951, when he said: 'It has never been the rule in this country—I hope it never will be—that suspected criminal offences must automatically be the subject of prosecution. Indeed, the very first regulations under which the Director of Public Prosecutions worked provided that he should intervene to prosecute, among other cases: "wherever it appears that the offence or the circumstances of its commission is or are of such a character that a prosecution in respect thereof is required in the public interest".' That, said Sir Hartley, was still the dominant consideration, and he continued: 'So, under the tradition of our criminal law the position is that the Attorney-General and the Director of Public Prosecutions only intervene to direct a prosecution when they consider it in the public interest so to do.'

So it is that the essential question is whether in all the circumstances a prosecution is required in the public interest. One cannot state any one general all-embracing principle upon which difficult decisions have to be made. One has to look at all the facts and circumstances of each case. There must, however, be some general considerations to be taken into account in making a decision, while guarding against these becoming too inflexible. Among these is the question whether a prosecution would in all the circumstances be oppressive, perhaps because of the staleness of the alleged offence or because the real vice at which the particular provision of the criminal law was aimed had not been achieved, although the letter rather than the spirit of the enactment had been contravened.

Perhaps the most important general consideration that I may refer to is certainty of conviction. This can never be guaranteed. The enforcement of criminal law would clearly be brought into disrepute if there were an inordinate number of unsuccessful prosecutions, and the public interest would certainly not be served thereby. This does not mean that every prosecution that is brought must succeed, or else that it should not have been brought. Obviously the reliability of the evidence when tested by cross-examination may be eroded, or a different slant put upon it when the evidence for the defence is given, and in the end a court may quite properly say that the prosecution has failed to satisfy it beyond reasonable doubt of the guilt of the accused, and hence acquit. This, however, does not mean that the prosecution should never have been brought.

In my view a prosecuting authority should only prosecute when, at the time when the decision has to be made, in its view the evidence, if it stands up, will establish the guilt of the accused. This decision

71

has to be taken, so far as the Department is concerned, without the opportunity of seeing or hearing the witnesses, and is based upon the statements of the witnesses, the report of the police which accompanies them and the assessment therein of the reliability or otherwise of the witnesses' evidence. Only if the prosecuting authority's view of the evidence at that stage is that there is a reasonable prospect of conviction, can a prosecution be warranted. A prosecuting authority should not, in my view, institute proceedings upon evidence that it believes is insufficient, albeit suspicious, to establish the case. A prosecutor's main duty is to prosecute, and to endeavour to see that the case is properly prepared or is properly and firmly but fairly presented, and that guilty people are if possible brought to justice. Side by side with this, he has a duty to endeavour to see that no innocent person is convicted, or even charged.

I did not regard myself as a dictator, and I rarely interfered with the ordinary course of events. An example of the sort of circumstances in which I felt compelled to intervene was the case of a young boy charged with theft. For some reason proceedings had been continuing for a grossly excessive time, and although I was told that the boy intended to plead guilty, I felt that it was monstrous that this matter should have been hanging over his head for so long a period. I therefore took over the case and dropped it on the grounds of unreasonable delay.

I should like to dispel once and for all the belief in some quarters that the Director of Public Prosecutions is specially subject to political direction. This just is not true—at least, as far as I was concerned during my stewardship. Very shortly after my appointment, a minor motoring collision occurred in which a vehicle driven by HRH Prince Philip, the Duke of Edinburgh, was involved. This was not, of course, the sort of matter that would normally have been dealt with by me, but because of the Duke's position, the case was referred to me by the police. Prince Philip had made it known that he wished to co-operate in the investigation of the accident by the police, and statements were taken from both him and the other driver—in each case under caution—rendering each statement admissible in evidence in the event of proceedings being taken against the person who had made it.

As it happened, after examining the evidence it was quite clear to me, and to counsel (whose opinion I took, and who so advised) that while it showed that the other driver (who in due course was prosecuted and convicted) was at fault, it would not support any proceedings against Prince Philip. However, the important fact is that the case was considered and decided irrespective of the eminence of the person involved, and that no pressure whatever was brought to bear on me.

When Ramsay MacDonald's government fell in 1924, following an alleged attempt to influence the Attorney and Director for political purposes to withdraw a prosecution, Stanley Baldwin ordered that under no circumstances was political pressure to be exerted in future, and that was certainly the position as I found it. I was responsible to four different Attorneys—Hobson, Elwyn Jones, Rawlinson and Silkin, two Conservative and two Labour—and never once was any pressure put on me to exercise my discretion in a particular way, not even when the activities of the Home Secretary himself came under review. Obviously, in sensitive cases where I had to consider where the public interest lay, it was my duty to keep the Attorney-General informed—secrets cases, for example, or those involving foreign nationals, such as Leila Khaled, to which I will refer later—and on such occasions I myself might seek his advice, but never his instructions, though under the Regulations he could have given instructions.

It is true that the Director is responsible to the Attorney-General, who is a politician and a member of and legal adviser to the Government, but that part of the Attorney's functions that consists of the overall supervision and control of the enforcement of the criminal law is entirely outside the political field, and is of a quasi-judicial nature. No one from the Cabinet downwards can give the Attorney any directions as to the bringing or not bringing of criminal proceedings in any particular case. Similarly, subject only to the Attorney's power to give the Director directions in this limited quasi-judicial field, no one is entitled to give him any directions or to seek to influence him as to the bringing or not bringing of criminal proceedings. This does not, of course, mean that an Attorney may not consult a department as to the likely effect—for example, the Foreign Office as to the effect on our relations with some foreign country—if criminal proceedings are or are not brought, as the case may be. This he would certainly be entitled to do before deciding whether such proceedings would be in the public interest. The ultimate decision, however, must be the Attorney's alone, and uninfluenced.

It was no easy task for me to follow a man of Sir Theobald Mathew's stature. He came from a distinguished legal family. His grandfather had been a Lord of Appeal, and his father a silk. He himself had been called to the Bar, but had practised for sixteen years as a solicitor before joining the Home Office. He had been Director continuously since before the end of the Second World War during a time of radical changes in the structure of society, and a time too of vastly increased work for the Department. He had been able successfully to keep his finger on the pulse of public opinion, without which no Director can function efficiently, for the law is not static. There is no point in prosecuting cases if the climate of opinion is such that no jury is likely to convict. The Director, like a judge, must move with the times, and keep abreast of current ideas concerning crime and punishment, economic and social theories and literary and artistic values. There have been important changes in the law during this century, including the abolition of hanging for murder and of flogging; also in the law concerning homosexuality and obscenity. There have been changes in the qualifications for jurors. If Mathew had continued to operate in the style of his predecessors I suspect that he would not have enjoyed the confidence of the public, and I was aware that I too needed to be alive to new thinking and to move with the times.

Mathew had a reputation as a first-rate administrator. He died in February 1964, and I succeeded him the following May. All the staff I inherited had been introduced by him to the Department, which was divided into divisions on a geographical basis, one for the Metropolitan area and others for the rest of the country. I had a Deputy Director, and there were Assistant Directors in charge of each division, under whom operated a professional officer known as the Assistant Solicitor and the Senior Legal Assistants and Legal Assistants. The main changes in my time were the setting up of two new divisions, one concerned with police matters and one with company frauds. Consequent on these new creations the Assistant Solicitors were put in charge of the divisions and Assistant Directors were upgraded and reduced in number to two, to have overall responsibility, one for London and one for the provinces.

The new structure was partly a response to the increasingly subtle methods of the modern criminal, particularly in the area of what my successor, Sir Thomas Hetherington, has referred to as 'company frauds and the other white-collar offences . . . the national and international conspiracies involving violent crime as well as the more sophisticated financial swindles'. It was also a response to the Police Act of 1964. In my first full calendar year there were nearly 1,200 references under the Police Act—an amazing additional work-load when it is remembered that only forty years earlier this was not far short of the sum total of all cases dealt with in a similar period by the Department. It is interesting to note that in my last completed year as Director the Department considered no fewer than 17,253 cases. Perhaps this says something about modern inflation! Incidentally, of these cases, proceedings were brought by us in 3,125 instances, involving 12,591 charges and 4,573 persons—a number of the remaining cases being left to the police or other authority to prosecute.

An additional work-load arose in 1973, when the principle of criminal bankruptcy was entrenched in the law, and a judge was empowered to order a convicted criminal to compensate his victim, where there was a loss of £15,000 or more. All such criminal bankruptcy orders were to be referred to the Director of Public Prosecutions, whose duty it was to decide whether the public interest required that the matter should be pursued at public expense, in which case the Director became the petitioner in bankruptcy proceedings. Obviously there was only point if there were some reasonable prospect of getting hold of money the criminal may have salted away, and this required careful investigation. The problem was that we had very inadequate accommodation in Buckingham Gate for our existing people, with as many as three professional officers in one room, and although in anticipation of these extra duties I had earmarked specialist staff, there was nowhere to put them. Because our activities were necessarily conducted amid strict security, we could not easily share accommodation.

Looking back at the matter, I am astonished at the lengths to which I went to secure more space for my Department. When the Home Office told me that the Home Secretary was proposing to make an order bringing in the criminal bankruptcy legislation as authorized by Act of Parliament, I said flatly that I could not undertake the additional work adequately in the existing building. In 1975 we were moved to Queen Anne's Gate, and even then I found the lady messengers sitting on chairs at the end of a corridor, with no room of their own, not even a window, before I did something about it.

I am often asked by members of the public how the Department operated. The answer is much like any other business, albeit within the framework of strict security. Some people think that I spent my entire day poring over pornographic books and pictures, that I was some sort of Director of Public Pornography. Although, of course, I did my duties in this respect, my time was not spent disproportionately in this manner. When a case came, for example, to the Department from the police it went to the appropriate division, and the officer in charge would allocate it to one of the Legal Assistants or Senior Legal Assistants, who would study it, prepare some written note, further consult the police as necessary, then refer back to the head of his division. In the majority of cases it was at that level that a decision was taken regarding proceedings, and if they were to be launched, whether the Department should undertake their conduct or whether this should be left to the police. It would not have been possible for me and the Deputy Director to see, let alone consider, every such case, and by and large it was left to the Assistant Solicitors to refer to us such cases as they thought were important—all very serious cases, such as treason and murder, all sensitive cases, particularly those likely to blow up in Parliament or on which it was advisable to consult the Attorney-General, all cases involving important questions of policy, and such like.

A great deal of our time was, as I have said, occupied in considering complaints against the police, and a number of prosecutions followed. There are those who would argue that our whole effort should be directed against the criminal fraternity, and that we should not weaken the resolution of the police by subjecting them to microscopic scrutiny, especially when such scrutiny is often at the instigation of known crooks. This is, however, something of an unfashionable view at a time when authority commands less and less respect. Many people seem nowadays to be on the side of the criminal. There is a tendency in my view to accept too readily excuses for the commission of crime, and to regard it as a disease requiring treatment rather than punishment. Everything is urged by way of excuse—that the criminal has come from a broken home, that his mental development has been totally retarded, that he has got in with bad associates, and so on. While not suggesting that any of these factors is unimportant, or should not be taken into consideration, I feel we are in danger of accepting excuses too readily. It is also a fact that the criminal is often glamorized in fiction and on the screen. It is an exaggeration, of course, to say that the criminal has become the hero and the policeman the villain, but there do seem to be some people with an apparent vested interest in encouraging such a belief.

A 'bent copper' is a very serious threat to our system of law and order, but the public should realize that a healthy police force is their surest protection, and should not always jump to the conclusion that just because a complaint is laid, it must have substance in fact. However, criminal behaviour by a policeman is totally unacceptable.

One case in particular caused me some concern, not least because of the way it came to our attention. It resulted in the trial and conviction in 1971 of two police officers, Detective-Inspector Bernard Robson and Detective-Sergeant Gordon Harris, on charges of corruption, and raised in issue the value of taped evidence. It all stemmed from an inquiry by a national newspaper when a man informed a reporter that he was being blackmailed by police officers who were threatening to produce manufactured evidence against him, and to charge him with a criminal offence unless he paid them money. This was, of course, a most serious allegation, and instead of reporting the facts immediately to the police, or direct to my Department, the newspaper first carried out its own investigation, and—with singular indiscretion, in my opinion—blazoned the story for all to read. They did this, moreover, the very day after they had given copies of their evidence to the police, and before any police investigation could even be started, let alone concluded, or any charge preferred.

Readers unfamiliar with this case, or who have forgotten it, may care to guess the identity of the newpaper in question. It was in fact *The Times*, and they got hold of the story in quite an amusing way. They actually advertised for a retired burglar—not, I hasten to say, in their own columns. It appears that the newspaper was preparing an article on how to protect one's home from thieves looking for antiques—an altogether admirable exercise—and who better, they thought, to advise them than someone who had actually been in the business of stealing from houses? Among about fifteen replies there was one from a person who claimed to have the right qualifications, and it was planned to rent a house and get him to burgle it.

But that is another story. What we became concerned with was that a person who had made contact with the newspaper in these circumstances introduced three young men to the reporter, to whom they made allegations about bribery and corruption in the police force. One of the men was 23-year-old Michael Perry, and he specifically mentioned the two officers who then became the target of the newspaper's investigation, which extended over a period of a month.

The two journalists principally involved made use of modern techniques. For example, they arranged for a microphone and recorder to be connected to the telephone in the house where Perry was staying with his mother. A microphone was also placed under the dashboard of his car, with a recorder in the boot, to make a permanent record of a meeting that it was hoped to arrange between Perry and one of the police officers. Perry himself was fitted with a throat radio microphone behind his shirt which was connected to a sound recorder in a near-by car, and another recorder was placed in his overcoat pocket. On another occasion, at a meeting in the Army and Navy Stores between Perry and Robson, a journalist was stationed near by with a recorder in his holdall. An earlier meeting between Perry and the two officers was observed by reporters, one of whom used a ciné-camera with a zoom lens. Perry was also provided with marked money.

Although it is fair to say that none of the marked money was ever traced back to the two accused men, the evidence of the tape recordings was damning if admissible in a court of law, and indeed a large part of the subsequent trial was devoted to this issue. For two weeks there was a trial within a trial, involving distinguished counsel (including James Comyn, Q.C., and Israel Finestein, Q.C., for Robson; and Roger Frisby, Q.C., for Harris). A great attack was made on the tapes and there was considerable difference of opinion between experts as to their originality and authenticity. The defence claimed that noises on the tapes indicated interference. When, however, Mr Justice Sebag Shaw decided to admit them—for reasons he gave after the trial—the conviction was almost inevitable. Robson, a senior Scotland Yard officer, was sent to prison for seven years, and Harris for six.

Conviction of the officers was made more difficult by the way *The Times* behaved. The newspaper eventually brought their evidence to the police, but whether they were right to test it first is a matter of opinion. I am quite convinced, however, that they were wrong to publish it at the time. If the police had ignored it, no one could have quarrelled with the newspaper publicizing it. Instead *The Times* immediately splashed it on both the front and centre pages, which had the result of forewarning the suspects of the evidence against them.

Investigative journalism no doubt has its proper place in the scheme of things. It is a growing phenomenon in all the media, and often it serves a very useful purpose, but it is not a substitute for the law. Newspapers should not seek to assume the function of the police unless they have good cause to believe that the latter are falling down on the job. If someone believes he has been swindled he should go to the police, who have a duty to investigate, rather than to a newspaper, whose main interest is to increase circulation. The police have machinery for investigation, and are paid to investigate.

In this particular instance, apart from advertising to the police officers the matters they might be called upon to answer, the publicity could have resulted in a difficult position with regard to the trial. Indeed, had it not been for the considerable delay in bringing the case to trial, partly to allow time for the examination of the tapes by experts for both the prosecution and the defence, it might have been very difficult after such publicity to find an unprejudiced jury.

Be that as it may, the case of Robson and Harris raised the important question of the reliability of tapes. Tapes will be of doubtful value if every time they are used in evidence their authenticity may be challenged. If experts are going to dispute whether a tape is the unaltered original, or whether it has been interfered with, tapes are not the positive proof of what was said which they might appear to be. It has been widely advocated recently that all statements made to the police should be recorded, but this is not necessarily the panacea that some people suggest. There are obvious advantages in recording a statement, but one of the alleged advantages is certainly not borne out by the case of the two police officers. While there remains the possibility of tampering with a tape, it is open to as much question as a 'verbal'. Juries do not always believe what an accused is alleged to have said to the police when it is disputed, and it is by no means certain that they will give greater credence to a tape recording.

In any case, it is very often what a person says to the police when first challenged that may be most important. It may be practical to record an interview in a police station, but if a policeman on the beat stops someone whom he believes to be acting suspiciously at two o'clock in the morning, must he carry a miniature recorder in his buttonhole? Will it otherwise be claimed that his evidence is unreliable because it is unrecorded, in which case one can take notice of nothing said before reaching the police station? I am very concerned lest by introducing tape recordings wherever possible we create different classes of evidence giving rise to different credibility.

It goes without saying that corruption in the police force is a matter of the most serious concern to the community. If we cannot place our trust in the very people whom we employ to maintain law and order, the rule of law will be set at naught and anarchy will ensue. Corruption in public life is also a dreadful cancer that needs to be cut out of the system. It is this that gave such importance to the series of prosecutions in my time as Director associated with the name of John Garlick Llewellyn Poulson.

When his name first came to public notice, Poulson, although not himself a qualified architect, was head of one of the largest architects' practices in Europe, with offices in Pontefract (where he lived), London, Middlesbrough, Edinburgh, Lagos and Beirut. He was a well-known figure in Yorkshire, where he had interests in politics— he supported the National Liberal Party—in sport and in the Methodist Church. His main interest was his business, of which—and before he became involved in corruption—he had every right to be proud, for he built it up from modest beginnings. He had had the idea to cut costs by providing a comprehensive service. He made it unnecessary to consult architects, engineers and surveyors separately. He employed experts in all these fields, thereby saving his clients considerable time and trouble. This perhaps, more than anything else, was the secret of his success.

On 11 February 1974, after a widely publicized trial that lasted over fifty working days, Poulson and William George Pottinger were found guilty of conspiracy to corrupt, and of six charges of corruption. Pottinger was a very senior civil servant. On 4 March 1974 Poulson and Ernest George Braithwaite pleaded guilty to six charges of corruption. Braithwaite had been Secretary of a Regional Hospital Board. On 15 March 1974 Poulson and Graham Tunbridge each pleaded guilty to a charge of conspiring together to commit corruption, and to five substantive charges of corruption. Tunbridge was employed by the British Transport Commission. On 24 April 1974 Andrew Wilsher Cunningham and Thomas Daniel Smith were tried on a number of similar charges involving Poulson in another case that attracted great attention. Cunningham was probably the most powerful man in County Durham, and wielded immense influence in local government. Smith—popularly known as T. Dan Smith— was an immensely influential figure in regional and local government in the north-east of England, notably in Newcastle. At his trial with Tunbridge, Poulson had asked for two offences to be taken into consideration, in relation to both Maurice Vincent Kelly and William Henry Sales. In April 1974 Kelly pleaded guilty to one count of conspiracy with Poulson and six counts of corruptly receiving bribes. In May 1974 Sales was convicted on five counts charging corruption and involving Poulson. Both Kelly and Sales were employed by the National Coal Board.

The common denominator in this immensely complicated series of trials, involving the Civil Service, local authorities and nationalized industries and services, was John Poulson himself. In the Tunbridge case one of the counts on which Poulson was convicted was that of corruptly giving a cheque for £200 as an inducement to or reward for Tunbridge assisting or showing favour to him in relation to the proposed redevelopment of Cannon Street Station in London. An inducement mentioned in one of the charges concerning Braithwaite was the free use of certain premises. Kelly admitted that Poulson had paid for four separate holidays for him, two in England and one each in France and Spain, and that he had provided him with a motor-car. Sales admitted accepting carpets and curtains and bottles of port and champagne.

These examples—some, of course, comparatively trivial—give the flavour of a number of Poulson's activities. He claimed, doubtless with some justification, that he was by nature a generous man given to charitable actions, although many felt that his generosity was meant to yield dividends.

It is worth looking slightly more closely at his relationships with

Pottinger, and with Cunningham and Smith. The substantive charges on which Poulson and Pottinger were convicted alleged that Poulson had made gifts to Pottinger, or caused gifts to be made to him, to secure favours in connection with building projects in Scotland. Pottinger was at the relevant times either Under-Secretary in the Scottish Development Office in charge of planning in the Highlands, Assistant Under-Secretary of State at Whitehall concerned with Scottish Office affairs, or working at the Department of Agriculture and Fisheries for Scotland. Specifically, the gifts were a suit and overcoat value £167 14s. 0d., two holidays value £1,753 4s. 3d., a Rover car or the use of such a car, and two cheques totalling £3,650. These charges were of a representative character, because there was evidence of other gifts having been made also, which were covered in general terms by the conspiracy count. It was not sought to relate any particular gift to any particular benefit.

The Crown case was that Poulson—who had first met Pottinger in 1963—soon realized that the latter was a man of power and influence who could assist him greatly, and that his gifts were meant to secure Pottinger's support should it ever be needed. (In a significant letter he wrote in 1970, Poulson explained that Pottinger could influence a great many people to give him work, and that it was Pottinger who had finally obtained extra fees for him in connection with a project concerning Edinburgh schools. While not suggesting that there was anything improper in this, this shows the importance that Poulson attached to Pottinger.) The defence argued that the gifts were made out of genuine friendship by a naturally generous man, and that Pottinger in his public capacity did nothing that he would not in any case have done to assist his benefactor.

It is relevant here to refer to Estacode, a document that sets out the rules of conduct by civil servants in the performance of their official duties. Paragraph 61 of Estacode categorically forbids the acceptance by a civil servant of a gift or reward by virtue of his office. In circumstances where refusal of a gift may cause offence, it is expressly provided that an immediate report must be made to his superiors. Pottinger made no such report, in the belief, he said, that there was no reason to disclose gifts made by a friend.

Cunningham and Smith pleaded guilty to a number of charges involving either Poulson, Smith or both men, in making gifts to Cunningham for the purpose of influencing him to favour Poulson in one or more of his, Cunningham's, various capacities as an officer of the Felling Urban District Council, the General and Municipal Workers Union, the Northumbrian River Authority and the Durham County Police Authority. Three of the gifts, value £1,338 14s. 4d., concerned holidays in Estoril and Brighton. It was stated that Cunningham and his family had actually enjoyed nine paid holidays in six years. The sums involved in other counts were not very great, but the pattern was there for all to see. The Crown contended that Cunningham and Smith used their enormous influence to secure lucrative contracts for Poulson, who in turn rewarded them handsomely. Since 1962 Smith had been acting as some sort of consultant for Poulson, and it was said that he employed a number of people in local government whose task it was to use their influence on Poulson's behalf. His greatest achievement from his benefactor's point of view was in securing the support, as early as 1963, of a man as potentially helpful as Cunningham, whose power and influence may be judged by a list of the public offices he held.

He was among other things chairman of Durham County Council from February 1963 to May 1965; chairman of Durham Police Authority from 1964 to 1973; chairman of the Northumbrian River Authority from 1964 to 1968; chairman of the North East Joint Regional Airport Committee from 1963 to 1973; and chairman of the Tyneside Passenger Transport Authority from 1969 to 1973. He was also a member of the National Executive of the Labour Party, and chairman of its Finance Committee, Staff Negotiating Committee and Northern Committee—quite a man for Poulson to have on his side.

But for a time it appeared that perhaps Cunningham was not the biggest fly in Poulson's web. Allegations were bandied about concerning Members of Parliament, including no less a figure than Reginald Maudling himself, who at one time was only a step away from becoming Prime Minister of this country. It was subsequently proved that he and others had received money from Poulson in connection with their services, and of course there was nothing improper in that. What may have been improper—although it was certainly not illegal—was that in promoting Poulson's interests in the House of Commons they failed to disclose their own financial involvement with Poulson. This of course is a matter for Parliament, and indeed the Royal Commission on Standards of Conduct in Public Life—the Salmon Report of 1976—drew attention to the fact that the criminal law does not apply to the bribery or attempted bribery of a Member of Parliament in respect of his Parliamentary activities, and recommended that consideration should be given to a change in the law in this particular respect. I can disclose that the matter of Mr Maudling's possible corrupt involvement with Poulson was considered by my Department, and we were advised in this respect—as we were in relation to all matters concerning Poulson—by two very distinguished and experienced Queen's Counsel, one of whom subsequently became a High Court judge but has unhappily since died, and the other who has recently been appointed a High Court judge, and the conclusion reached by them (with which I fully agreed) was that there was insufficient evidence to justify criminal proceedings being taken against Mr Maudling. It is only fair to say that he at all times denied that there had been any illegal behaviour on his part. I should like to add that no political pressure of any sort was brought to bear on me at any time with regard to this matter.

It would be tedious to go into detail about the various trials arising from Poulson's activities, if only because so much of the evidence was repetitive. Readers will be able to form their own views about the seriousness of the matters with which Poulson and others were charged. I have heard it argued that corruption is both rife and inevitable, and that Poulson was merely one of the unlucky people who was found out, but that was clearly not the view of the learned judges who dealt with these difficult matters. Poulson himself was sentenced to a total of seven years' imprisonment. Smith received a sentence of six years, and both Cunningham and Pottinger had their five-year sentences reduced to four on appeal.

CHAPTER 6

The Terrorists

THE USE or threat of violence with the aim of achieving political ends
has existed both nationally and internationally throughout history,
but it has most regrettably spread and substantially developed
throughout the world in recent years. Its development so far as the
United Kingdom is concerned has been such as to necessitate the
passing by Parliament of temporary statutes creating offences and
giving wide powers to the Secretary of State designed to deal with—
and so far as possible to prevent—terrorism in its various forms. The
principal statutes that came into operation with regard to this during
my tenure as Director of Public Prosecutions were the Prevention of
Terrorism (Temporary Provisions) Act, 1974, re-enacted with
amendments by an Act similarly entitled in 1976, and the Hijacking
Act, 1971, relating to the hijacking of aircraft. All prosecutions for
offences under these Acts require the consent of the Attorney-
General, and consequently in practice are submitted by the police to
the Director of Public Prosecutions, and after consideration in the
Department are forwarded to the Attorney with its advice. The
ultimate decision, however, lies with the Attorney-General.

There are some who appear to consider that acts of violence,
whether against individuals or property, by the use of guns or the
planting of bombs or incendiary devices or kidnapping, should not be
regarded as acts of terrorism if the crimes are committed in an endeavour to achieve political ends. Whatever may be said in respect of
states ruled by despots, and in which no elections, or no free elections,
are held, no freedom of speech or expression of opinion is allowed and
dissidents are punished by imprisonment or banished with or
without any proper trial, acts of terrorism allegedly for political ends
cannot possibly be tolerated in countries democratically governed,
where free elections are held, freedom of speech is permitted and the
liberty of the individual is properly protected by the courts.

84

Indeed, the 1976 statute to which I have referred expressly defines the meaning in that act of 'terrorism' as 'the use of violence for political ends and includes any use of violence for the purpose of putting the public or any section of the public in fear'. What is inexcusable is terrorist activity by unrepresentative minorities seeking to impose their will on the majority to whom it is anathema. What possible justification can there be for groups like the Red Brigades in Italy or the Baader-Meinhof gang in Germany arrogantly to seek to subvert the chosen way of life of the Italian and German peoples, when Italy and Germany are today democratic countries where political change is possible without resort to force?

I am no authority on Irish history, and I am only expressing a personal opinion when I say that, even granting that the Roman Catholic minority in Northern Ireland may have a number of legitimate political grievances, the latter are surely not of a nature and on a scale even to start to justify the dreadful bombing campaign that has been a feature of the past dozen years or so. If the aim of the killers is to unite Ireland, how can they insist when the majority of the electorate in the North have demonstrated time and again that they wish to remain a part of the United Kingdom, and when even successive governments in the South have spoken out against terrorist activity as a means of achieving this end?

The truth is that the IRA and its political wing, together with those factions who have similar aims, are a comparatively small and unrepresentative group who are seeking to achieve by terrorist means what they cannot achieve politically via the ballot box in either part of Ireland. They have no mandate from anyone except themselves. They seek personal power without having the excuse of the freedom fighter that he can see no possibility of encouraging change peacefully. Indeed, they call themselves an army, and have rejected gradual and peaceful change in favour of the bomb, which spreads its horrors indiscriminately. A bomb cannot tell a Catholic from a Protestant or a sympathizer from an enemy, however carefully or selectively it may be placed.

Be that as it may, neither I nor any officer in my Department would—or for that matter could—ever have allowed personal feelings to determine the actions we took when faced with IRA terrorism in England. No matter how serious the offence, we had to be satisfied as always that there was sufficient evidence on which a reasonable jury was likely to convict, without which there was no way in which a prosecution could have proceeded. Fortunately for me, Northern Ireland had its own Director of Public Prosecutions.

The IRA did not, of course, confine themselves to Ireland. In an attempt no doubt to influence the British people to demand the withdrawal of their forces from the province, or perhaps merely to publicize their cause, they carried out a series of dreadful attacks in England—notably in London, Birmingham and Guildford. It was my duty as Director of Public Prosecutions to deal with these serious matters, and I propose to give an account of one of the resultant trials. I have chosen to deal with the Birmingham bombings as being representative of all the cases, and also because the trial had a most interesting sequel.

The trial of nine men actually took place at the Crown Court at Lancaster, on the application of the defence, because it was felt that there might be problems about giving the accused a fair hearing in Birmingham, which was where the victims were killed who were the subject of the murder charges. Their deaths, and injuries to 162 other people, resulted from explosions in public houses in the city on 21 November 1974. It is always highly inconvenient and expensive to transfer a trial from where most of the witnesses live, but probably no crimes committed in peacetime have aroused a greater sense of public outrage—most strongly, of course, locally—and the judge felt he had no option in the matter. As he himself put it, 'even if a Birmingham jury had, as they probably would have, given these nine a perfectly fair trial, if they had been convicted by a Birmingham jury they would never have believed that they had had a fair trial'. Additionally, the judge went out of his way in his summing-up to warn the jury about allowing the enormity of the crime to induce in their minds an emotional response or reaction of anger and indignation. 'The only proper attitude of mind to the decision of such questions', he told them, 'is an attitude of dispassionate detachment.' Judges are always giving this sort of advice, and I believe that it says a great deal for the fairness of our system that every consideration of this nature was, as usual, afforded the defendants in so dreadful a case.

The indictment consisted of twenty-one murder charges against six defendants, Hugh Callaghan, Patrick Joseph Hill, Robert Gerald Hunter, Noel Richard McIlkenny, William Power and John Walker. There was a further count against these same people, together with Michael John Murray and Michael Bernard Sheehan, of conspiring to cause explosions. Sheehan was separately charged with possessing explosives. Only one of the principal accused—Hill—had any sort of criminal record, and his offences were comparatively minor. He was a painter by trade, as were Hunter and Power; all three had come to England in the early sixties, and were unemployed at the time of the bombings. McIlkenny and Walker had arrived in the fifties and worked at the same firm, as millwright's mate and crane-driver respectively. Callaghan, the eldest of the accused, had been in England since 1947, and had been out of work since 1971.

Their ages ranged from twenty-nine to forty-four. The police believed that they were part of a conspiracy that resulted in eleven bomb incidents, mainly in the Birmingham area, during the first three weeks in November 1974. There were three attacks late on Guy Fawkes night, or early the following morning, of which two involved high explosives and one an incendiary mixture. One bomb, causing widespread damage but fortunately no injuries, went off at Conservative Party headquarters in Birmingham; another, where the bomb failed to ignite, was left outside the Inland Revenue offices in Wolverhampton. There were no fewer than five attacks on the night of 14–15 November, of which three were with high explosives and two with incendiary devices. The first of these incidents took place at the RAF Association club in Northampton; later a bomb exploded at the Conservative Association offices in Solihull; another bomb went off at the Central Telephone Exchange in Coventry.

Although considerable damage was caused, the only death arose as a result of the Coventry explosion. The experts believed that a high-explosive bomb had detonated prematurely, killing James McDade, whom the police believed to have been another conspirator who was in the course of planting the very bomb that ended his life.

The type of target involved may be significant. Of the eight first attacks, two were on the offices of a political party, one on an Air Force club, one on a tax office and one on a telephone exchange. The reader can form his own view about the significance, if any, of the choice. The other attacks were on business premises, a timber yard and car-repair firm. A branch of Barclays Bank was a target of one of three attacks on 21 November. Two unexploded bombs were discovered there and made safe by the heroic men of the Bomb Squad. They know the risks they take, and theirs is true bravery. Unfortunately, the same night saw two terrible and tragic explosions. Having previously selected targets where, and times when, there was comparatively small danger of loss of life, the bombers decided—and it can only have been a deliberate decision—to attack two crowded public houses.

At 8.18 p.m. a nitroglycerin bomb exploded in the Mulberry Bush public house in the Rotunda Building, Birmingham, killing ten people and injuring thirty-six, some very seriously. Within four minutes a high-explosive bomb went off a few hundred yards away at the Tavern in the Town public house in New Street, killing eleven people and injuring 126. The damage at both places was of course very substantial.

The experts who examined the scenes, basing their conclusions upon common features of design and upon the components used, traced a direct connection between the bombs planted on the night of 21 November and two of the previous bombs; they also established a probable connection with three of the previous bombs, and a possible connection with one other. In other words, there was a direct or probable scientific connection between eight of the eleven attacks, and the police were convinced that all the attacks were connected. One of the bombs recovered from outside the bank was manufactured in the Irish Republic, and the coincidence of dates and venues was such that the police were satisfied that the bombings were also the work of the same group of people.

The IRA sometimes issued warnings when bombs were about to explode, presumably with the object of saving innocent lives, and the nature of the attacks in early November 1974 suggested that some care was being taken to damage property only. Why suddenly there should have been deliberate assaults on crowded places, which must inevitably have resulted in loss of life, is uncertain. Some people close to the events believed that the bombs in the two public houses were planted in revenge for the death of McDade, although the logic of that belief is somewhat doubtful, McDade having caused his own death.

Without adequate warning, there was no way in which the public houses in Birmingham could have been attacked just after eight o'clock at night without the certainty of deaths and injuries. What else could this have been but deliberate mass murder, unless there had been some terrible mistake? Suggestions to this effect were made by some of the accused. Hunter, for example, said 'This was never meant to be. It has all gone wrong,' and it is only right to point out that some sort of warning was telephoned to the *Birmingham Post and Mail*, from a call-box by a man with an Irish accent, seven minutes before the first explosion. Whether the message was official (in which case it was deliberately misleading) or whether it was conveyed privately by someone only partly privy to the affair who was acting unofficially, is a matter of speculation. What is indisputable is that the warning was too late, and insufficiently explicit—indeed, inaccurate in part—for it referred to two bombs, one at the Rotunda, without specifying the Mulberry Bush, and one at the tax office in New Street, whereas the bomb in New Street went off at the near-by Tavern in the Town. If a serious warning was intended to have saved lives and to have avoided murder, it would have needed to be much more specific, and to have been given sufficiently early to enable the areas to be evacuated. Both explosions actually occurred as police officers, alerted by the newspaper, were on their way to the supposed scenes.

There was considerable evidence of association between all nine defendants and the dead man McDade. There was also evidence to demonstrate sympathy with the IRA on the part of most of the accused, who admitted to Republican sentiments but who affected to condemn terrorism. Most significant was a statement by Callaghan in which he purported to attribute ranks to the principal accused. According to him, Walker was a brigadier, Hunter a captain and he, Hill, McIlkenny and Power were lieutenants. (For the record, he later said it was McIlkenny, not Hunter, who was the captain.)

A most telling document was a funeral notice found in Walker's house. It referred to 'Volunteer Lieutenant James McDade, Northern Irish Republican Army, died on active service 14.11.74', and concluded with the exhortation, 'Support us in our struggle for which many have died'. Walker sought to explain this away by saying that he had picked it up casually in a public house, and that until he had read it he had had no idea that McDade was an IRA terrorist.

There was evidence that Hunter, McDade and McIlkenny, among others, had been seen calling at Walker's home over a period of time, sometimes carrying plastic bags. McIlkenny and Walker had been seen looking at a number of clocks together; Walker had been heard to tell McIlkenny that Sheehan had been foolish when he had angrily threatened to blow up a man's house, since such a threat might have attracted the attention of the police. Walker had been very upset by McDade's death and helped to make arrangements for the funeral and, according to one witness, he had explained what might have gone wrong with the bomb. Most damning, if a workmate of Walker was to be believed, on the day of the bombings Walker had advised him not to visit the city centre that evening.

The evidence suggested that the six accused men met at New Street railway station in Birmingham in the late afternoon of 21 November, when certainly McIlkenny and Power bought tickets. The police believed that the men then dispersed in order to plant the bombs. Walker was allegedly seen near the Rotunda Building at about 7.50 p.m., and shortly thereafter the six men were observed again at the railway station, where all except Callaghan boarded a train. They arrived eventually at Heysham and passed through the barrier. McIlkenny, Power and Walker had travelled on consecutively numbered return tickets, and Hill and Hunter on consecutively numbered single tickets. They were arrested before they were able to board the boat to Belfast. Callaghan arrived home late in a distressed condition, saying that he had been at the Tavern in the Town just before the explosion. He was arrested the following day.

The six men were subjected to scientific tests. Hill and Power were found to have traces of nitroglycerin and ammonium nitrate on their hands. Walker had faint traces of ammonium nitrate on his. No traces were found on the other men, so it seemed possible that Hill and Power had had the actual handling of the bombs. Power in fact had made a written statement in which he admitted that he had been involved, and said that he had been given a bomb to plant by Walker. Hill, on the other hand, denied having had any hand in planting bombs. The most he would admit to was involvement with the other accused and some knowledge of what was intended.

After initial denials, McIlkenny made a written statement admitting participation with the other five, and in the bombings of 21 November. Hunter, who became hysterical when first interviewed, refused to make a statement, but some of his oral answers could have been construed as confirming his guilt. Callaghan made a written statement in which he confessed to taking part in the planting of the bomb at the Mulberry Bush.

If Callaghan were correct, Walker was the senior member of the conspiracy. When first interviewed, Walker went some way towards confirming his part in the affair. He later admitted handling the constituents of high-explosive bombs. When confronted with the statements of McIlkenny and Power he made a written statement, admitting his part and involving the other five accused and the dead McDade.

There was no doubt that the police had a formidable case, but it had still to be proved in a court of law before a judge and jury. One can think of many countries where people accused of the offences would have received very short shrift, but that is not the British way. The lengthy proceedings extended over nine weeks, from 9 June to 15 August 1975. The judge, Mr Justice Bridge, was himself ill and unable to sit for five days.

Some of the statements made, or alleged to have been made, by the defendants were pretty damaging to their cause, and eight sitting days were occupied in an attempt to have them excluded as being inadmissible. According to the police, all interrogations had been conducted with perfect propriety, and there had been no infringement of the Judges' Rules. All statements in writing had been taken under caution, and had been properly signed. As far as oral admissions were concerned, they had either been noted at the actual time or recorded shortly afterwards, as was common practice, by two officers comparing their recollections. No violence or threats had been made to any of the prisoners.

That was not, however, the prisoners' story. All gave evidence of either gross personal violence against them while in police custody or of outrageous threats as to what would happen to them and their families if they refused to confess. They further claimed that their alleged confessions were substantially fabricated or were complete distortions of what in part they may have said.

One side or the other had to be lying. Many allegations against the police were, in the words of the judge, 'of the most bizarre and grotesque character'. For example, the defendant Power had claimed to identify a certain police sergeant as one of five policemen who had assaulted him. He alleged that the officer had been present when there had been a threat to throw him out of the window. The sergeant was also supposed on a different occasion to have pulled him up by the hair, saying, 'You will never see your wife again.' It was proved, however, that the sergeant could not possibly have been present at the time and place of the latter incident.

Another extraordinary allegation was made by McIlkenny, who said he had been made to stand against a wall while police officers fired a revolver at him at point-blank range. There was a click, and an officer pretended he had made a mistake, saying the gun should have been loaded. The trigger was then pulled another three times, and on each occasion there was a report, but blank cartridges had been used. The same policeman was then alleged to have said, 'Next time it will be for real.'

The experienced judge, who had the advantage of seeing all the witnesses before forming an opinion as to where the truth lay, clearly did not believe these sensational stories. He was, however, most concerned by a bruise near Walker's left eye and by marks on the chests of Hill, Hunter and Power. Two police officers gave evidence that while being led to a car on 22 November, Walker, whose head had been covered with a coat, had struck his head on the car, thus presumably sustaining the injury, but the officer who was driving at that time had no recollection of any such occurrence. The same officer flatly contradicted Walker's story that he was the victim of a deliberate blow on the eye while in the car which rendered him unconscious. The judge preferred Walker's statement, made in the presence of a solicitor and a police officer, that he had fallen. As for the chest injuries, the judge decided that they had probably been self-inflicted for the purpose of supporting a challenge to the alleged confessions.

The result of the trial within the trial was that the judge was satisfied that all the confessions had been made voluntarily, and that they were admissible in evidence. The arguments, of course, had taken place in the absence of the jury, who were unaware of the judge's conclusions. The whole matter was canvassed again before the jury, who could have ignored the admissions had they believed they were other than voluntary. The important fact, however, is that the admissions were put before them and, if accepted, they were very damaging.

Before considering their verdicts the jury were able to give full weight to the defendants' allegations and the police denials. All the men accused, except Callaghan, complained before the jury of gross violence and brutality, in certain cases amounting to torture. Two of them, for instance, said that their feet had been burned with lighted cigarettes. All except Hunter complained of threats, including threats to cause death by being thrown out of an upper window, into a lake or out of a fast-moving car on the motorway. One threat was that the IRA would be informed that one of their number had 'squealed'. A particularly nasty allegation was made that a police officer had sought to induce confessions by saying that angry mobs were clamouring for vengeance against the accused's wives and families outside their homes in Birmingham, and that the police would with-draw protection.

At 12.28 p.m. on 15 August 1975 the foreman of the jury rose to answer the Clerk of the Court. One hundred and twenty-six times in succession he replied 'Guilty' to the clerk's questions. The six main defendants had been convicted individually on all twenty-one murder charges. On the judge's directions the jury were discharged from giving verdicts on the conspiracy charge against the men found guilty of murder. Murray and Sheehan were convicted on the con-spiracy charge, and Sheehan for possessing explosives.

The sentence, of course, for six men was the only one now prescribed by law—imprisonment for life in respect of each count. Occasionally a judge sees fit to suggest that a convicted murderer serve a minimum sentence, but Mr Justice Bridge made no such recommendation. What he did say was that the verdicts were based on the most overwhelming evidence he had ever heard. Sheehan was sentenced to nine years for conspiracy and a concurrent five years for possession. Murray, the only defendant who freely admitted his membership of the IRA, also received nine years, to be served con-currently with a twelve-year sentence he had earlier been given after another trial for a precisely similar conspiracy. He had virtually refused to participate in the proceedings, and in sentencing him in what in practice was a most merciful manner, the judge addressed him as follows: 'Because you have maintained silence throughout the case and prohibited your learned counsel, who acted for you under Legal Aid, from addressing the jury, and *because I wished to make it clear above all that that was not going to prevent you from having a fair trial*, I felt obliged to say on your behalf yesterday what could be said on your behalf which had been left unsaid by your own counsel on your own instructions.' The italics are mine. They make their own point.

Neither the judge nor, I think, the jury gave much credence to the extraordinary allegations of police misconduct, but Mr Justice Bridge was deeply concerned at the possibility of maltreatment on the part of certain prison officers. 'No doubt', he said, 'in due course further inquiries will be made and further steps will be taken in that regard.' It was following these remarks that my Department initiated a police investigation which resulted in the prosecution at Birmingham Crown Court of fourteen prison officers on charges of assaulting the six bombers in Winson Green Prison.

Since all the officers were acquitted—a decision with which I have no quarrel—I do not propose to deal at any length with the allegations. We felt that the interests of justice required a prosecution to be launched, although we were aware that the evidence of convicted prisoners was of doubtful value. In particular we decided not to call the convicted bombers themselves. They were not the type of witness whose evidence was likely to be received with much sympathy by a jury, and no doubt, by continuing to claim also that they had been assaulted in police custody, they might have tried to use the proceedings to reopen issues that had already been decided. Undoubtedly they did receive certain injuries, and different courts apparently concluded that such injuries were not the result of assaults by policemen or proved to have been by prison warders, so how they came by them has never been satisfactorily resolved. Many people may say that the terrorists got what they deserved, but no one concerned with the administration of the law in this country can possibly condone assaults on prisoners. I take some pride in thinking that so fair is our system that we seek to protect even those whom we have reason to detest.

I never cease to wonder at the extraordinary arrogance of small groups of people who think they know better than the rest of us how the world should be run. Some of them—the most fanatic—seek nothing more than power, and I suspect that many anarchists if they had the chance would be the first to jump in and fill the vacuum that their chaos had caused. Others—the more idealistic—misguidedly set themselves up as representatives of what they see as the downtrodden masses, without realizing that the same masses support neither their policies nor their methods.

As I have indicated earlier, revolutionary tactics have no place in a parliamentary democracy, where there is not only the possibility of change but where ideas are constantly evolving. Anyone who is dissatisfied with the structure of society in our own country has only to observe how it has changed during this century, or for that matter during the comparatively short time I was Director of Public Prosecutions, to realize that there is no need for violence in order to achieve change. Change comes about naturally. Yet the history of the post-war world is replete with examples of revolutionary groups, with international terrorist links, seeking to impose their own tyranny in place of what they see—or pretend they see—as an existing one.

Apart from the IRA, our own very special terrorist problem, we in this country have, thank God, been largely spared the terrorist horrors that have plagued near-by Italy, for example. However, there was a terrible manifestation of terrorism between 1968 and 1971, mostly associated with the Angry Brigade. This was a name they gave themselves in communiqués they issued to the media. The only thing I can say in their favour is that they were very young, and that they attacked property rather than people. What distinguished them from the IRA, apart from their political aims, was that they luckily killed no one and injured only one person, but of course there was the risk of death to anyone who might have been present when one of their bombs exploded.

I must also add that the police found what they believed constituted a death list containing 170 names, including my own, although this was a matter hotly at issue at the trial of eight people subsequently accused in connection with twenty-five explosions or attempted explosions. It was denied that there had been any thought of assassinations. The explanation, according to certain of the defendants, was that they were intensely interested in the power structure in this country, and that they were engaged in a form of counter-survey of people at the top, intending to expose abuse of power wherever they discovered it: in the courts, among the police, in big business, in government, among property-owners and in industrial relations.

Be that as it may—and in retrospect, this explanation may have been the true one, since no one was killed—the police took it seriously enough, and afforded protection to the many people who were potential targets. I well remember being informed by the Metropolitan Police that I was on the list and that neither I nor my wife should dismiss the threat lightly. Police officers with guard dogs were at my house around the clock, and when I went to work I was met on arrival at Waterloo Station by a plainclothes officer who escorted me to my office in Buckingham Gate, and back again at night. I am not sure what one man could effectively have done if there had been a genuine attempt to kill me, but at least I went about my work in the knowledge that his presence made it more likely that my murderer would be caught. In the circumstances, all one can reasonably do is to get on with one's job and hope for the best. It cost me sixpence extra for the additional passenger every time I took a taxi from the station to the office, but that seemed a small price to pay for protection.

If that seems a facetious comment to make in such serious circumstances, I can only say that some sense of humour is needed to approach what became known as the Angry Brigade trial, for it lasted from 30 May 1972 until 6 December of the same year. It would require a book of its own—and a long one at that—to tell the whole story of the six months or more in court, which must have been a protracted ordeal for all concerned—for the judge, Mr Justice James (later Lord Justice), for the jury, for counsel and for the eight accused. I can do no more in this context than refer briefly to aspects of the case that seem to me of general interest.

There were four men and four women on trial, in itself a symptom of the increasing part played by women in all walks of life. John Barker, Christopher Bott, Hilary Creek, James Stuart Christie, James Greenfield, Catherine McLean, Anna Mendleson and Angela Weir were charged with conspiring to cause explosions likely to endanger life. There were ten other charges in the indictment, but this was the main one. Christie had been sentenced to twenty years' imprisonment in Spain for an offence involving explosives. At the age of eighteen he had travelled to Madrid, with explosives and detonators taped to his body, having openly said in a television interview that the only way to end the régime in Spain was to kill General Franco, the country's head of state. He had been released after only three years, and had received considerable publicity, but he was the only defendant who may have been well known to the public. All the accused pleaded not guilty. Barker, Creek and Mendleson defended themselves; the five others were represented by distinguished counsel.

The Angry Brigade first made their existence known in a communiqué, numbered 1, posted to *The Times* on 4 December 1967. It included the words 'Fascism and oppression will be smashed. Embassies, judges, hired pigs. Spanish Embassy machine-gunned

Thursday.' In fact, some bullet damage was discovered at the Embassy a day or two later, but the defendants were not charged with any incidents prior to 1968. There were explosions, or attempted explosions, between 3 March 1968 and 18 August 1970 at the Embassy, at branches of the Bank of Spain in London and Liverpool, twice at a branch of the Bank of Bilbao, at an Iberian Airways office and in luggage labelled for an Iberian Airways plane. (Two men were arrested and convicted in respect of one of the bank attacks, and had on them letters signed 'International First of May Group'.) There were also two Italian targets—the Italian Trade Exhibition Centre in London, on 9 October 1970, and the office of the Italian Vice-Consul in Birmingham on the following day.

The other incidents took place at an American forces club; at Paddington Station; at the home of Sir John Waldron, Metropolitan Commissioner of Police; at the home of the Attorney-General; in the passenger lounge at Heathrow Airport; in BBC vans outside the Albert Hall the night before the 'Miss World' competition; at the Department of Employment and Productivity; at the home of a Minister, Robert Carr; at the Ford Motor Company; at Biba Boutique; at Tintagel House; at the home of the chief executive of Ford; at the home of another Minister, John Davies; and at a Territorial Army drill hall.

Following the assault on the American club, Reuters received a letter signed 'First of May Group, Revolutionary Solidarity Movement'—indicating a connection with the Bank of Bilbao attackers—saying, 'Please transmit to the Pentagon and White House killers.' It is possible that there was more than one group at work, and considerable time was taken at the trial in investigating alleged similarities between the different incidents, but the Angry Brigade boasted about their responsibility for several of the most noteworthy explosions. On one occasion they issued their communiqué— number 4, in fact—under the name 'The Wild Bunch', so it is not impossible that they may also have used 'First of May Group' as one of their aliases. This particular message was sent to Sir Peter Rawlinson following the attack on his Chelsea house. The writer had the arrogant effrontery to inform the Attorney-General of England and Wales that 'You can dream up the law and order you like, but remember you are subject to our justice.'

The incident at Mr (now Lord) Carr's home in Barnet was on 12 January 1971, the day of a big demonstration against the government's Industrial Relations Bill. Communiqué number 5 was most interesting. 'We are not mercenaries,' it announced. 'We attack property, not people. Carr, Rawlinson, Waldron would all be dead if we wished. . . . British democracy is based on more blood, terror and exploitation than any empire in history. It has a brutal police force whose crimes against the people the media will not report. . . . We have started to fight back and the war will be won by the organised working class with bombs.' A month later, communiqué number 6 declared, 'Our attack is violent. Our violence is organised. . . . Where two or three revolutionaries use organised violence to attack the class system, there is the Angry Brigade. Revolutionaries all over England are already using the name to publicise their attacks on the system. . . . so must organised violence accompany every point of the struggle until, armed, the revolutionary working class overthrows the capitalist system.' Communiqué number 7 stated unequivocally, 'Two months ago we blew up Carr's house . . . It is Ford's tonight.' There was in fact an incident that very day at the Ford Motor Company works.

The explosion at the Biba shop in Kensington occurred on 1 May 1971. Communiqué number 8 described it as a 'Special May Day present', and said 'The only thing you can do with modern slave houses called boutiques is wreck them.'

Just how dangerous these activities were may be the subject of argument. There can be no doubt that a group of people calling themselves the Angry Brigade was engaged in a conspiracy to cause explosions, including many, if not all, those mentioned above. Indeed, communiqué number 7 admitted to further attacks, mostly on Conservative Party offices, which formed no part of the prosecution case. Although they claimed not to be killers, and in fact killed no one, in the very next breath they spoke of organized violence.

'Who do you think the Angry Brigade are?' asked communiqué number 9, and then provided its own answer. 'The Angry Brigade is the man or woman sitting next to you. They have guns in their pockets and anger in their minds.' The point was whether the eight defendants were members of the Brigade. Four of them—Barker, Creek, Greenfield and Mendleson—lived at an address in London where the police claimed to have found explosives and detonators, and there was strong reason to believe that one or more of the communiqués had been run off on a duplicating machine in the house. There was considerable evidence of association between the various defendants, and they made no secret of their political views, from which a jury could reasonably have inferred at least some sympathy with certain of the aims of the Angry Brigade, if not necessarily with its methods.

The scientific evidence, indicating similarities between the various incidents, was strongly challenged by the defence. The police were accused of improper conduct, of inventing statements, of perjury, of vicious assaults on Barker and Greenfield, and of planting the explosives and detonators in the house where four of the defendants lived. There were also complaints that this was a political trial, in the sense that it was because of their political views and activities that the eight people were accused. The defence was certainly pursued with particular vigour, and I make no complaints about that, although I confess to having been surprised that one of the counsel should have asked in open court the judge's permission (which was refused) to give a cake to Anna Mendleson on her twenty-first birthday, which took place while the case was being tried. The accused were mostly young, intelligent and not wholly unlikeable, but I felt that this was a misguided attempt to create sympathy for one of them.

The jury retired at 1.10 p.m. on Monday, 6 December 1972. They returned for five minutes at 11.35 a.m. the following morning to seek help from the judge on a point that was worrying them. They returned again at 11.15 a.m. the next morning to say that they could not reach a unanimous decision, and the judge told them that he would accept a majority verdict on which ten of the twelve were agreed. They finally came into court at 5.10 p.m. on Wednesday, 8 December. The defendants Bott, Christie, McLean and Weir were acquitted on all charges. The defendants Barker, Creek, Greenfield and Mendleson were found guilty on the main conspiracy charge and on four lesser charges, by a majority of ten to two. Greenfield was acquitted unanimously on two lesser charges, and Mendleson on one. The jury added a rider to their verdict, asking the judge to be lenient with the convicted four.

I have referred to this case because I believe it to be an admirable example of British justice in operation. Unless one believed that the police had planted explosives and invented stories, there was what the judge described as 'overwhelming evidence' against the convicted four, but it took over six months to prove the case in court. There was no automatic conviction for anyone. Compare our system with that obtaining in some countries, where if newspaper reports are to be believed secret trials are over almost before they have begun, and where the unfortunate accused are often executed before the verdicts have been announced to the world and before they can appeal to a higher authority. I wonder which system those who seek to overthrow our way of justice would prefer for themselves.

Mr Justice James sentenced the four conspirators to ten years each on the main charge, and to lesser concurrent sentences on the minor charges. He said that he would have given them fifteen years but for the jury's recommendation. 'The philosophies which you subscribe to . . . are those which are set out in the various Angry Brigade communiqués,' he told them. 'Your participation, as found in this conspiracy, arose because you objected to the orderly way of society. One of the most precious rights we have is that an individual should hold his own opinions and be able to express them; and when one finds others who set out to dominate by exercising their opinions in preference to all others, to the extent of enforcing them by violence, in these circumstances it undermines that most precious right.'

There are no doubt matters open to criticism in our system of law, but as long as it affords the care and consideration that were shown to the IRA bombers and the Angry Brigade, there is nothing vitally wrong. The fair rule of law is our best protection against the growth of terrorism in our midst.

CHAPTER 7

Under attack

'THE SIZE and ramifications of this criminal enterprise made it one of the most serious with which the police have ever had to deal.' So said Lord Justice Lawton in the course of judgment in what, for convenience, I shall call the Wembley robbery appeal. Unfortunately, the distinguished judge saw fit to criticize my Department quite severely.

It was the very seriousness of the enterprise in question that determined my course of action. In December 1972 a man named Derek Creighton Smalls, known as Bertie, was arrested on suspicion of involvement in a robbery at Wembley the previous August, when Barclays Bank in the High Street had been raided by armed and masked men and over £138,000 was stolen. One of the raiders had fired a shot, but fortunately no one was injured by it.

This was only one of a series of similar crimes that had begun in October 1968 with the theft of £72,000 from a branch of the National Provincial Bank in Brighton. Later there were further raids on banks and business premises, as well as on security vans carrying money. In all, over £1¼ million was stolen! The raids were carefully planned, and the criminals who participated were ruthless men, some at least of whom not only carried guns but were prepared to use them, resulting in at least one person being wounded. One of the most serious attacks was on a bank in Ilford in February 1970, netting nearly £240,000, when ammonia was squirted in the face of a security guard.

The police formed the view that these crimes were the work of a particular gang which had enough members to enable them to use different personnel on different jobs. I believe in the circumstances that Lord Justice Lawton's description of the gang's operations was in no way exaggerated.

The police were not entirely without success. Three of the gang were arrested and convicted in connection with the Ilford robbery, but that still left between four and six unaccounted for, since at least seven men, and possibly nine, had participated in that particular venture. One or two others were arrested in the normal way and charged with crimes without it being realized that they were connected with the general enterprise.

It was only when Smalls was arrested following the Wembley robbery that the police learned the whole story. On the very day he was arrested he said to Detective-Sergeant Marshall: 'You give me outers and bail now, and I'll give you everything on these jobs you told me about.' Ten days later he offered to tell what he called 'the inside story' in return for a certain guarantee. It was then, of course, that the matter came urgently to the attention of the top people in my Department. Here was a man who was not just what in criminal jargon is known as a 'grass', but who was to be named by the Press as a 'supergrass'—the first of his kind. He was willing, in return for some sort of immunity, to spill the beans in no uncertain way.

It now became necessary for us to consider where the public interest lay—always our cardinal test. The police said that Smalls was offering them a wonderful opportunity to smash major organized crime. Without his evidence it would have been impossible to prosecute only one or two people. With it the whole gang might be put behind bars for many years.

It was in these circumstances, and after the most anxious consideration, that we decided to grant immunity to Smalls. The terms of the immunity were contained in a long letter from an Assistant Director to Smalls's solicitor dated 2 April 1973. Briefly, we agreed not to offer any evidence against him on a criminal charge in respect of any offence other than homicide which Smalls might disclose to Commander Yorke or his designated police officers, on the understanding that he would make full disclosure of his own criminal activities and those of his associates. We also agreed, among other matters, to arrange for the protection of his family and, upon termination of the evidence that he might be required to give, secretly to escort him, his wife and children to a place of his choice.

Following this arrangement, Smalls admitted his part in no less than twenty armed robberies, and implicated twenty-six other persons. In practice he was arraigned at the Old Bailey on 13 July 1973, on three counts charging him with robbery and one of conspiring 'with other persons to rob other persons'—admittedly, to use Lord Justice Lawton's description, 'one of the oddest conspiracy counts ever to be put into an indictment'. The prosecution offered no evidence, and Smalls was found not guilty. He was taken

101

immediately to the magistrates' court to give evidence against the twenty-six people who had been arrested as a result of his confessions. All were committed for trial. The indictment contained forty-nine counts.

For convenience, J. C. Mathew, who we briefed to lead for the Crown, successfully applied to have the indictment presented in three separate trials. They were long and complicated. The first lasted sixty-seven days, the second for twenty-five and the third for twenty-six. As a result, sixteen of the accused were convicted. Appeals were subsequently allowed in the case of three, so the final result of granting immunity to Smalls was the conviction of at least eleven criminals who we would not otherwise have been able to touch, and of course the breaking up of the gang.

I do not propose to give an account of these trials except to say they were another illustration of the fairness of the British legal system and of the admirable care and attention by solicitors, counsel, judge and jury to the issues. Mathew's opening speech in the first trial lasted nine hours, for example—not six days as stated by Lord Justice Lawton, by the way; the summing-up took six days, and the jury were out for the best part of three. It was the appeal by fifteen of the convicted men that most concerned me, largely because of the strictures of Lord Justice Lawton in his judgment. Argument was advanced, of course, at all these trials, and at the appeal, about the admissibility and value of the evidence from a man who had been granted immunity from prosecution in respect of his part in the enterprise, and it was contended in the Court of Appeal that Smalls should not have been allowed to give evidence at all. It had long been established that accomplices were competent witnesses, but here was an accomplice who had unusually powerful inducements to give evidence. If he had failed to repeat in court what he had said in his statements to the police he could still have been prosecuted for many of the crimes to which he had confessed, and further, he would have been in danger of losing police protection for himself and his family. He had been far more powerfully motivated, for example, than a witness who hoped to receive a reward for information leading to a conviction.

Although the Court of Appeal accepted that Smalls's evidence was admissible, and that the juries had been given adequate warning about the need for corroboration, Lord Justice Lawton was clearly unhappy. 'It is in the interests of the public,' he said, 'that criminals should be brought to justice; and the more serious the crimes, the greater is the need for justice to be done.' Describing Smalls, however, as 'one of the most dangerous and craven villains who had ever given evidence for the Crown', he quoted from Hale's *Pleas of the Crown* and specifically referred a particular passage to my attention. Writing over three hundred years before these events took place, Chief Justice Hale had given it as his view that 'more mischief hath come to good men by these kind of approvements by false accusations of desperate villains than benefit to the public by the discovery and convictions of real offenders.'

There is certainly room for argument about the propriety of granting immunity to a criminal to obtain his evidence against other criminals, and I have explained that in this particular and most exceptional instance, I had felt that the public interest lay in so doing. I regretted in the circumstances that Lord Justice Lawton should have dealt with my conduct and that of the Department in very unfavourable terms. He recorded his 'surprise' that what he called the 'ineptly worded' letter to Smalls's solicitors should have been sent. 'Above all else the spectacle of the Director recording in writing, at the behest of a criminal like Smalls, his undertaking to give immunity from further prosecutions is one which we find distasteful.' Although he agreed that undertakings of immunity from prosecution might have to be given in the public interest, referring to the letter he said, 'Nothing of a similar kind must ever happen again.'

I was in hot water, and the Lord Justice's strictures were widely reported. Coming from a judge of whom I had the highest opinion, I was considerably worried about whether I had after all done the wrong thing. Fortunately for me, the Court of Appeal certified that there was a point of law of general public importance, and the unsuccessful appellants were able to apply to the House of Lords for leave to appeal. It was in the House of Lords that both Lords Salmon and Dilhorne commented unfavourably on the instruction that I must not again follow a similar course. 'What I think is a little disturbing', said Lord Salmon, 'is that if the comment of Lord Justice Lawton was not justified, it should be left standing, because it might put considerable inhibition on the Director in future, if exactly similar circumstances occur.'

Lord Dilhorne went further. 'I am wondering', he said, 'to what extent it is right for any court to give directions to the Director as to how he should conduct his business. The Director of Public Prosecutions works under the Attorney-General. I would have thought it quite wrong for it to come from any judicial authority at all. He may be condemned for what he has done, but he must not be told what he has got to do in the future.'

No one in any walk of life, certainly no one in the public eye, can expect to escape criticism. Sometimes it is justified, sometimes not, and I am not so thin-skinned that I cannot accept it gracefully, I hope, whether I believe I am right or wrong. I was surprised, however, at the degree of publicity given to Lord Justice Lawton's criticisms, which seemed to serve as a focus for anyone who wanted to attack the Department. I took the view—and I still do—that it was right to grant immunity to Smalls. One's only defence against criticism is a knowledge that one is doing one's best as conscientiously as possible, and perhaps I was over-sensitive on this occasion.

There had of course been numerous precedents for allowing an accomplice or conspirator in a particular case to turn Queen's Evidence for the sake of securing the conviction of the principal criminal. Testimony from so-called supergrasses, of whom Bertie Smalls was the first, was greatly different in scale, often involving a whole series of crimes and criminal activity. Evidence from super-grasses subsequently became a feature in several criminal trials, usually resulting in far lighter sentences for them than they might otherwise have received, and I understand that the police believe that supergrass testimony has assisted in a large measure for smashing organized crime in London. That is the justification for what I did in the Smalls case, and my action in that matter was entirely exceptional.

There was one other occasion when I found myself under attack, from no less a figure than David Steel, M.P., Leader of the Liberal Party. This was over the Department's handling of the case concerning Peter Hain. Before dealing with that extraordinary business, I will refer briefly to the case of Andrew Newton, which was the forerunner of one of the most dramatic legal processes of the century, involving no less a person than Steel's predecessor as leader of the Liberal Party, Jeremy Thorpe. The trial in which Thorpe and his co-defendants were acquitted on charges that included conspiracy to murder took place after I had ceased to be Director of Public Prosecutions, and so does not properly have a place in my story, but I was of course Director when the prosecution of Newton revealed the tip of a very sensational, if highly improbable, iceberg.

At this remove, the facts of the Newton case are less interesting than the circumstances surrounding them. On 16 March 1976 Andrew Gino Newton, an airline pilot, appeared at Exeter Crown Court before Mr Justice Lawson on charges of possessing firearms, and one of destroying property contrary to the Criminal Damage Act—the property in question being a dog. He pleaded not guilty to the two most serious charges but guilty to the remainder.

A strange story emerged based on the allegations made by Norman Scott, aged thirty-six, who described himself as a writer and who had made a statement to the police on 26 October 1975 in which he said that he had completed an autobiography that included details of a homosexual relationship he had had over a period of years, following which he had received a number of phone calls offering him lucrative employment as a fashion model. At about the same time he had met a man called Peter Keen in a public house in Barnstaple, and some three weeks later in the local market. On the second occasion Keen got out of a car, approached Scott and asked whether he might speak to him. Scott refused and walked away, but the man followed, saying 'Look, you've got to talk to me, you're in a great deal of trouble,' then seized him by the arm and said, 'I don't think you really realize this, but you are going to be killed. A gentleman has been paid over four figures to kill you. He's coming from Canada and I want to help you. I want you to come with me now.' Keen, according to Scott, went on to say that a lady was waiting to see Scott, and that she was the wife of the person with whom Scott had had the homosexual relationship.

Scott agreed to go with him, and to take with him any relevant documents. He put a copy of his manuscript and copies of letters in a briefcase, but was then told that the lady did not wish to be seen. Instead, Scott allowed himself to be persuaded to discuss matters with Keen. They landed up eventually in a local hotel where, during a conversation lasting from three to four hours, Keen said that he was being paid to protect Scott, and that if Scott were to go to a particular solicitor and make a statement saying that all was untrue, he would receive a large sum of money. Scott said that this was tantamount to blackmail, and it was left that Keen would telephone him again.

He duly did so, several times, on one occasion calling himself Andrew instead of Peter, but Scott was reluctant to arrange another meeting. Scott agreed, however, to see Keen again, having been told that 'our friend from Canada is in the country. I must see you.' The rendezvous took place on 24 October and Scott took with him a Great Dane bitch called Rinka. They went in Keen's car, after eight o'clock at night, Keen driving very shakily, and they stopped at the very top of the moors at a remote spot. The wind was howling. Scott got out of the car and the dog jumped over the back seat and followed Keen out also. Scott caught hold of the chain around her neck, and then heard an unexpected sound. Rinka fell dead. 'You've shot my dog,' Scott shouted. 'Oh no, not my dog!'

Keen twisted Scott's right arm behind his back and held something —presumably a gun—to his head, saying, 'It's your turn.' Scott could feel the blood from the dog on his hands. There was a strange sort of noise at his head, but nothing happened. Keen's hand was shaking as he went back to the car. Scott did not know whether to run or stay.

Keen came back towards him with his arm pointed at him. Scott started to run away, but thinking of the dog, retraced his steps. Keen levelled his arm at him again, then turned back to the car in obvious frustration and drove off. Scott stayed with the dead Rinka for five or ten minutes until a car came along which he stopped. 'Oh, please,' he told the driver, 'he's shot my dog and tried to shoot me!'

Scott made it clear that he never actually saw the gun, but his belief was that Keen had shot the dog and tried to shoot him, but that the gun did not work the second time. The only alternative explanation, if the story was to be believed, was that Keen had been trying to frighten him. There was considerable corroboration for Scott's story, and a post-mortem on Rinka established that the poor creature had indeed died as the result of a bullet-wound.

Newton was subsequently to admit that he and Keen were one and the same person. He eventually admitted shooting the dog, but said that he had done no more than point the gun at Scott, which he agreed was loaded, at a distance of four or five feet. He had made no attempt, he said, to pull the trigger, his object having been to frighten a blackmailer and to secure the return of a letter and a photograph.

By way of explanation, he told a bizarre and incredible story about writing a letter, and enclosing a photograph of himself in the nude, to a girlie magazine. 'I thought I was writing to a bird,' he told the police, but apparently Scott turned up at his address, having somehow got hold of the supposedly incriminating evidence! Thereafter Scott, he said, had been blackmailing him.

At the trial Scott strongly refuted the allegations, and after three hours' consideration the jury convicted Newton on the main charge of possessing a firearm with intent to endanger life, for which offence he was sentenced to two years' imprisonment, and to smaller concurrent sentences on three lesser charges, including the one concerning the dog. It may be of interest if I record that seven months later Newton wrote from prison to the Clerk of the Court, requesting the return of a colour photograph of himself 'in my birthday suit'.

The whole affair was puzzling. If Scott were believed, there may have been an attempt to murder him, but on the evidence available it seemed unlikely that such a charge would stand up, and explanation that he was merely trying to frighten may have been nearer the truth. Scott was alleging an association in the past with prominent members of the Liberal Party, and it was difficult at the time to know what credence to give to what he was saying. In terms of prosecuting Newton, it was in any case irrelevant whether the truth was that the latter had induced Scott to go out onto the moors because he was connected with those helping Thorpe, or whether as he claimed, he was merely trying to get back the photograph.

There were rumblings of future trouble. Soon after the shooting of Rinka a question was asked in Parliament, and on 3 February 1976 Cyril Smith, the Liberal Member, during an interview on *News at Ten* said he had been told that a sum of money had been paid to Scott by Tory Central Office. This brought forth a demand from Sir Michael Havers, Q.C., M.P., the present Attorney-General, to the Attorney-General for the matter to be investigated by my Department. Representations about the affair were also made to us from other sources—though not, I hasten to say, from Mr Thorpe or any of his political colleagues—but there was nothing precise as far as hard evidence was concerned at that stage, certainly nothing that seemed relevant to Newton. It was only later that things started to come out which suggested that the stories being canvassed by Scott might be less unlikely than had at first appeared. It is only right to say, however, that there was no traceable connection at the time between Newton and Jeremy Thorpe or his friends.

Newton had been charged on 20 November 1975, and partly because of the nature of Scott's allegations, the file on the case was submitted to the Department by Avon and Somerset police on 10 December, asking us to assume responsibility. The Devon and Cornwall police were independently investigating Newton's complaint that Scott had been blackmailing him, and their report was received on 6 January 1976, and we immediately decided that the case against Newton should proceed. There was never any doubt as to the proper course of action, once we knew the facts—or such facts as were available.

There was no attempt at a cover-up, and no attempt to protect Jeremy Thorpe. One or two suggestions were made to this effect. The magazine *Private Eye*, for example, saw something sinister in the fact that, as they thought, we had asked Devon police to investigate an aspect of the case while another police force had charge of the Newton prosecution. I take this opportunity to explain that although the Avon and Somerset police were dealing with the case—for the simple reason that the incident actually took place within their territorial jurisdiction—matters relating to Norman Scott and Jeremy Thorpe were naturally investigated in Devon, where they were centred. It was a matter of practicality, nothing else.

The same magazine sought also to make something of the fact that Jeremy Thorpe's father was a King's Counsel on the Western Circuit where I learnt my law. I do not believe he was on that circuit; anyway, I certainly never knew him. The comment reflected an allegation by Norman Scott at the Thorpe trial that Thorpe had said to him, 'You can't hurt me . . . the DPP's a friend of mine.' From the context, since Scott was reporting a conversation he said had taken place at a time long before my appointment as Director, Thorpe must have been referring to Theobald Mathew—even if Scott had been correct in his recollection. In evidence, however, Scott actually referred to me by name, but he later retracted when it was pointed out that, having regard to the date, he must have been mistaken in referring to me. For the record, I knew Jeremy Thorpe—but not his father—as a member of the Western Circuit, and on one occasion I was instructed to lead him in a civil case that was settled out of court, but he was hardly a friend, and I cannot say that I knew him socially. One thing I can say with confidence is that my slight acquaintance with him personally in no way affected my behaviour, or that of the Department, in dealing with matters relating to him.

When Peter Hain was alleged to have stolen a bundle of £5 notes of the total value of £490 from a bank, and tried for this offence, the case—as would be expected—attracted much publicity. But I refer to it here only since certain politicians following his acquittal sought my resignation, and even as to one of them my dismissal, as Director of Public Prosecutions. I want, however, to make it quite clear that I do not wish in any way to impugn the verdict of the jury acquitting him. They found him not guilty after a protracted and careful consideration of all the evidence adduced both by the prosecution and by the defence, and I entirely accept as correct the conclusion which the jury reached, and that the case was one of mistaken identity by those who claimed to identify him. I feel confident, however, that readers of this book will appreciate (though some politicians appeared not to do so) that because a person has been rightly acquitted of an alleged offence, it does not necessarily follow that this person should not have been prosecuted. As I explained previously, when a case is submitted by the police to the D.P.P. for decision as to whether a prosecution should be initiated—or if it has already been commenced, whether it should be continued—those in the Department, including the Director himself, like counsel when they are instructed, do not and should not see and hear witnesses as to the facts. They make their decision on the written statements of the witnesses and any assessment of their reliability given by the police in their accompanying report. Obviously, if the case comes to trial the reliability of the evidence of the witnesses for the Crown may be eroded under cross-examination, or a different slant on the case may be given by the evidence adduced on behalf of the defence, and the

accused may be rightly acquitted, notwithstanding that the proceedings may have been perfectly properly initiated and brought to trial.

This case was referred to my Department five days after the police had charged Mr Hain with stealing the money, and their report with witness statements was submitted to us two weeks later. It was therefore on the evidence which we had before us that we had to decide whether the case should proceed.

The relevant facts as given in the statements initially submitted to us by the police for consideration were as follows:

On 24 October 1975, very shortly before one o'clock in the afternoon, a young man went into a branch of Barclay's Bank in Upper Richmond Road, Putney, and asked a lady cashier to change a £10 note (which he produced to her). While waiting for change, and apparently on the spur of the moment, he snatched a bundle of £5 notes from the counter, value £490, and ran out of the bank. He was chased by an accountant employed in the bank, and some young boys in the High Street saw the chase and ran behind them to find out what was going on. As the accountant gained on the man the thief threw the stolen money on the ground, saying 'All right, here you are,' and made off while the accountant picked it up. At this point the boys caught up with the accountant and then endeavoured to assist him in looking for the thief in various side-streets, but were unsuccessful. The last that the accountant saw of the thief was as he ran away down a road called Werter Road, and similarly the last that the boys saw of him at that stage was as he ran down that road and turned out of it when he reached the bottom.

About five minutes or so afterwards a man (admittedly Peter Hain) was seen by the boys to hurry out of a car in Werter Road and enter the local branch of W. H. Smith by the side-entrance. Two of them claimed immediately to have recognized him as the thief they and the accountant had been chasing, one of them saying 'We realized it was the same man that we had first seen—the man being chased, in the white check shirt. The man was dressed as before [he gave in his statement a detailed description of the man's clothing]. He was definitely the same man.' A second said 'I immediately recognized him as being the man who a few moments earlier had been chased along Werter Road.' The third boy was less positive, saying 'I thought the man was the same as the one being chased, but at that time I wasn't quite certain so I went to W. H. Smith's to make sure . . . and then I saw that he had glasses on: they had dark rims. He was dressed the same as the man being chased. To me he looked exactly the same except I did not see his face properly.' The boys followed him into the shop and told the assistants and a trainee manager what had happened and pointed to Peter Hain. They were advised to tell the police if they were sure. This they did, having noted the number of the car. As a result of this the man was traced and arrested, and taken to Wandsworth police station. He was none other than Peter Hain himself, whose home was in Fawe Park Road, quite near both to the bank where the theft had occurred and to Werter Road, down which the thief was chased.

When interviewed at the police station Hain remarked 'This is a fit-up. It's because of who I am.' On being told about the theft he said 'What on earth has that got to do with me?' In response to the evidence of the boys, he asked 'Is this a joke or something? This is absolutely incredible. You must be joking.' He said he had not even been to the bank. He was a public figure, and it would have been the height of stupidity for someone in his position to commit such an offence. He was later to say—and in this he was supported by members of his family—that at the time of the offence he was about to do shopping elsewhere. He had gone to Smith's to buy typewriter ribbons, and had hurried in because he had left his car on a yellow line. He maintained his innocence at all times. He told the police that he left his house at about 12.50, went to his mother's house two doors away to ask if he could do any shopping for her, then went in his car to the side-entrance to W. H. Smith's in Werter Road, and that he had returned home by about 1.10 p.m. This was confirmed by his solicitors on his behalf in a Notice required by statute of the alibi on which he was intending to rely. This stated that he left his home at approximately 12.50 p.m., and after briefly visiting his parents' home he entered his Volkswagen at approximately 12.55 p.m. and drove to Werter Road, where he left his car in the vicinity of W. H. Smith's shop. He returned to his car after making a purchase there and drove back to his home, and that he estimated that he was away from home for ten to fifteen minutes.

The defence later called a fifteen-year-old boy who said that he had been ahead of the chasing group until their quarry had turned and given him a look that scared him, so that he gave up the chase. He had seen the thief's face clearly three times, and the man was not like Peter Hain. He claimed that his friends had only gone to the police to get the afternoon off school and get a lift back in a police car. They all denied this, and it seems somewhat inconsistent with their being so motivated that they should have followed Peter Hain into W. H. Smith's shop, to tell the attendants what they said had occurred and to have sought advice (which was given them) as to what they should do. With reference to the fourth boy's statement that he had seen the thief's face clearly three times, and that he was not like Peter Hain, I should perhaps mention that two of the other three boys stated that the man whom they were chasing was wearing glasses, described by them as square ones with dark rims round the edges. It was when he looked back (one said four times; the other, three) that they noticed this. Peter Hain, of course, was admittedly wearing such glasses when he ran into the shop.

The police did not arrange for any of the three boys to go to an identification parade. This was no doubt because they had seen and identified Peter Hain as he ran into the shop, and a repeated identification of him at a parade would have been of little if any value. As for the adults, however, the accountant did not positively identify Peter Hain at an identification parade. The cashier from whom the money was stolen made a positive identification of Hain at a parade, and said that the only difference was that his hair was now more 'pushed up', adding that she had no doubt about the correctness of her identification.

Another cashier picked out somebody else on the parade who was quite unconnected and merely assisting by standing as one of the men on the parade.

A lady customer at the bank who had just drawn some money from the cashier from whom the notes were subsequently stolen was not able to make a positive identification. She added, however, that she only got a glimpse of the man when he was in the bank. A man later came forward after reading an appeal for witnesses by Hain's solicitors in a national newspaper, and said that he had seen the thief in the bank. This man was a customer intending to withdraw some money, and while he was writing a cheque for this purpose saw a man go up to the cashier and speak to her. He then heard the cashier yell out something like 'Hey', when he looked round and saw the man running out of the door. He attended a parade at which he said that he did not recognize anyone, but added 'On the other hand, I never really got a good look at the man in the bank in the first place.'

As one would expect in the case of a sudden and unexpected occurrence of this sort the witnesses did not purport to give exact times. There was, however, a remarkable consistency and agreement in the times which they did give, and it was clear from the statements of the witnesses who saw the thief at the bank and being chased in the street immediately afterwards that the theft had taken place between about 12.50 p.m. and 1 p.m.

Similarly, it was clearly the accused's case that he left in his car to go to purchase the typewriter ribbons at about 12.55 p.m. and that he arrived back at approximately 1.10 p.m. It followed therefore that he admittedly was away from his home unaccompanied and not far from the bank at just about the time that the theft occurred.

There then was the position as to identification at the time when my Department had to decide whether the prosecution which had already been commenced should proceed.

Mr Peter Hain had been identified positively and expressly without doubt by the cashier at the bank as the man who had stood immediately in front of her at the counter in daylight and had grabbed the bundle of £5 notes which were lying in front of her. She had previously on the day of the theft given a description of the man and made up a photo-fit picture of him by selecting various component features from a visual-aid handbook, both of which were considered reasonably to fit Peter Hain.

I should mention that on the day on which he was to stand on an identification parade the *Evening Standard* had published a photograph of Peter Hain with a statement that he was due on that day to appear on an identification parade. This resulted in contempt proceedings being taken and a substantial penalty being paid.

The cashier said, however, that although prior to attending the identification parade she had seen on a desk at the bank a folded newspaper with a headline something like 'I am not a bank robber' she did not touch the paper and certainly did not seen any photograph of Mr Hain.

Of the three schoolboys aged twelve who had taken part in the chase, two said they had recognized Peter Hain immediately and with certainty when he got out of his car and ran into a W. H. Smith's shop. The third was less positive, but had identified him in the terms which I have already indicated.

Further, the man whom these four witnesses identified in this way turned out to be a person who not only had been out from his home unaccompanied in the immediate vicinity of the bank at just about the time of the theft but who was back in Werter Road—true, in a car, wherever it might have come from—only a few minutes after the thief had been chased and had dropped the stolen money in that road.

On the other hand, the accountant who had chased the thief through the streets was unable at the identification parade positively to identify Peter Hain, nor was any of the other witnesses who had seen the thief, either in the bank or being chased through the street immediately outside, able to do so. One, indeed, as I have said, picked out a person who was not in any way a suspect, and had merely been asked to assist by being one of the men standing on the parade.

As I have said, there was later called for the defence a fourth boy, who said that he had been ahead of the chasing group, and that the man being chased was not like Peter Hain. The defence solicitor supplied us with a copy of the statement which he had taken from this boy, but not as far as I can remember after this length of time, until after the committal proceedings when the case was sent for trial. If my recollection is right as to this, therefore, it was not part of the evidence we had before us when we decided that the case should proceed, but even if it had been, it would not, I think, have affected our view that the case was clearly one which should be tried by a jury.

Positive evidence of identification, provided that it is in circumstances in which it appears to be reliable, is evidentially of greater value than evidence of a negative nature merely indicating that witnesses are unable positively to identify anyone, particularly if they had only a fleeting glance.

The fourth boy, of course, went further than merely failing to identify anyone by giving evidence that the man whom he chased was not like Hain. His evidence had therefore to be considered together with the evidence of those who had affirmatively identified Peter Hain. Just as they might be mistaken, so might the fourth boy, and one must consider their evidence and his in the light of all the circumstances, including their conduct. The fourth boy apparently became scared and gave up the chase. As I have said, I confess that I did not find his suggestion that the other three boys purported to identify the person in question, and went to the police only to get a half day's holiday (and hopefully a ride in a police car) at all convincing.

In Hain's favour was the fact that his fingerprints were not found on the recovered notes. What other prints were there were all eliminated, but there was actually one print that did not match that of any of the bank personnel. (Further, his fingerprints were not found on the £10 note which had been left by the thief, but I do not know what if any prints there were on it.) There was also talk of the whole business having been set up by South African interests anxious to damage a powerful enemy. I understand that one man did later claim to have seen dossiers that indicated a classic frame-up. According to his story, a double was flown to Britain from South Africa, and the theft was timed by two-way radio, alerting the double that Hain had left his home to go shopping. I do not know whether this person was available as a witness, nor how far he could have given any admissible evidence.

It is pertinent in view of the criticisms subsequently levelled by the politicians to point out that Mr Hain was represented by very experienced advocates. Prior to the committal proceedings a copy of the statements made by each of the Crown's witnesses was supplied to the solicitors, who had the opportunity to ensure that the committal proceedings were in a form which would enable them to submit that the evidence was not sufficiently strong to justify the accused being committed for trial. They did not, however, do this. Similarly, but even more important, at the trial Mr Hain was represented by exceedingly experienced leading and junior counsel, who could at the end of the prosecution's case have submitted that the evidence was not sufficient for it to be safe for the case to be left to the jury to decide, and that it should not therefore proceed further. Had they thought that such a submission was justified I feel confident that his counsel would have taken this course. However, no such submission was made. Similarly, even without any such submission being made, it would have been open to the judge of his own accord, had he thought it right to have done so, to have directed the jury to acquit on the ground that the evidence was so weak that it would be unsafe for the trial to proceed further. He did not do so.

The trial opened at the Old Bailey before Judge King-Hamilton, Q.C., on 30 March 1976. The issues were thoroughly canvassed, and leading counsel for the defence spoke of the great dangers of identification based on fleeting glimpses. There was no section of the criminal law, he said, in which there had been more proven miscarriages of justice than in the case of mistaken identity. The judge too warned the jury as to the special care that should be exercised before convicting on evidence of identification, because of the risks of mistake being made by witnesses in such cases.

The jury retired to consider their verdict on 9 April. After four and a half hours they could not agree, and the judge then told them that he was permitted now to accept a majority verdict if it was one on which at least ten agreed. After a further retirement they came back with a verdict of not guilty, which met with cheers in the gallery. I wish again to make it abundantly clear that I do not quarrel with the verdict in any way, but I do strongly dispute the criticism levelled by the politicians at myself and my Department following the acquittal. Mr David Steel, M.P., sponsored a motion 'That this House calls for the resignation of the Director of Public Prosecutions.' This was signed by five members in addition to Mr Steel—a total of three Liberal and three Labour Members.

One of Mr Steel's co-signatories, Labour Member Neil Kinnock, went even further. He said that the Hain trial threw 'into great doubt the capacity of the Director of Public Prosecutions because it had been quite apparent throughout this affair that this case should never

114

have come to trial.' Quite apparent to certain politicians, perhaps, but not by any means to all of them, for a proposed amendment to Mr David Steel's motion was put down by Sir Frederic Bennett and signed by six Conservative Members. This amendment sought to substitute after the word 'House'

> notes that more honourable Members have joined the Right honourable Member for Walsall North in seeking the resignation of the Director of Public Prosecutions; assumes this follows the Hain acquittal; congratulates Mr Hain on having the good fortune to live in a country where accused people are often found innocent; notes his latest knocking campaign without surprise; waits expectantly to hear adverse comment from him on countries with legal systems where accusations are tantamount to guilt; . . . .

I was grateful for this support, but I regretted that a decision as to whether people should be prosecuted should apparently have become the subject of party politics. Such decisions should be above any party political considerations, and so far as I was concerned, were always kept completely free from them.

I maintained at the time, and I still maintain, that the prosecution of Peter Hain was justified, although I accept of course that he was mistaken for somebody else. Had action not been taken on the evidence available, there might well have been accusations of a cover-up. Indeed, in a letter to *The Times* published on 13 April, following the acquittal, the late Rt. Hon. Sir Eric Sachs (formerly until his retirement, Lord Justice of Appeal), referring to what he called 'unfounded criticism' of me, wrote (after referring to the course which the trial had taken): 'It is thus plain, without in the slightest impugning the verdict, that the Director's appraisal was correct when holding it was his unpleasant duty to continue the proceedings: had he done otherwise he would have been in breach of his duty.'

A decision to prosecute does not imply that a person is necessarily guilty of the offence charged, but that there is a case to answer. Someone had undoubtedly committed the offences, and there were witnesses who claimed to identify Peter Hain. However unlikely it was that someone in his position, so much in the public eye, would seek to steal from a bank, there was virtually no option but to proceed. Mr Hain himself would, I assume, be the last person to suggest that there should be one law for the famous and one for others.

One felt that a degree of political capital was being made out of the

Hain case. The Home Secretary and the Attorney-General faced questions in the Commons about the cost of the prosecution and about police procedure, and there was a call for an inquiry into the handling of the case. The Attorney expressed himself as satisfied that my decision that there was a prima facie case, suitable for trial by jury, was a reasonable one. When asked by David Steel to dismiss me, the Home Secretary's answer was simply 'No'.

People can look alike, and there are many people who have doubles or near-doubles. This makes it all the more necessary to be careful in cases where the issue of identification is central, and just as a court will always look for corroboration when rape is alleged, so it may be dangerous to rely on evidence of identification alone. Peter Hain was unfortunate in that a theft was carried out by someone who resembled him so closely as to confuse people, but I think one would have to be very prejudiced to agree with him that his trial was, as he put it, 'a farcical prosecution'.

One useful by-product of the Hain case was that it further directed public attention to the problems of identification. In the previous year the Court of Appeal had overturned convictions based on evidence of identification, and Lord Widgery had made the important observation that misidentification was the most serious chink in our armour when we say British justice is the best in the world. (I used similar words myself when I gave evidence to the Devlin Committee, quoted in their Report, to the effect that identification was the Achilles heel in our criminal law.) A committee had been set up under the chairmanship of Lord Devlin—before the commencement of the Hain case—to examine the question, and following publication of its report (in which it recommended that proceedings should not in future be taken on evidence of identification alone) the Attorney-General announced in the House of Commons, on 27 May 1976, that he and I had reviewed the whole area of identification evidence and procedure and had agreed on certain guidelines for the future. Later that year the Court of Appeal—a five-judge bench—in R. v. Turnbull and others laid further guidelines to be observed by trial judges when identity is in issue. They did not wholly agree with Devlin, and, while stressing the special warnings that must be given to a jury as to the danger of mistake in the case of identification evidence, they gave examples of instances where it would be perfectly proper to proceed, and indeed to convict, on evidence of identification alone. It will be understood that at the time we were considering the Hain matter we did not have the benefit of the Devlin Committee's report and the guidelines later laid down by the Court of Appeal, but even had the Hain case arisen subsequently, I think that, taking into account the Turnbull judgment in the Court of Appeal, we would have been unlikely to have come to any different decision regarding prosecution. The application of these guidelines to a case of identification by several persons in relation to separate incidents may well be different from several-persons' identification at the same time in relation to one incident.

The Hain case was perhaps a classic example of mistaken identity, but I was concerned (though only indirectly) with an even more extraordinary case where identity was the issue, and once again a prominent figure was involved. Now, I can well believe that there may be many men around who look not unlike Peter Hain, but I venture to express the opinion that there are few who could have been mistaken for the late Sir Gerald Nabarro, M.P.

Nabarro sported a moustache as famous as that of Jimmy Edwards, so how could he possibly have been mistaken for a woman? Yet that was what was claimed. In the early evening of 21 May 1971 a stream of traffic was travelling north on the Southampton to Ower road when a Daimler-Jaguar car, with the well-known number-plate NAB1 belonging to the flamboyant Sir Gerald, arrived so fast at a round-about that, unable to negotiate it in the normal way, it went around it in the wrong direction, narrowly avoiding a collision with an oncoming lorry, which was forced to drive off the road onto the side.

Unfortunately, the lorry-driver was never traced, but there were two apparently reliable witnesses. One, an engineer named Jones, said that he had noticed the rogue Jaguar in his mirror, overtaking cars until it pulled in immediately behind him and then tried to overtake him when it was unsafe to do so, forcing him to brake and swerve on to the nearside verge. By the time he was able to regain the road the other vehicle was about six cars ahead of him, still over-taking, until it reached the roundabout, where he witnessed the dangerous manoeuvre. The other, a film editor named Ambrose, said that he was approaching the roundabout when he saw in his mirror a car approaching fast. When he was about four vehicles away from the roundabout, and there was no adequate room for anybody to pass, he was surprised that the car overtook him at speed, forcing him and the vehicles in front of him to brake, and in such a way as to have been unable itself to regain the correct side of the road.

Mr Jones felt that he had been involved in so serious an incident of bad driving that only his experience had saved him from an accident. He stopped Mr Ambrose and asked him if he would act as a witness. He then reported the matter immediately at Totton Police Station.

Both men had independently taken the number of the dangerous car. Jones stated that the driver was a man, and was almost certain that the front-seat passenger was a woman. Ambrose stated that the driver was a man in his fifties with a moustache, and he was certain that the passenger was a woman. In due course both men gave evidence in court that Sir Gerald Nabarro, M.P., was the driver.

Nabarro was not the sort of man to have been easily mistaken for somebody else, and the converse was of course true. He was a personality who was not averse to publicity, and his face was familiar to many people who watched television or read newspapers. With his prominent moustache, he could hardly have been mistaken for a woman, and in any case the two witnesses were positive about the driver being a man. What on earth were the police to think, therefore, when following the dispatch to Nabarro of the statutory notice of intended prosecution his secretary Mrs Margaret Mason telephoned them to say that she had driven the car on the occasion in question, and that she could remember no incident that might have caused her to be prosecuted?

I do not mean to be facetious when I say that his secretary did not have a moustache and that she could not have been mistaken for a man if she had been seen full face, or even in profile. (One feels bound to add, however, that if the witnesses only identified the driver as being a man when they were looking at the car from some distance behind, they could readily have been mistaken.) She was interviewed by the police, and stuck to her story, but she declined to make a written statement. Nabarro was later seen by a senior police officer, to whom he claimed that he had been asleep in the car at the crucial time, and that his secretary had been driving.

There was a complete conflict of evidence. It would seem highly improbable that Nabarro and his secretary could both be mistaken in their recollection, and the possibility had to be faced that either the witnesses were mistaken or he and his secretary were both lying.

In the event Nabarro was summoned for dangerous driving and for driving without due care and attention. He elected to go for trial, as he was entitled to do on the charge of dangerous driving, and the case was heard on 24 January 1972 at Winchester Crown Court before Mr Justice Bridge. J. Spokes appeared for the police, and Petre Crowder, Q.C., for Sir Gerald.

Mr Jones and Mr Ambrose gave their evidence, and persisted in their account of the events. Nabarro was called in his own defence, and repeated his story, which in turn was confirmed by Mrs Mason, who said that she had been employed by Sir Gerald as his driver for about a month before the alleged incident. She alone had driven the

118

car that evening. Support for this version came from Mr McNair Wilson, M.P., on whose behalf Nabarro had addressed a meeting during the afternoon. He had seen Sir Gerald and Mrs Mason leave, and according to his recollection Mrs Mason had been driving the car. There was a possibility that Sir Gerald and his secretary-driver had changed places after stopping at an antique shop soon after their departure, but they both denied this.

The judge put the issue squarely to the jury. Either the prosecution witnesses were mistaken or Sir Gerald and Mrs Mason were giving false evidence. 'It is no use', he said, 'shutting one's eyes to the implication of that.'

After 2 hours and 35 minutes the jury were unable to reach a unanimous verdict. The judge then instructed them regarding a majority verdict, and by eleven to one, after a further retirement, they brought in a verdict of guilty. Nabarro was fined £250 and disqualified from driving for two years. 'This was not', Mr Justice Bridge told the convicted Member of Parliament, 'an error of judgment. This was a deliberate and outrageous piece of driving.'

Exactly a week later Sir Gerald applied for the suspension of the driving disqualification, but Mr Justice Croom-Johnson dismissed the application. The Court of Appeal, however, in June 1972 ordered a retrial on the basis of new evidence. The Court was told by his counsel, Mr Petre Crowder, Q.C., that the day after his conviction Sir Gerald was interviewed on the B.B.C.'s radio programme *World at One*, and that as a result a number of witnesses came forward. He also told the Court that there was no dispute that the car was being driven dangerously—the sole issue was the identity of the driver. After the Court had heard the evidence from five new witnesses, Lord Widgery, the Lord Chief Justice, said after consulting the other two judges, 'It is abundantly obvious that there is here a matter to be debated before the court' and ordered that there should be a new trial, and that the previous conviction be quashed, and that Sir Gerald's driving licence should be returned to him. The new trial took place at the Guildhall, Winchester, the following October, almost nine months to the day after the first trial. The police were now represented by Sir Joseph Molony, Q.C., leading J. Spokes, and Petre Crowder, Q.C., again appeared for Nabarro, who once more asserted that his secretary had been driving the car.

On this occasion Mrs Mason was not called to give evidence. This gave rise to speculation as to the reason for this, and some appeared to think that it was because it was thought that she at any rate might have changed her evidence as to the driving of Sir Gerald's car. I note from the Press that he is reported to have said following his acquittal that 'Legal advice was that she should not be called.' I do not of course know the reasons for this advice, which was entirely a matter for his legal advisers, but there are several good and valid reasons why it should have been given, and I do not think—and should have been surprised to learn—that it was because it was thought that Mrs Mason might have changed her evidence about the driving of the car. The jury at the second trial returned a unanimous verdict of not guilty after an absence of 2 hours and 50 minutes. Since at this trial—presumably in accordance with what counsel had told the Court of Appeal—there was no dispute as to the car having been driven dangerously, this verdict must have been on the basis that they were satisfied that Sir Gerald's secretary was in fact driving the car at the material time and place, or at least that it had not been proved beyond reasonable doubt that she was not doing so. It is only fair to her, therefore, to remember this and to regard it as vindicating her in the evidence she gave at the first trial in respect of the driving of the car.

I should make it clear that the prosecution was not launched by my Department but by the Hampshire Constabulary. The Hampshire police had been in touch with us about the case in August 1971, but beyond offering advice about the charges we did not intervene in the matter, and the conduct of both trials was entirely in the hands of the police and their legal advisers.

I mention this because some people seemed to assume otherwise, and at least one prominent Member of Parliament and several private citizens wrote either to the Attorney-General or to the Lord Chancellor or direct to us about the case, and I was obliged not only to explain the facts but to decide whether to pursue the matter further. There were as far as I can remember some who seemed to think that since Mrs Mason was not used as a witness for the defence, she should have been called by the prosecution. It is unnecessary for me now to go into any detail with regard to this, but there are of course a number of reasons why the prosecution would not be expected in the circumstances to call and rely on her as a witness, and I would have been most surprised if they had done so. Obviously, they could only have even contemplated doing this if she altered her previous evidence. If she had altered her evidence as to who was driving they would not wish to call as a Crown witness someone who had considerably altered her evidence given previously.

In any event, the question as to the witnesses whom he should call was entirely a matter within the discretion of prosecuting counsel Sir Joseph Molony (unhappily since deceased), whom I knew well, and greatly admired. He was one of the most skilled and experienced counsel on the Western Circuit, and I should certainly always have had complete confidence in his judgment on a question of this sort.

As to other aspects of the case, my general advice was that the issues had been most fully and adequately examined in the courts, and that no useful purpose would have been served by further interviewing Mrs Mason or any other of those concerned.

CHAPTER 8

Matters of security

I HAVE explained why immunity was granted to Smalls in return for his evidence. Had he killed anybody, I should undoubtedly have taken a different view about him, because I cannot conceive that it can ever be in the public interest not to prosecute a murderer—provided, of course, there is sufficient evidence to present to a judge and jury. The public interest has to be considered even more carefully in cases involving national security. The question of granting immunity to Professor (Sir) Anthony Blunt in respect of his activities in relation to the Soviet Union was dealt with during the inter-regnum before I assumed the Directorship, and I only became aware of it at a considerably later date. However it would appear that there was in any event no evidence against him at this time other than legally inadmissible confessions provided by himself as a result of an inducement.

Occasionally a case arose which if it were mishandled could have adversely affected the country's relations with foreign governments. An example was the arrest of Leila Khaled, a Palestinian Arab woman, following the attempted hijacking of an Israeli aircraft in 1970. She and a companion known both as Arguello and as Diaz boarded a Boeing 707 airliner belonging to El Al Airlines at Schiphol Airport, Amsterdam. The plane was en route from the Netherlands to New York. Soon after departure, Khaled and her accomplice tried unsuccessfully to capture the aircraft and force the pilot to divert it to Amman in Jordan. This involved the use of both guns and grenades. According to Khaled herself, eleven minutes after departure she and Arguello rushed towards the flight deck, she with a grenade in each hand and he with a revolver and a grenade. They were confronted by the purser, named Eisenberg. Arguello demanded that he open the cockpit door, and fired at his legs. At the same time Khaled was forcing one of the air hostesses to knock on the cockpit door, threatening if the door were not opened to shoot a steward named Vider, who was in the forward area.

Eisenberg communicated with Captain Bar-Lev by telephone. 'It's a hijack,' he said quite simply, 'with a gun and grenades. Two people.' The flight engineer then looked through the cabin door on the Captain's instructions, and was able to confirm that he could see a man with a gun and a grenade. The Captain thereupon immediately informed London Airport. He was asked to repeat his message, and did so. The time of the message was all-important. It was received a few seconds before 12.50 p.m., at which point the air traffic control officer (who was watching the radar screen) noted that the aircraft was just over the town of Clacton-on-Sea—or in other words, in British air space.

At 12.51 Captain Bar-Lev informed London Airport that he was pursuing an emergency descent. He then caused the airliner to dive, so as to throw whomsoever was outside the cockpit off balance. Certain members of the crew then bravely tackled their two attackers. In the fracas steward Vider was shot in the stomach, but was fortunately not killed. Khaled actually pulled out the pin from one of the grenades, but miraculously it had a weak spring and failed to explode. Unaware of this, Purser Eisenberg held both her hands tight to try to prevent an explosion.

Arguello fired seven shots from his gun, and it was presumably one of these that hit Vider. The male attacker himself was shot four times—there were security guards on the plane—and within a minute both attackers were overcome and tied up. The Boeing made an emergency landing at London Airport, and although at first the crew were reluctant to deliver up the hijackers, they eventually did so. Arguello died from a wound through the heart before he could reach hospital. Khaled was taken into police custody.

It seemed beyond dispute that she had been involved in the commission of a number of offences against British law. The steward, Vider, had been shot by Arguello, and she could have been charged as having been a party to Arguello's attempt. There had been an attempt to steal the aircraft—contrary to Section 12 of the Theft Act of 1968, by the way! There was also the possession of ammunition with intent to endanger life, and the possession of explosives for an unlawful object. Some consideration was even given to the possibility of a charge of piracy. We had first to establish, however, whether the offences had been committed within our jurisdiction. With a plane travelling at over 400 m.p.h., there was some slight doubt as to where precisely the attempted hijacking had taken place. At such a speed, two or three minutes could make the difference as to whether the aircraft had actually passed into British air space. There was a possibility that the attempt had been commenced outside our jursidiction, but that it had continued within it.

Having examined all the facts, I came to the conclusion that there was sufficient evidence to support the belief that certain offences had been committed while the plane was in British air space, and by Article 1 of the Convention of Paris, 1919, every Power has sovereignty over the air space above its territory. It was a question, therefore, of what charges, if any, should be made. The matter was complicated because the Israeli authorities sought Khaled's extra-dition to Israel. The El Al Boeing was, of course, an Israeli aircraft, and by virtue of the Tokyo Convention Act of 1967, Israel also had jurisdiction.

A deceptively easy option would have been to hand Khaled over to the Israelis, saving us the time and expense of prosecuting her and the cost of maintaining her in prison if she were convicted and sentenced to a term of imprisonment. Even had we wanted to do this, however, inevitably she would have claimed that her offences were of a political nature and that it would have been oppressive to have sent her to Israel. Exactly what constitutes a political offence raises a number of very complex questions, and if indeed we had decided that Israeli jurisdiction should take precedence over our own, we would undoubtedly have incurred the wrath of the Jordanian Government and of many Arab nations. It was impossible to satisfy both Israel and Jordan.

Khaled was a member of the Popular Front for the Liberation of Palestine, which to the Israelis was a terrorist gang whose members were prepared to use terrorist methods to achieve their ends. Goodness knows what would have happened if Khaled's grenade had exploded in the pressurized aircraft, and how many innocent lives would have been lost. The Israelis argued that to repatriate a fanatic, who was prepared to sacrifice her own life for her cause, would only serve to encourage further acts of terrorism. Unfortunately, we could not look at her case in isolation, for it became linked with the blowing up of three aircraft in Jordan and the concomitant safety of their passengers and crew who were taken hostage by a guerrilla group, whose demands included the release of Khaled.

I have already explained that the Director of Public Prosecutions is answerable to the Attorney-General, and must in the last analysis take instructions from the Attorney, should he seek to give them. This does not in practice mean that the Director is in any real way inhibited in his ability to make decisions. I cannot conceive of circumstances, for example, where the Attorney would seek to interfere with the day-to-day operations of the Department, although of course he would from time to time consult with us about matters that might conceivably require his response in Parliament. Indeed, we would ourselves have drawn to his attention any matters that seemed to us peculiarly sensitive.

I never felt that I lacked the independence to make my own decisions, and in my whole stewardship I never had reason to feel that there was interference from the law officers. In this particular instance, involving political issues, I was only too happy to be able to lean on the Attorney-General. The matter required delicate handling at the political rather than the legal level, and I did not regard myself as the best person to decide what was in the public interest. Prosecution of Khaled for possession of explosives required by statute the consent of the Attorney, although I did not need his consent for a charge of attempted murder, but in a matter of this nature, raising as it did our relations with foreign countries, I was content to seek his advice as to whether the public interest here would be served by prosecution. There were also complicated considerations as to whether alternatively Khaled should be extradited to Israel or repatriated to Jordan, and this was a matter to discuss with the Home Secretary, who was responsible for extradition, and the Foreign Secretary.

'The Khaled Case,' to quote the main leader in *The Times* of 11 September 1970, 'is caught up in matters of high diplomacy, and takes its place in the balance between peace and war in the Middle East.' Three aircraft, one a British VC10, were blown up at Dawson's Field in the Jordanian desert. The passengers and crew, including eight who were British, were held hostage in or near Amman, and demands were made to the governments of the United States, West Germany, Switzerland, Israel and Britain for the return of a number of people, including Leila Khaled, who were held for terrorist activities in those countries.

A co-ordinating committee was set up representing the five nations who were all concerned primarily for the safety of the hostages, although there were naturally differences of opinion as to how best to deal with the problem. The Israelis, for example, were the least inclined to compromise, and they rounded up a number of Arabs, presumably in the hope of increasing their bargaining powers. There was much public discussion at home, such eminent politicians as Enoch Powell and Duncan Sandys maintaining that the law should take its normal course.

All along the British Government made it clear that they could not countenance any sort of arrangement that would involve the return of only some of the hostages. It was not enough that women and children should be released. All hostages must be treated similarly, regardless of sex, nationality or religion. Negotiations were proceeding on this basis when the situation appeared to get out of hand, and it seemed to the Government that there would be a very real threat to the lives of the hostages unless Leila Khaled were released. She had already been treated somewhat specially on instructions from the Home Secretary, who allowed her to be detained at Ealing police station instead of in Holloway Prison. Now Palestinian extremists were said to be on the rampage in Amman, and a serious riot was feared.

In these circumstances a committee of eight senior Ministers met, including the Prime Minister, Edward Heath, and they let it be known that they were prepared to return Khaled to an Arab country as part of a satisfactory settlement of the hostages issue. The Attorney-General announced that he would not be recommending a prosecution. In the result Khaled was allowed to leave the country and all the hostages were freed.

There was something of an outcry in certain circles, where it was felt that pandering to terrorism could only encourage further problems of this nature. I have much respect for this view, as well as for the view that the safety of innocent hostages must always be safeguarded as far as possible. There are some issues where there is no exclusive right and no exclusive wrong, and I was pleased that my part in the proceedings was a modest one of advising on the legal situation.

Arab, and more recently Islamic, militancy has been a feature of recent years. No longer are these people content to fight their battles on their own home ground. They regard the foreign streets of London and elsewhere as their rightful battleground, on which to demonstrate and even kill. I intend no comment about the justice or otherwise of their causes when I point out the problems they create for those whose duty it is to protect our security and uphold our law. Hijackings, kidnappings and the taking of hostages are a particularly nasty and insidious form of activity, and unfortunately they are on the increase, given sanction even by the government and people of one particular Middle Eastern country. Such crimes raise very difficult issues, for the safety of innocent people is often involved, and this has to be balanced against the encouragement that is given to such activities by capitulating to the demands of terrorists and criminals who were manifestly willing to exploit the seizure of hostages to achieve their ends.

What looked at one time to be another sensitive problem, involving Black militancy, at least one foreign government and even, it was rumoured, the Mafia, was known as the Spaghetti House siege. The techniques employed on that occasion, as also in the matter of the Balcombe Street siege involving IRA men on the run, were later to come in useful during the siege of the Iranian Embassy in 1980. The police, whose handling of the Spaghetti House affair was quite admirable, learned many valuable lessons at the time about how to deal with situations of this nature.

It all began on a Saturday night, 27 September 1975, at the head-quarters of a company that ran a chain of restaurants in central London which specialized in Italian cuisine. Most, if not all, the directors and managers of the group were of Italian origin, and it was the custom on Saturday nights for branch managers to meet at their Spaghetti House restaurant at 77 Knightsbridge, there to discuss the week's business and to count the takings for that particular day before depositing them in the night safe at Barclays Bank, Hyde Park Corner, about 250 yards away.

On the night in question nine managers assembled, including the General Manager, Giovanni Mai. Having held their meeting, they put the money they were planning to bank into two cases and switched off the lights as they were about to leave the restaurant. As they reached the glass doors to the street three Black gunmen confronted them. Two carried pistols, and one was armed with a sawn-off shotgun. One man had a balaclava pulled down over his face, with slits cut out as eyepieces. They demanded the takings.

Mr Mai and another manager, Alfredo Olivelli, dropped the cases containing the money and kicked them under the restaurant tables. The gunmen shepherded the managers back into the room and ordered them downstairs into the basement self-service area. The nine Italians and the three Blacks descended the stairs in single file, led by the General Manager.

The area was in darkness, which was unfortunate for the gunmen, since Mr Mai, unseen by them, was able to escape up another set of stairs into the restaurant and out into the street.

The gunmen had apparently not had time to count heads, and were unaware that one of the Italians had got away. They ordered the others to remove their jackets and empty their pockets, taking charge of the proceeds. Then two of them forced the manager Mario Roscelli at gunpoint to return upstairs and open the safe, but they must have been disappointed, for all they found were two small packages containing £40 each, presumably uncollected wage packets for two waiters. As Mr Roscelli and the two gunmen were about to rejoin the others in the basement the police arrived, alerted by Mr Mai from the near-by Berkeley Hotel.

It was now early on Sunday morning, 1.53 to be precise. The gunmen could not understand what had gone wrong with their plans, and how the police had come on the scene. Roscelli was pushed forcefully down the stairs, dropping the wage packets in the process, and in considerable panic the gunmen drove the Italians as hostages into a basement storeroom, where all eleven men, managers and gunmen, were virtually prisoners behind locked doors. The Spaghetti House siege had begun.

At about 2.30 Superintendent Dean arrived and spoke to the gunmen through the door. He was told to leave and come back at four o'clock, which he did. He then spoke to a man who identified himself as Franklyn Davies and who demanded the attendance of the Home Secretary. Dean returned an hour later and was met by a demand for a radio. It was then that the first of a series of written notes was pushed under the door. It was in the form of a poem, and read: 'We are tired of hustling on the street, scraping every day for meat. We want to live, black and free. Try making a world where everybody's happy. The very first time I had a taste of relative freedom, I had a gun in my hand, and I said to the man "Now you understand."' (The word 'relative' was in capitals and underlined; the word 'gun' appeared in capital letters within a square, presumably for emphasis.)

It was by no means clear what sort of people the gunmen were, and it was difficult to assess their intelligence. The obvious explanation was that they were common criminals who had embarked on an enterprise that had gone wrong, and support is lent to this view by the fact that Davies had been released from prison only five months previously after receiving concurrent sentences totalling ten years for offences including robbery while armed and robbery with violence. On the other hand, they seemed to be making some sort of political statement, and it may be significant that one of the other gunmen had no previous record, and the third had only minor convictions. Be that as it may, the political angle became more apparent when a senior official arrived from the Home Office at about seven o'clock and was confronted with three demands: the release of 'the Cricklewood eleven'—not a cricket team but a reference to a group of people currently on trial at the Old Bailey; the release from prison of two men convicted in respect of what was known as the 'Brockwell Park fracas'; and the dropping of charges against the 'Luton Dollar Road seven'. These were all cases where Blacks were involved, and the gunmen insisted that their demands be acknowledged in a letter signed and stamped by the Home Secretary.

Meanwhile the police called in experts who set in motion a monitoring system that enabled them to hear what was happening in the storeroom, and later in the day they were joined by a psychiatrist. They also provided a small transistor radio, as demanded, which they placed outside the door, and which was taken in by one of the hostages.

By 8.30 a.m. Sir Robert Mark, the Commissioner of the Metropolitan Police, had arrived at the scene and a note was passed asking for a tin-opener—there were obviously tins in the restaurant storeroom—and drinks in the form of coffee, orange juice and water. There was also a request for cigarettes ('Senior Service', 'Marlboro' 20, 'Dunhill' 20, 40 'Benson & Hedges' were specified!) A similar message the following day, for eight packets, was accompanied by four one-pound notes, the money contributed by the hostages, according to the writer.

At the request of the hostages, the intervention of the Italian Ambassador was sought and a number of conversations took place throughout the morning and early afternoon between the Italian Consul-General and the gunmen. These resulted most encouragingly in an agreement to release Mr Olivelli, who, aged fifty-nine, was the oldest of the hostages, probably to ensure the release to the media of a statement prepared by the gunmen and handed by Davies to Olivelli as he was freed at 4.40 p.m.

This statement, signed by Davies, began: 'We are part of a new Black Liberationist Army. We came to the Knightsbridge Spaghetti House with two principal aims: A) to finance the operations of our organisation. B) To demand a halt to police repression of Black people.' The statement referred again to the case of the Cricklewood eleven and went on: 'After these demands have been met, we want a car to take us and our hostages to Heathrow Airport. There we demand an aeroplane to be waiting to take us to a destination of our choice.' The threat was then made that 'If our demands are not met, we will be forced to shoot our hostages one by one.'

There was no way the authorities could take anything but a very serious view of such a threat, but throughout the rest of the day, and the following day, Monday the 29th, contact was kept up and conversations continued. The Italian Ambassador delivered a letter in which he said that he was aware that the hostages had not been ill-treated so far, and in which he appealed for their release. It was returned immediately marked 'Rejected'. He, however, was given a letter for the Home Secretary in which the gunmen said they would never surrender to the police. They intended to leave as free men, 'either dead with our hostages or alive into a waiting minibus which will take us straight to an aeroplane at Heathrow. When it is decided that we are to leave here with our hostages and our guns, you have our absolute word as black, proud men that we will not shoot unless the police fire first. We are freedom fighters, not cold-blooded monsters.'

The same letter referred to life in the storeroom as 'becoming impossible'. 'By continuing to "sit it out",' they wrote, 'you are playing with the lives of these unfortunate men, three of whom are already in need of medical attention!'

It was shortly after this that the Italian Consul-General asked for the release of the sick men, promising personally to contact Roy Jenkins, the Home Secretary, in Blackpool. When this undertaking was broadcast on the radio the gunmen made a gesture by releasing Mr Cenicolla, who was taken to hospital. There were signs that their bark might have been worse than their bite.

On Tuesday the 30th, more was discovered about the gunmen and their associates. A Black woman, claiming to be a supporter of the Black Liberation Front, arrived with a representative of the Nigerian Embassy. Davies had been brought up in Nigeria, and the woman may have been a friend of his who had approached the Embassy in an effort to help him. She claimed to know the identity of the gunmen, and gave their first names as Bonsu (otherwise called Tony), Frank and Wesley. Frank, of course, was Franklyn Davies. The police suspected that Bonsu was Anthony Munroe and the third man Wesley Dick.

Since the start of the siege the police—whose conduct throughout is deserving of the highest praise—had been making inquiries about Davies. These inquiries also appeared to implicate an Italian named Lillo Termine.

While these inquiries were proceeding, the gunmen continued to issue their statements. They described themselves as the 'Martyrs of Knightsbridge', as 'three black men surrounded by over two hundred enemy guns' and 'the soldiers of the people, the niggers of the street'. They went on:

> We have progressed to a certain stage, but now we are running on the spot. To go any further forward it is necessary to demonstrate we are willing to die for our cause. . . . We cannot beg for freedom, we have to take it. . . . We are the new breed of Black people, Proud, Revolutionary and Free. Today we have to take our freedom, the same way the Babylonians took us out of Africa and put us in America and the West Indies to become their slaves. We have to take our freedom the same way these people take our lives every day. Black people have been

dying for years for the WRONG reasons. Death in the struggle for liberation of Black people is death of the highest order.'

By the following day, Wednesday, 1 October, the police were prepared for a long siege. They continued to converse with the gunmen and to meet their requests for water, coffee and cigarettes. Still the notes were pushed under the door. One, signed 'Major Davies', was addressed to the government and people of Italy. 'We three men', it said, 'are a cell of the Black Liberationist Army, a newly formed and highly secret urban guerrilla organisation which is loosely affiliated to the Black Liberation Front and various other groups. We have no quarrel with the eight men we took hostage. Our only purpose in life is to defend the interests of the Black community in the area in which we live. This means that we have occasionally to confront the British state, and all its organs, in particular the police force which has been notorious in the oppression of our people.' I am reminded irresistibly of the communiqués issued by the Angry Brigade. It is almost as if these people went to the same school. This document claimed: 'We entered the Knightsbridge Spaghetti house with the intention of raising £20,000 for our organisation.'

These letters revealed a mixture of intelligence and muddled thinking, perhaps according to which of the gunmen was writing or to his state of mind at the time. Some of them were on scraps of paper or paper napkins, and I have edited them very slightly for spelling and for reasons of clarity. They must undoubtedly have interested the psychiatrist who was in attendance. Perhaps more worrying to the police was a letter to the President of the Italian Republic which one of the Italians was permitted to send out, or perhaps was instructed to write. It indicated that the hostages believed that they would be killed if concessions were not made.

Thursday, 2 October, was a decisive day. The police had been keeping observation on a house in Acton where the suspect Termine lived. He arrived home at 4.15 a.m. and was immediately detained. He admitted being concerned in the initial robbery attempt, and made a full confession. Ten hours later the police detained a club-owner in Soho. Though he denied that he had been involved in the plan to rob the restaurant, he admitted he knew Termine and the gunmen. It was now decided to make use of the fact that the men had a radio, and that they listened regularly to news broadcasts. The news that the club-owner and Termine had been arrested and charged with conspiracy to rob the Spaghetti House was given out on a nine o'clock bulletin that evening.

It had a dramatic effect on the gunmen, who according to the hostages were visibly shaken. In the early hours of the following morning, the sixth day of the siege, the atmosphere in the storeroom changed completely. For the first time the electric light in the room was extinguished. This was just before three o'clock. The gunmen were heard squabbling among themselves, and it appeared that some development was imminent. Davies apparently was arguing the case for surrender; the others were holding out.

At 3.55 a.m. Davies asked to speak to Commander Payne and gave him the wonderful news that it had been decided to release the hostages. A few minutes later they came out and were taken to hospital for a check-up. They told the police that Davies was armed with the shotgun and that the other two men had the pistols. The police continued their dialogue with the men. 'Well, Sir Robert, you've finally won,' Davies said, though he was not in fact speaking to the Commissioner. Shortly after four o'clock the doors opened and, on orders from the police to give up their weapons, the shotgun and one automatic gun were thrown out.

Suddenly there was a loud bang. Dick and Munroe called out that Davies had shot himself with the remaining gun. The two men were instructed to leave the storeroom and lie on the floor. They obeyed, and were quickly handcuffed. Davies was found lying in a corner of the room, seriously wounded but still alive, a revolver in his hand. He was examined by a doctor and rushed to St George's Hospital, where a bullet was found to be lodged in his liver. It was decided not to remove it at the time, but his life was saved.

It was impossible to interview him for six days, but eventually he was charged with conspiring to rob, with attempted robbery, with having a firearm with intent, and with false imprisonment. At his subsequent trial at the Central Criminal Court he was found guilty on three counts, and was sentenced to fifteen years for the attempted robbery, ten years concurrently on the firearm charge, and six years consecutively for the false imprisonment—a total of twenty-one years. This was a very severe sentence, even for someone with his record, and in his favour was the fact that he had persuaded his colleagues to surrender, but I agree most strongly with the additional sentence for holding people hostage. Dick was sent to prison for a total of eighteen years and Munroe for seventeen, reflecting the Common Serjeant's serious view of this particular criminal enterprise. Termine, who pleaded guilty to conspiring to rob, was in fact the only accused to be found guilty on this charge, and he was sentenced to six years. The club-owner was acquitted.

It was estimated by the police that it would have taken eight months for one man to transcribe all the conversation they monitored during the six-day siege, but at no time did the gunmen discuss their motives. This was undoubtedly a case of a robbery having gone wrong. If Mr Mai had not escaped and raised the alarm the siege would never have occurred, but that does not help us to assess the reason for the attempted robbery. Was it to obtain £20,000 for the so-called Black Liberationist Army or was it an ordinary criminal enterprise? The facts that Davies had a criminal record and that Termine (who was not a Black man) was involved argue for the latter, and I incline to the view that this was merely a case of criminals seeking sympathy by introducing political overtones.

It looked at one stage, however, as though the siege might have very serious implications. The involvement of Italians inevitably gave rise to rumours of a Mafia connection, but there was absolutely no evidence of this. There may have been other cases where one suspected some Mafia influence, but I can only say that, at least during my term as Director, there was very little evidence of any organized Mafia activity in this country.

The Spaghetti House case also raises the issue of the attitude of the police to Blacks. The gunmen were accusing the police in their letters of injustice and prejudice. Unfortunately, there is—for reasons that it would be inappropriate to examine here—a considerable degree of crime associated with young Blacks, and the police have a duty to deal with it. It is my experience that they do so in exactly the same way that they deal with all crime. I qualify what I say, however, to this extent: undoubtedly cases do arise occasionally where there may be an individual antipathy, but such antipathy, I am convinced, is no more widespread in the police than among civilian members of the population.

A much more real threat to our security than the Spaghetti House affair was the behaviour of David James Bingham and his wife Maureen. Theirs was a somewhat sad story that might never have come to light but for David Bingham's voluntary confession. He was a sub-lieutenant aboard HMS *Rothesay* in Portsmouth at the time, when his conscience compelled him to inform the ship's senior officer that he was, and for some time had been, an agent for the Soviet Union. He admitted having photographed naval secrets, which he then passed on to the Russian naval attaché. I cannot, of course, even now give details of the information that he handed over, and in his defence it was later stated that he had done his best to minimize the value of such information, some of which was no more than could be discovered by a diligent reader of the local press; but in the opinion of one expert, some of the information was almost beyond price. For this valuable service he received the princely sum, over a period of eighteen months, of £2,810!

The facts behind his treachery were curious, to put it mildly, for this was not a case of the Russians seeking to subvert a British serviceman, but of the man himself volunteering the information. Nor was it a case of someone acting from political convictions. All Bingham wanted was paltry sums of money to pay his household expenses, his hire-purchase commitments, and to buy a new car. The circumstances in which the Russians were approached were almost comic. According to Bingham, he was discussing his awkward financial situation with his wife, who jokingly suggested that they should approach the Russian Embassy for help. Not long thereafter, he wrote a note which his wife delivered to the Embassy in London. According to him, she had gained admission and had told a man there that her husband wanted to work for the Russians to pay off his debts; she was told that she would receive an invitation to a function, which she should attend. In due course the invitation arrived, she went and was questioned about the debts. She was then instructed to tell her husband to go to a certain address in London, and when he did so he met his contact Lory Kuzmin, an attaché at the Embassy.

Mrs Bingham had more than one story to account for her visit to the Embassy, but if the version is to be believed which she told a *Daily Mail* reporter, she went there and knocked on the door. It was opened by a man who told her that no one was available to see her, but who invited her to return the following day, which she did. She then saw someone named Ivan, who questioned her, and she went back yet again the next day with a letter from her husband. This improbable sequence of events—if you want to spy for the Russians, knock on the Embassy door and ask for Ivan—appears surprisingly not to have been too far from the truth. At all events, her visit to the Embassy was the prelude to her husband's involvement in a strange relationship with Kuzmin.

Bingham first met Kuzmin in February 1970. He rang the bell of the house to which he had been directed, went up in the lift and was met by the attaché, who took him into a room where there was food and vodka. He was asked to show his naval identity card. Kuzmin indicated that it was unwise to talk in case the conversation might be recorded. He turned up the radio and a large part of the interview was conducted by writing messages. Bingham was handed some church notices and instructed that in the event of an emergency he was to post them to an address in west London and go to a place near Guildford in Surrey.

There was something amateurishly funny about the whole

business if Bingham's story was to be believed, but then came the serious part. Kuzmin told his new recruit to buy a camera, but positively not in Portsmouth, and to photograph certain documents. They were to meet ten days later outside Guildford Cathedral. Kuzmin handed over £600, £500 being to pay off some debts and £100 for the camera. On 14 March 1970 Bingham purchased a camera and a film for £72 15s. Shortly afterwards he kept his rendezvous outside the cathedral. Kuzmin asked to see the receipt for the camera.

Bingham was then further instructed about what was useful to the Soviet Union, emphasis being laid on anti-submarine detection equipment. He was to leave the film of whatever documents he photographed beneath a broken car door that had been thrown into the bushes in an isolated spot not far from Guildford. This was to be done at an agreed time on a particular Saturday evening, or at the same time on the following Saturday if he was unable to do so on the first occasion. He was then to go to a particular telephone box and there leave an empty cigarette packet. Once that had been done a parcel containing money would be left for collection by him at another appointed place.

Surely no novelist would invent such a plot, but Bingham went to work in deadly earnest. There was yet another comic twist when, at his first attempt to leave material for Kuzmin, he was unable to locate the abandoned car door, so he sent his wife, who was more successful. Indeed, according to his statement, his wife met both Mr and Mrs Kuzmin at the scene, and Kuzmin pointed out to her what looked like a large grey stone beneath the car door, but which in fact was a putty casing, which she took home. The casing covered a parcel that contained a film which when developed gave further instructions. Why Kuzmin should have gone to the trouble to prepare a film when there were also written instructions in the package is somewhat obscure. The written instructions were notes about another 'drop', as it is called, in October.

During the first part of September Bingham attended a course on torpedo and anti-submarine matters and was issued with documents that included Allied naval manoeuvring instructions. He photographed these documents, using a 500-watt bulb, in his bedroom at home. He then put the film in a polythene bag, together with a note about the extent of his current debts, and placed them in the putty casing. He went with his wife, so he confessed, to the dropping place and left the parcel in the manner arranged. He then drove to the spot where Kuzmin had arranged to leave a parcel for him, and he left the cigarette packet in the telephone box. Kuzmin's parcel contained a sum of money and instructions to go in December to a place in New

Malden on an enclosed map. He was to wear a green tie, and when approached and asked the way to the golf clubhouse, was to reply, 'It is a quarter of a mile in that direction.' If no one approached him, he was to repeat the exercise the following Saturday. And so it went on.

On one occasion he received a postcard directing him to a farm where he picked up a parcel containing a film ordering him to improve his photography! When the police searched Bingham's house they found typewritten instructions, of which the following is an example:

> Dear Friend. Thank you for the material. We hope that everything is all right with you and your family. Timetable for 1971: February 27th from you via place 1 (tree), April 24th from you place 2 (hollow), June 19th from us via place 3 (gate), August 28th from you place 4 (bridge), October 16th meeting in Sutton (Sandy Lane) at 7pm before which you put the parcel into place 5 (telegraph post), December 18th from us place 6 (post). The reserve for both parties place 7 (door) . . .

—and much more in the same cryptic vein.

He had received these particular orders at the meeting in New Malden at which he was given £1,000, his largest single reward. More than half of this was intended to pay for his new car. All the places mentioned in the orders were identified by Bingham to the police, and they were all in the Guildford area. Without this documentary proof of his activities one might perhaps have been forgiven for doubting Bingham's confession, revealing as it did such a strange chain of events and bizarre method of operation.

There came a time, despite the money he had been paid, when Bingham was being pressed by his creditors to the point at which he delivered one of the church notices with which he had been supplied in case of emergency. It resulted in a meeting with Kuzmin, who said he had no money on him, but would meet Bingham the following week. He added that Bingham would have to justify an additional payment by supplying information of great importance. It was following this encounter on 27 July 1971 that Bingham photographed a particular Naval Intelligence Report which contained the conduct of the British fleet in time of war.

This was his most serious offence. The value of this information to the Soviet Union was said by a witness to have been incalculable.

Two days later he pawned his camera. Four days later he went with his wife, he said, and delivered the film to Kuzmin, who had no money at the time but promised to let him know when it would be available. He also said that his wife told him that she had written to the Russians for money while he was aboard ship, and he alleged that she made an abortive journey to London for the same purpose. On 13 August, he received a letter from a finance company to say that unless he paid them £232 by the 21st, they would inform the police that he had sold a car that was subject to hire purchase. He was obviously in desperate financial straits, but on the 21st he visited the finance company and paid them in cash. He had picked up £300 the previous day, after putting more pressure on Kuzmin. With the money was a note asking him to stick to the agreed programme.

Ten days later, having pawned the camera without which he could not provide further information for his paymasters, and having reached a point at which he felt he had to unburden his soul, Bingham made his confession. His trial was at Winchester Crown Court in March 1972. Mr Justice Bridge presided.

There was ample evidence to corroborate the confession, and in any case Bingham pleaded guilty to all charges. He had enlisted in the Royal Navy at the age of sixteen as a boy seaman, and was only thirty-two at the time of his trial. His was a tragic case of a man who had foolishly got into the clutches of a foreign Power and had no road of escape except by way of confession and imprisonment. Despite a very powerful plea for leniency from his leading counsel, and despite the fact that he had made a clean breast of the whole business, Mr Justice Bridge was bound to take a very serious view of his conduct. He was sentenced to a total of twenty-one years' imprisonment.

CHAPTER 9

What is obscene?

ON 7 JANUARY 1966 solicitors acting for publishers Calder and Boyars Ltd wrote to me to say that they proposed to publish a book (a copy of which they enclosed) entitled *Last Exit to Brooklyn*, by American author Hubert Selby Jnr. They described it as 'a work of very serious intent which is certainly not likely to appeal to those of prurient interest'. They requested, however, that if I did decide to prosecute, I should bring the proceedings under Section 2, rather than under Section 3, of the Obscene Publications Act, 1959, and added that such proceedings would be vigorously defended.

A prosecution under Section 2 entitled the defendant to trial by jury, whereas there was no such right if proceedings were launched under Section 3, in which case a magistrate could, if he found a book obscene, order its forfeiture.

The publishers, it seemed to me, were inviting me to give them a clearance to publish the book with impunity. Whatever may have been my personal views about the work, I did not regard myself as a literary critic, but more important, I was not prepared to assume the mantle of censor. If Parliament wanted books to be treated in the same way that plays and films once were, it was up to Parliament to extend the powers of the Lord Chamberlain's office or to appoint a Book Censor—a course of action against which, I suspect, this particular publisher, and indeed any publisher, would have fought strenuously.

In any case, the law was far less certain in matters of alleged obscenity than I would have wished, had it been my duty at that time to decide whether the book in question actually offended against the law—or, to apply my Department's test, whether conviction was likely to result from prosecution. A very non-committal reply was therefore sent one week later. I included the words, 'If you find—as I am afraid you will—that this is a most unhelpful letter, it is not because I wish to be unhelpful but because I get no help from the Acts'—a comment, incidentally, with which Lord Justice Salmon later said that he felt considerable sympathy.

I doubt very much whether my Department would have initiated proceedings against the book but for the circumstances that arose later which forced our hand. Indeed, in the following June, the Attorney-General, in answer to a question from Sir Cyril Black, M.P., told the House of Commons, after consultation with me, that he had no intention of prosecuting in respect of this book. Sir Cyril then decided to take matters into his own hands, as he was perfectly entitled to do, by launching private proceedings under Section 3, with the result that the magistrate ordered the forfeiture of three copies of the book which had been seized.

It should be explained that a decision by one magistrate is not binding on another. The Chief Metropolitan Magistrate had pronounced the book obscene, but his jurisdiction was strictly limited, and there was nothing to stop the book being circulated elsewhere in the country. The publishers were, however, in danger of having to contest other proceedings without having the opportunity to go before a jury, and they informed me in writing that they intended to continue publishing the book, despite the magistrate's verdict, and said that they would defend any proceedings I chose to take under Section 2. Whether or not this was an invitation to prosecute, we decided to take action—'perhaps not surprisingly' in the circumstances, again to quote Lord Justice Salmon. One benefit arising from prosecution might be that we would have the first thorough opportunity under my Directorship to test Section 4, which provides that a person shall not be convicted under Section 2, or suffer an order for forfeiture under Section 3, 'if it is proved that publication of the article in question is justified as being for the public good on the ground that it is in the interest of science, literature, art or learning or of other objects of general concern'. It also permitted the admission of expert evidence as to 'literary, artistic, scientific or other merits'.

The trial took place over nine days at the Old Bailey before Judge Rogers. The publishers were represented by John Mortimer, Q.C., and Cyril Salmon; J. Mathew and M. Corkery appeared for the Crown. It was regarded by both sides as a case of outstanding importance in its field, and indeed it was said that the outcome might affect not only the future of literature in this country but also the right to free speech.

The old order changeth, yielding place to new, and never more quickly, perhaps, than in the public attitude to moral issues during the period in which I was Director of Public Prosecutions. A society that had expressed shock when Shaw's Eliza Dolittle was allowed to use the word 'bloody' on the stage was becoming used to far stranger words in print following the unsuccessful prosecution against Penguin Books Ltd, the publishers of D. H. Lawrence's *Lady Chatterley's Lover*, and the words of Mr Justice Stable in his summing-up in the case of Regina *v.* Martin Secker & Warburg Ltd had done much to liberalize the position, at least for serious writers. The law, however, was still imprecise—which is one of the problems of obscenity—and it fell to my lot to have to test the law in at least four major instances, of which the case of *Last Exit to Brooklyn* was the first.

Perhaps the most famous prosecution of the century in respect of alleged obscenity in a book had occurred following publication in 1928 of *The Well of Loneliness* by Radclyffe Hall. The subject of the book, lesbianism, was taboo at that time, and although it would hardly raise an eyebrow today, Bodkin, who was then Director of Public Prosecutions, may well have been reflecting public opinion of the day in taking the view that open discussion of female homosexuality would tend to undermine society. He was not without powerful support, even in literary circles. No less a figure than Rudyard Kipling agreed to give evidence for the prosecution. It is interesting to note that the metropolitan magistrate who ordered the book's destruction in forfeiture proceedings refused to hear evidence from experts, and he was upheld in his decision by the London Sessions Appeals Committee.

The prosecution of *Lady Chatterley's Lover* occurred in 1960 when Mathew was Director. There had been earlier forfeiture orders made in respect of the work, and the Director was faced now with the challenge of an unexpurgated edition for the first time in paperback at a low price. It has been said that Mathew was very hesitant to take proceedings, and I am sure that he only did so in the belief that he too was reflecting public opinion. The jury took a different view, however, and in contrast to Kipling, no less a literary figure than E. M. Forster gave evidence for the defence.

I found myself without much choice in the case of *Last Exit to Brooklyn*. The meaning of obscenity under the Act of 1959 is expressed as follows: 'an article shall be deemed to be obscene if its effect . . . is, if taken as a whole, such as to tend to deprave and corrupt persons who are likely, having regard to all relevant circumstances, to read . . . it'.

What is meant by 'deprave and corrupt'? What weight is to be given to words like 'tend' and 'likely'? What are 'all relevant circumstances', and exactly how does one interpret 'taken as whole'? Who are the persons likely to read the article? If even lawyers disagree about the interpretation of the Act, what is a jury to make of it? It is in these circumstances that the directions of the judge are of vital importance, and one can sympathize with Judge Rogers in his quite difficult task, particularly since the judge had little guidance from authority regarding a defence under Section 4. Expert evidence was now admissible and witness after witness—thirty in all—went into the box to support the view that the book was a work of literary merit (as indeed they had done in the case of *Lady Chatterley*). It is far easier, it appears, to find prominent people who will come forward to praise a book than it is to obtain the evidence of people prepared to say that they find the book harmful, and although the Crown produced witnesses to rebut the expert evidence for the defendants—including the Rev. David Sheppard, the famous cricketer who was later Bishop of Liverpool—the weight of expert evidence was on the side of the publishers. This was to be a feature of several subsequent cases, and there were occasions when it was a matter of judicial comment. People were never slow to bring complaints to my attention, but ask them to give evidence and they would run a mile.

I do not propose here to describe the contents of *Last Exit to Brooklyn* beyond saying that it painted a shocking picture of low life in a deprived section of a big city. It was never suggested by the prosecution that the book was other than a serious book, or the publishers other than serious publishers, but John Mortimer for the defence conceded that the purpose with which the book was written was irrelevant if in fact, taken as a whole, it tended to deprave and corrupt a significant number of those likely to read it. He argued strongly, however, that there was no such tendency, that in fact readers of the book could only be filled with compassion for the characters and feel revulsion for the conditions in which they lived. Far from encouraging readers to violence, homosexuality and drug-taking—which were features of the book—it would positively discourage them.

It was a difficult case, and the jury were out for almost three and a half hours before they returned to court to ask the judge whether they had first to decide whether the book was obscene before considering the defence of public good. Judge Rogers correctly said that this was so. One can well understand the difficulty that the jury must have felt in regard to this when one has in mind the definition of obscenity in the Act. They first had to consider whether the prosecution had proved beyond reasonable doubt that the book tended to deprave and corrupt the people likely to read it. If they came to the conclusion that they were not sure, that was the end of the case. If, however, they decided on the evidence that readers would be depraved and corrupted, they then had to proceed in considering Section 4 to decide whether, notwithstanding this, publication was for the public good—in this particular case largely on the grounds of literary merit, the onus now being on the defence to prove this proposition as a matter of probability!

The jury were out another two hours before they convicted the publishers, who were fined £100 and ordered to pay £500 costs. They cannot have found their task easy, trying to balance their own commonsense view of what was obscene with all the expert evidence as to the book's literary, sociological or ethical merits, particularly as they were given a minimum of guidance from the judge as to how to deal with the defence under Section 4. This was in fact one of the grounds of the successful appeal by the publishers which came before Lord Justice Salmon, Mr Justice Geoffrey Lane (now Lord Chief Justice) and Mr Justice Fisher. While sympathizing with the judge, who was dealing with laws that had been tested only infrequently, the Court of Appeal decided that the jury's verdict could not stand. In the course of his judgment Lord Justice Salmon made the following pronouncement: 'The jury must set the standards of what is acceptable, of what is for the public good in the age in which we live.'

The difficulty that my Department encountered in cases of alleged obscenity, where the law, even as amended in 1959, was less precise than we could have wished, was that in considering whether there was evidence of a nature likely to result in conviction we had virtually to outguess the jury—and juries could be notoriously unpredictable in issues of this sort. In practice, we were very unlikely, therefore, to institute proceedings against books of serious intent published by reputable publishers. As I have said, but for the result of the proceedings taken by Sir Cyril Black, M.P., we would not have taken action in respect of *Last Exit to Brooklyn*. There were instances, however, of publications which seemed to us more obviously to offend against the Obscene Publications Acts, where the chances of conviction were good, and which should properly be considered by a jury. Certainly the most notorious of these was the famous *Oz* case.

An entire book has been written about the case. The magazine *Oz* was a manifestation of what came to be known in some circles as the alternative culture. It was one of a number of so-called 'underground' magazines that sprung up, particularly in the United States, in an effort to give expression to minority opinion, and to provide different reading matter from what was currently available. These magazines were usually less reverent in their treatment of current themes and much more amateur in approach than the established journals, but that in itself was a matter of concern only to their readers. The right of expression is a vital freedom, and it is only in extreme cases that the law should be involved to limit that right, as for example in the case of libel.

As Director of Public Prosecutions I would have applied precisely the same test in deciding whether to launch proceedings under the Obscene Publications Acts against a so-called 'Establishment' newspaper as I would against a so-called underground one. The law, of course, does not recognize the distinction, and indeed neither description is really accurate. *Oz*, perhaps the most famous British underground journal, was in fact published quite openly. The issue of *Oz* that fell foul of the law was actually the twenty-eighth, entitled 'Oz School Kids Issue', and if it had been published as a supplement by *The Times*, I have no doubt that my department would have taken precisely the same attitude towards it. I stress this because it is sometimes claimed that decisions to prosecute for obscenity are made on political grounds, whereas no such considerations were ever taken into account.

The only reason that proceedings were taken in respect of *Oz* was that it seemed perfectly apparent that the School Kids Issue contained matter that any reasonable jury would find to be obscene within the meaning of the Obscene Publications Act, 1959.

This particular issue purported to have 'been put together with the help and inspiration of about twenty people, all 18 or under, mostly still at school'. In the words of its own editorial introduction, the magazine 'was hit with its biggest dose of creative energy for a long time', and 'on the whole everyone who worked on the issue enjoyed the chaotic anarchistic anti-authoritarian way' in which it was prepared. It was not, however, the anarchistic or anti-authoritarian content that exercised our attention but the obscene way in which this content was often expressed.

The cover, front and back, showed a number of naked young women, at least four of whom appeared to be engaged in lesbian activity. On page 10 there was a drawing of a schoolmaster with his trousers down, playing with himself sexually while groping a young boy, presumably one of his pupils. On page 14 two short essays advocated that we should have the same sexual freedom as animals, including the right to copulate in public. Following this was a cartoon in six strips showing the lovable Rupert Bear sexually inspecting and then assaulting an elderly lady! On page 28, under the heading 'Suck', there was what I suppose was meant to be an extract from an imaginary book about oral sex, in which a girl places an ice cube in her mouth to increase the man's pleasure. The Small Ads section contained advertisements for bizarre books, photographs of nude boys and men, Swedish pornography films, personal stimulators, dirty postcards and leather underwear. About one of the sixteen-year-old contributors, it was said that she had 'many obscene ideas but can't put them down'; about another, that he enjoyed 'drawing cartoons of a perverted nature'. It will surprise no one that there should also have been a liberal sprinkling of four-letter words.

These are examples of some of the contents to which objection was taken, and I have listed them to stress that although there was an editorial plea in the magazine to 'give us the freedon to smoke, to dress, to have sex, to run school affairs', this was not a political case, as it has occasionally been presented, of an authoritarian Establishment seeking to suppress a revolutionary journal, but quite simply an attempt to uphold the law. The twenty-eighth *Oz* may all have been good dirty fun to some, but this was an issue prepared largely by schoolchildren and although the issue also contained several worthy contributions, it must surely have been the likelihood that it should circulate among schoolchildren. Several complaints were made to the police, who referred the matter to my Department, and it may not surprise too many people that one of the counts in the indictment accused the four defendants—Oz Publications Ink Ltd and Richard Neville, James Anderson and Felix Dennis—of conspiring with a number of young people 'to produce a magazine containing divers obscene, lewd, indecent and sexually perverted articles, cartoons, drawings and illustrations with intent thereby to debauch and corrupt the morals of children and young persons within the Realm'.

There were further counts in the indictment, respectively accusing them of an offence under Section 2 of the 1959 Act, of publishing an obscene article, and of having certain obscene articles in their possession for publication for gain.

The case was tried at the Central Criminal Court by Judge Argyle. It opened in June 1971 and lasted over five weeks. It truly was a 27-day wonder. Brian Leary appeared for the Crown; John Mortimer, Q.C., led for the defence. The Old Bailey had never seen a trial quite like this. The defendants were intelligent and versed in the ways of securing publicity and the support of like-thinking people. Their attitude to the proceedings paradoxically was both respectful and defiant, and there were times when the court was in danger of being turned into a circus. There is always a problem with a case of this sort, and had it not been a strong judge presiding over the trial, he could on occasion have lost control of it, even though the defendants were acting within their legal rights. Some might think that the court became a meeting-place of the old world and the new, of the conventional and the unconventional.

The case raised two interesting points of law. The first was whether a magazine should be treated as a book which had to be considered as a whole, or whether the jury could look at individual items in isolation and pronounce the whole publication obscene on the basis of any one of them. In fact, for the purpose of the trial, both the prosecution and the defence as well as the judge treated *Oz* as a book, but the Court of Appeal later decided that this was a wrong proposition. In the words of Lord Widgery, the Lord Chief Justice, 'A novelist who writes a complete novel, and who cannot cut out particular passages without destroying the theme of the novel, is entitled to have his work judged as a whole, but a magazine publisher who has a far wider discretion as to what he will, and will not, insert by way of items is to be judged under the Act on what we call the "item by item" basis'. The second point concerned the expert evidence on behalf of the defendants which took up twenty days of the trial. Much of it was directed to show that the School Kids Issue was not obscene, and the Court of Appeal stated unequivocally that it was wrong to admit expert evidence as to obscenity. 'We are not oblivious of the fact', said the Lord Chief Justice, 'that the people, perhaps many people, will think a jury, unassisted by experts, a very unsatisfactory tribunal to decide such a matter.' Expert evidence could be called to establish the defence of public good under Section 4, but the question of obscenity must be left exclusively to the jury.

This particular jury were not satisfied that there was an intention to corrupt public morals, and they acquitted all defendants on the first count, but they were convicted on the other charges. From these convictions they appealed.

John Mortimer, Q.C., argued successfully in the Court of Appeal that the judge had misdirected the jury with regard to the definition of obscenity by perhaps giving too wide a definition to the word. He was also supported by the court (the Lord Chief Justice, Mr Justice James and Mr Justice Bridge) in his contention that the judge had failed to give adequate direction to the argument advanced for the defendants that, far from tending to deprave and corrupt, certain of the contents were so disgusting as to deter people from following their example. Mortimer had used the 'aversion' argument in the *Last*

Exit to Brooklyn case, and he had established it as a pillar of any future defence in an obscenity trial. He had actually called an expert witness in the court below, a doctor who was a highly qualified psychiatrist, who gave evidence that aversion therapy was widely used in mental hospitals, but was also effective in the case of healthy people.

The appeals from the convictions to which I have referred were allowed. When allowing them the court contrasted the meaning to be given to the word 'obscene' in the Post Office Act 1953, in which it could properly be given its ordinary meaning, and its meaning in the Obscene Publications Act, where it had been precisely defined.

Felix Dennis addressed (presumably facetiously) a question to the Lord Chief Justice after the court had allowed the appeals except on the one count. 'When we were granted bail,' he said, 'we had to sign a piece of paper that we were not allowed to work on any underground newspaper or basically anything which might be tending to produce obscene matter. Does it mean we cannot go back to work?'

However, it will be appreciated that the appeals in both the *Last Exit* and *Oz* cases were allowed because the Court of Appeal found that there had been misdirection by the judges as to what was involved in the statutory provisions, but the court stated on both of these occasions that they were not ruling as to whether the publications were in fact obscene within the statutory definition in the Obscene Publications Act.

I have already touched upon the difficulties involved in deciding whether or not proceedings should be instituted in cases of this nature. These difficulties are, I consider, inherent in the very approach to this delicate (or indelicate) subject, and can be considered broadly under two headings, legal and psychological. In the first category, the primal difficulty, that I have already stressed, is the securing of a satisfactory application of the definition of obscenity as it is given under the 1959 Act. Cases have failed, misdirection has occurred, and all this has arisen from the sporadic yet vey real reluctance of juries to accept material as being in fact depraving and corrupting.

The second category of difficulty that I would advance is the psychological. Admittedly in some respects this is an unreal distinction, and the two categories merge impalpably into each other. It is not to be denied—although one would use this judiciously as a defence—that times do in fact change, and we change with them. One would not wish to emulate the wilder vagaries of the Victorian age, when trousers were commonly characterized as unmentionables. Since her first appearance in an obscure play, Mrs Grundy has been a figure of not unmerited derision, and the perennial desire not

146

to hamstring the Press or to fetter the human spirit is a not ignoble one. There has been instance upon instance—and not in the written word alone—where a great artistic endeavour would have faltered and died in the close confines of a narrow prudery. There is even an argument, as in *Lady Chatterley's Lover*, that what is by the consensus of the majority a strictly minor work by an author of acknowledged stature should still retain its esssential place in the canon, if only to mark a vital stage in that author's development (which of course includes regression). Far be it from me to cavil at works—however misguided some might think them—that integrate but do not advocate. By this I mean that it is one thing to express, with a degree of delicacy and verisimilitude the sentiments of a Mellors or with possible compassion but with certain fidelity the low life of a great city, but it is quite another matter deliberately to advocate and to set out as attractive a policy that cannot but strike at the roots of human society, based as it still is on familial concepts and upon countless necessary gradations of respect and self-respect. Huxley's World Controller speaks to us of the evils of inhibition and self-restraint, and with any luck if we follow his precepts we may achieve a brave new world indeed—and might even find it good!

I have touched upon these literary and social factors in order to emphasize once again that I am well aware that the world has moved on, as the world must always move on, that the fetishes and shibboleths of one generation will differ from those of another, that the values of free expression are undoubted values, even though one might argue that the true writer may in fact be improved by these non-literary obstacles that he has to overcome. These are all matters with which Section 4 concerns itself, and as the Penguin prosecution made abundantly clear, depending as they do in part on subjective estimates of literary value, they are nebulous and not entirely under the jurisdiction of the law. But where the law can properly concern itself, and must concern itself, is in the issue of the tendency to corrupt, and the provisions of Sections 2 and 3. Defences under Section 4 will arise from time to time, and it is inevitable that the law will have on occasion to balance its consideration of legal facts and implications with the views of literary and other pundits. It is accustomed, after all, to the necessary reception and assessment of evidence from experts in many disciplines when these disciplines impinge upon a question to be considered, even though it may be thought that they offer far more objective evidence than do their artistic congeners.

In one very interesting case while I was Director, John Mortimer, in raising a defence under Section 4, argued very forcefully that

147

where there was a large body of well-qualified evidence from serious and disinterested witnesses in favour of a book's literary or other merits it was almost perverse to disregard such evidence. The judge's comments on this 'attractive submission', as he put it, are interesting. He said that a 'counting of heads' had no part in reaching a decision, and that he had been driven to the conclusion that most of the defence witnesses were so uncritical of the book in question, and unrestrained in their praise of large parts of it, that they were at times less convincing than they might otherwise have been. In this connection I would remind the reader that the Court of Appeal has held that it is correct for a jury to be told that before even considering a defence under Section 4, they must be satisfied that the publication is obscene—namely, that it will tend to deprave and corrupt those who are likely to read it.

There is no doubt that there is in our day a vast quantity of material that most people will find themselves able to identify as pornography. This material is usually almost devoid of literary merit, pathetic in its infantile story line, monotonous in its mechanistic plots, filled with characters interchangeable except for the small consideration of gender, trashy in its presentation as in its conception. It can be distinguished from the small amount of doubtful material that has some pretence to literary form and merit, but Section 4 has resulted in extravagant claims being made for even the worst rubbish. As Director of Public Prosecutions I got very little help from the Obscene Publications Act, and it does not surprise me in retrospect that although we obtained convictions in the *Last Exit* and *Oz* cases, for example, these convictions were upset in the Court of Appeal.

Only one other case is perhaps worth mentioning as an indication of how we operated. It did not overtly concern children. If ever a book deserved the description 'For Adults Only', it was *Inside Linda Lovelace*, about which many complaints were made to us. Miss Lovelace had achieved notoriety as a result of her starring role in the film *Deep Throat*, the first film of its kind, intended for a minority audience, that in fact achieved considerable commercial success in the United States. In a very real sense, it broke through the porn barrier, if I may use the term. Films, I should point out, did not come within the scope of the Obscene Publications Acts of that time, but in any case *Deep Throat* had not been shown to the general public in this country. As its title suggests, it was concerned largely with oral sex, and perhaps the best way I can describe Miss Lovelace's book is to say that it was in the nature of a sexual autobiography. As one might expect from a lady who was prepared to be seen on the screen indulging in sexual acts, it was very explicit. It was also published in paperback form at a modest price that put it within easy reach of a very wide public.

Inside Linda Lovelace was perhaps a logical development of our so-called permissive society. The book flew the flag of complete sexual freedom. It did not matter what was said or how it was said. The publisher wrote a preface in which he described the author's philosophy thus: 'Sex serves life and therefore is good; inhibitions and prohibitions serve death and are therefore evil.' The author herself proclaimed that 'good sex contributes to a better world . . . I want to see the day,' she wrote, 'when sex will be an accepted thing and violence will be outlawed . . . I read recently that a *New York Times* study of violence on TV revealed that by eighteen each American child has witnessed 2,200 murders on the family tube, but not one natural act of love.' These opinions might well be supported by many people who objected to the book as a whole. 'You may consider my views dirty, sordid, immoral,' she said, 'but what I've written about has been going on since the beginning of civilisation . . . I don't consider any sex act dirty.' Elsewhere she triumphantly proclaimed that 'my God is now sex. Without sex, I'd die. Sex is everything. . . .'

That is her point of view, and to give her her due, the book had a number of commendable features, such as her comments about the horrors of drug-taking. Perhaps she saw herself as the great sexual liberator, seeking to free us all and initiate us into the secrets of fullest participation. The problem was that she had little respect for other people's sensitivities. The book dealt with such subjects as pornographic film-making, defilement of young girls, lesbianism, sodomy, sadism, and masochism, bestiality, and bizarre sexual behaviour, and in language and with an explicitness that many people found shocking. Perhaps it was her aim to shock the reader into heeding her message, perhaps indeed the book was written with high purpose rather than just to make money. I prefer to give her the benefit of the doubt. Nevertheless, I formed the clear view that a jury would be most likely to find that it was obscene within the meaning of the Acts, and I found it difficult to believe that a defence under Section 4 was likely to be convincingly supported.

Proceedings were issued against the publishers, John Hanau and his firm Heinrich Hanau Ltd, and the case came up at the Old Bailey before Judge Rigg. Brian Leary and F. H. Cassels appeared for the Crown, and John Mortimer, Q.C.—who we have seen had exceptional experience in this field as well as in others—led Geoffrey

Robertson for the defence. This was 1974, eight years after the *Last Exit to Brooklyn* trial, and we were aware in the Department that attitudes had changed even in this short time. The verdicts of juries in cases of this nature were very inconsistent, and it almost seemed that juries were only willing to convict where there was encouragement to extreme behaviour, such as sex with children. One distinguished barrister advanced it as his opinion that jurors were now adopting the view that there was very little that tended to deprave and corrupt a significant number of people likely to read a book or article.

This in fact was an important issue at the trial, where the prosecution contended that there was a danger of this particular book reaching young readers who might easily be depraved by it. The adult's greater familiarity with unusual sexual matters might have immunized him, just as an ambulance-driver might be less affected by a corpse. The jury actually returned to court (after being out for over two hours) to say that they were equally divided, and that there was no prospect of agreement among them. The judge sent them back, and they then asked specifically whether, in order to convict, they would have to find that a significant number of readers would be depraved by the book, or whether it was enough that anybody would be depraved. The judge told them that the Act left that matter to the jury.

The publishers were acquitted. Once again it appeared to me that a prosecution had come unstuck on this question of what constituted a significant number. The result, of course, was that sales of the book rose far higher than they would have done had there been no trial. The same, I am sure, was true of *Last Exit to Brooklyn*. This was the danger of an acquittal. If we prosecuted unsuccessfully, all we would achieve would be to give free advertisement to a book, and the publishers would proceed to make very substantial profits. The public interest, therefore, increasingly required us to be more and more careful in our judgment of whether a jury was likely to convict. Perhaps it was during my stewardship that major trials for obscenity began to become things of the past.

CHAPTER 10

Murder most foul

As DIRECTOR of Public Prosecutions, I arranged that every case in which a prosecution for murder was contemplated should be brought to my attention. Cases involving the security of the State apart, murder is still the gravest crime. Of course, there are murders and murders. There is a world of difference between a deliberate intention to kill and a domestic homicide arising out of loss of self-control, between ruthless killing in the course of a criminal enterprise and a homicide arising out of substantial provocation albeit that it was insufficient to reduce it to manslaughter. Following the abolition of capital punishment, however, some of the onus in considering the consequences of a prosecution had been lifted from my shoulders. In this particular sense only, murder had effectively been downgraded.

During the period in which I served there were at least three cases that caused me to wonder whether we had been right to remove the ultimate penalty. I was so concerned about one of these that I spent the first three days of the trial at Chester Assizes. This was in April 1966, and was the trial of Ian Brady and Myra Hindley on three charges of murder; Hindley was separately charged with being an accessory after the fact of one murder. No more evil circumstances had ever been put before a British court in my experience, and my concern arose partly from the fact that the chief prosecution witness, David Smith, would certainly be represented to the jury by the defence as an accomplice. Indeed, Brady and Hindley sought not only to implicate Smith but to transfer the blame to him. I remember wondering, looking at them as I sat in court, and knowing the strength of the evidence that was to be called for the Crown, how such wicked people could look so ordinary.

The prosecution case was immensely formidable without Smith, but had he not contacted the police the whole dreadful business might never have come to light, and we needed his direct evidence as to certain events. He was by no means a lawyer's idea of an ideal witness. He was a close friend and associate of the accused couple, he admitted that he shared Brady's contempt for other people, made no attempt to hide his dislike of work and gave his views on God and religion in what the trial judge described as 'extreme and blasphemous form'. More important, perhaps, although he was only seventeen when he first exposed the horrors that were to shock the nation, he had previous convictions for violence, and he said that he had been conspiring with Brady to carry out a robbery. He had also apparently been offered a substantial sum of money by a newspaper for his story in the event of Brady's conviction, so it was naturally said that he had a vested interest in a verdict of guilty.

On his own admission he had been present when one of the murders was committed. He described himself as a frightened and passive spectator, but it was suggested by the defence that he had actively participated in the events that led to death.

This was the young man on whom we had to rely, but it only served to emphasize the horror of the crimes that someone like him—in other respects a friend and collaborator of the accused—should have felt it necessary to bring their activities to a stop. 'I could not have lived with myself if I had not done so,' he said when asked why he had gone to the police.

He contacted the police in fact just after six o'clock on the morning of 7 October 1965. A few hours earlier seventeen-year-old Edward Evans had been killed with fourteen blows to the head from an axe; an attempt may also have been made to strangle him. The police constable who took the call arrived four minutes later at the telephone box from which Smith had rung. He was at once approached by Smith and his wife. Smith was carrying a carving knife and a long screwdriver, which the officer took from him. He was obviously agitated and upset, and later said that he had brought the weapons as protection. He was taken to the police station, where he made a very long statement.

Within two hours, as a result of this statement—which alleged that Brady boasted about other deaths also—Superintendent Talbot went with no fewer than twenty-five policemen to the house where Brady and Hindley lived, and where Smith alleged that Evans had been killed. The large number of police was partly because of the seriousness of the allegations, but also because Smith had said that there were loaded firearms in the house. Despite this, the Superintendent went in alone. He was met by Myra Hindley, who, obviously taken aback, lied and stalled. When told that the police had a report of an act of violence she said, 'There is nothing wrong here.' She was asked who lived in the house, and replied, 'Gran, myself and Ian.' The house was then searched and a bedroom door was found to be locked. Asked what was in the bedroom, she said firearms. When requested to produce the key she at first said it was at work.

At police insistence the key was eventually handed over. In the room they found a ghastly bundle, containing the trussed body of young Evans, his knees tied right up to his chest, ready for disposal in polythene wrapping inside a rug.

Brady was still in bed at the time, writing a letter to his employers to say why he could not be at work that day. He certainly did not tell them he would be otherwise engaged in burying a body. He was taken to the police station, and made a statement as follows:

> Last night I met Eddie [Evans] in Manchester. We were drinking when we went home to Hattersley [where Brady lived]. We had an argument and we came to blows. After the first few blows the situation was out of control. When the argument started, David [Smith] was at the front door and Myra called him in. Eddie was on the floor by the living-room door, and David hit him with a stick and kicked him about three times. Eddie kicked me at the beginning on my ankle, and there was a hatchet at the fireplace which I hit Eddie with. After that, the only noise that Eddie made was gurgling, then Dave and I began clearing up the blood. The gurgling stopped, then we tied up the body, that is Dave and I, nobody else, and Dave and I carried it upstairs. We sat in the house till three or four in the morning, then we decided to get rid of the body in the morning or the next night.

It will be noted that Brady was seeking to involve Smith and exonerate Hindley. For her part, Hindley refused to make a statement until she had seen Brady, and in fact never did make a statement. Her attitude all along was that whatever Brady said was right, and that her story was the same as his. Neither she nor he had done anything, and Smith was a liar.

The police made a major discovery in the car outside the house. It was a 'disposal plan' for the dead boy's body. Great importance attached to it, because the prosecution alleged that its contents were prepared before the killing; that it was evidence, therefore, that the crime had been premeditated. Brady explained that he had drawn it up between two and four o'clock in the morning, and that he had left it in his wallet under the dashboard when he went to lock up the car at 4 a.m. It was quite a detailed plan, which the prosecution felt was unlikely to have been put together in the tension and excitement following Evans's death. It even gave instructions, as for a military operation, about the checking and polishing of all buttons and clasps, even for brushing hair, cleaning shoes and wearing gloves! In evidence, Brady was to explain parts of it by saying that it referred to the cleaning of the axe before using it to dig the grave; that it provided for the carrying of loaded guns in case there was any interference when Evans was being buried on the near-by moors; and that it involved Hindley driving up and down the road, passing a given point every five minutes, while the burial was taking place. Brady, it transpired, did not drive, and this became an important consideration when assessing the extent to which Hindley was involved.

One short reference in the disposal plan read: 'Tick, Place P/B', and no one at first could explain this cryptic message. When asked Brady said it was a reference to Penistone Burn, where a payroll snatch had been planned for the following Saturday, and no greater significance was placed on it. It was to assume enormous significance within a fortnight, however, following the discovery by an observant police-man of a cloakroom ticket tucked behind the spine of a devotional book that had been given to Hindley on the occasion of her first communion seven years earlier. The ticket turned out to be a receipt for two suitcases that had been deposited at Central Station, Manchester, on the evening before Evans's death.

If 'Tick' referred to ticket and 'P/B' perhaps to prayer book—a thought that did not occur immediately even to the local police, whose admirable thoroughness in searching the house turned up this vital evidence—there was the closest possible connection between the death of Evans and what was in the suitcase. And it was the contents of the suitcases that turned what might otherwise have looked like a particularly unpleasant murder investigation into one of the horror stories of our time.

The suitcases contained what Brady called 'offbeat' material, including books, photographs and, most terrible of all, two copies of a tape recording. Why should this material have been removed from the house and deposited at the railway station the very day before Evans was killed, unless the youth's death was planned in advance and it was considered unwise to leave this evidence on hand in case any inquiries were made?

Seventeen-year-old Edward Evans disappeared in Manchester on 6 October 1965 and was dead within a few hours. Almost two years earlier, on 23 November 1963, twelve-year-old John Kilbride had disappeared without trace from Ashton Market. One year later, on Boxing Day 1964, ten-year-old Lesley Ann Downey had disappeared

154

in almost identical circumstances. Among the contents of the suitcases was a photograph taken by Brady of Hindley posing on young
John's grave, another of little Lesley's grave, others of the poor girl in
pornographic poses, and a truly terrible tape recording that no one
who has ever heard it is likely to forget. I felt sorry for the shorthand
writer who, in order to transcribe it, had to listen to it no fewer than
eight or nine times.

The trial of Brady and Hindley was before Mr Justice Fenton
Atkinson (later Lord Justice). The then Attorney-General, Sir Elwyn
Jones, appeared with W. L. Mars-Jones, Q.C., and R. G. Waterhouse
(both now High Court Judges) for the Crown. Brady's counsel were
H. E. Hooson, Q.C., and D. T. Lloyd-Jones; Hindley's G. Heilpern,
Q.C., and P. Curtis. It says a great deal for the British legal system
that two sadistic killers of the utmost depravity should have their
cases examined so painstakingly, so carefully. Both accused were
admirably represented, and the trial lasted fifteen days.

There was plenty of corroborative evidence to support what Smith
alleged, although there was no blood on the rugs in the room where
he said Evans had been murdered. This would hardly have been
possible if the rugs had been in position, as he claimed, but as the
judge pointed out, he may have been mistaken on this one point. To
whatever extent Brady and Hindley sought to implicate Smith—and
it must be remembered that he was only fifteen when the first child
was killed—they could not really escape from the facts of their own
misdeeds. There were striking similarities in all three killings. Three
youngsters had disappeared from public places, in the same general
area, within easy reach of where the accused lived. There was
evidence of abnormal sexual activity before death: John Kilbride's
underpants had been rolled down to his knees and knotted behind in
circumstances suggesting indecent interference; Lesley Ann
Downey had been stripped, cruelly gagged and treated disgustingly;
there were dog-hairs on Edward Evans's body, which could only
have been there if his trousers had been removed or taken down.
Two of the bodies were buried on the moors within a short distance
of each other. Moreover, photographic and other records had been
preserved which clearly linked the accused with the earlier murders
—preserved, according to Brady, because they were 'unusual'.

There was the same sort of pattern that had emerged in the notorious 'Brides in the Bath' case. There might have been an innocent
explanation for the drowning of the third wife, shortly after making a
will in the husband's favour, until it became known that his two
previous wives had suffered the same fate in almost identical circumstances. Similarly, young Evans's death could just conceivably have

been explained in Brady's own terms as something that had got horribly out of hand, a sort of monstrous accident, until Brady's involvement in previous deaths became known.

It seemed hardly possible to me on the evidence that a jury would fail to convict Brady of all three murders, but there could be some argument about the extent of Hindley's participation, particularly in the third killing. Her counsel applied unsuccessfully to the judge for a separate trial for her. She was younger than Brady—he was aged twenty-eight at the time of the trial—and apprently besotted with him. It could have been that she had acted under his influence. It was significant to me, however, that she reacted calmly to the same brutal events that turned the stomach of a young man with an admitted record of violence. When Smith called the police he was found to be shaking; when Hindley opened the door to them two hours later she behaved as though nothing were wrong.

Brady had met Hindley in 1960 when she joined the firm where he was employed. She became his typist, and later his friend and mistress. They claimed to have similar views on religion, politics and other matters. They had been living together with her grandmother for about eight months when he brought Edward Evans home on what was to be the poor boy's last day on earth. In so far as it was possible, Brady and Hindley both supported each other. Brady, in evidence, explained the presence of Evans in their house by saying that he had planned with Smith to 'roll a queer', and that he had met the boy, whom he knew to be homosexual, at Manchester Central railway station. He had decided 'that he was the one who would do for what Smith and I had been talking about earlier that night'.

The fact is that the boy did return home with him, driven there by Hindley, who had been waiting for Brady in the car outside the station. Whatever the reasons for Evans accompanying them, it is most unlikely to have been the one advanced by Brady. If he had in mind to rob a homosexual, why choose a youth of seventeen who was unlikely to have much money on him? I mention this unpleasant matter because it illustrates how Brady sought at every opportunity to involve Smith and to exclude Hindley. She was surprised and annoyed, he said, when he told her his friend Evans was going home with them; when he sent her to fetch Smith she asked why he could not wait until the morning; when Smith arrived and the struggle began she was not in the room, and it was only when Evans was lying face downward under the table in a pool of blood that he saw her standing by the door. She knew nothing about the plan to steal money from the boy, he insisted, nor about any plan to rob a bank or snatch a payroll, which he had discussed with Smith; most assuredly she was not involved with the killing of Evans in any way. Her own story was that she was in the kitchen while Evans was dying. 'All I am saying', she told a policewoman during the early investigation, 'is that I didn't do it. We are involved in something we did not do. We never left each other, we never do. What happened last night was an accident, it should never have happened.' She refused to say more. 'No,' she said, 'ask Ian. His story is the same as mine. We never left each other.'

Elaborating in court on the statement he had made to the police, Brady claimed that Evans had started the fighting by kicking and hitting him, admittedly because he had demanded that he put his cash and valuables on the table and then leave the house. He retaliated, and Smith joined in the resulting struggle. Brady admitted using the axe. 'The point was, when I had hit him, I thought he would shut up. I hit him again and it wasn't having any effect. There was blood appearing . . . I just kept hitting until he shut up.' It was really irrelevant to the issue before the court whether Smith had joined in, and the only question mark concerned the extent of Hindley's involvement. It should be pointed out that if Brady's story was correct, he was offering no explanation of how the dog-hairs came to be found on the dead boy's body. His story could hardly have been the whole truth, although it was virtually an admission of murder by him.

At the trial he completely denied any knowledge of the death of John Kilbride. He often took photographs on the moors, and the picture which the prosecution alleged was of Hindley posing on the child's grave was a casual snapshot of no particular significance, according to him. It was pure coincidence that he should have in his possession photographs of two different graves! For her part, Hindley said that he had chosen the spot for the picture, and that she had had no idea that it was the site of a grave, and indeed there was no other evidence against her on this point, nor indeed could it count against her that Brady offered no satisfactory explanation of the fact that he had written the name 'Kilbride' in an exercise book that had been found. It was in connection with this killing that Hindley was charged separately with being an accessory after the fact, since it seemed difficult to accept that, even if she knew nothing about the murder, she had not helped to dispose of the body. Some form of transport was needed to get the body to the moors, and the very closeness of her relationship with Brady (who could not drive) gave credence to the probability that she had at least driven the car.

Any doubts about the moral guilt of Myra Hindley must surely be dissipated by consideration of the murder of Lesley Ann Downey.

Brady, it appeared, was prepared to say anything that suited him. He thought nothing of claiming that Edward Evans had been selected because he was, he said, a homosexual, seeking thereby to involve Smith in a conspiracy to 'roll a queer'. Having denied any knowledge of the Kilbride case, he could not involve Smith in that murder, but he was not beyond alleging that the little girl aged ten had agreed to pose for pornographic photographs for ten shillings, and that it was Smith who had brought her to the house for that purpose. He never once said a word against Hindley, always against Smith: it was Smith who had the idea to take and sell the pornographic photographs, it was Smith who brought the child for that purpose, it was Smith who ordered her to undress, and it was Smith who took her away afterwards. The tape, however, that had been discovered in the suitcase at the station suggested an entirely different story, for Smith's voice never appeared in the recording.

Hindley's voice most certainly did. Brady's explanation of her presence was that he had insisted on her being in the room while the photographic session was taking place, 'as a witness in case something went wrong', and in case the photographs ever led back to them. Her presence would also help to put the girl at ease. Hindley claimed that she was a reluctant spectator, that in fact she was so embarrassed at the proceedings that she had to look out of the window because she could not bear what was going on.

The tape proved, however, that it was not a case of her merely doing nothing to stop the proceedings. She was an active participant, just as merciless in her treatment of the little child as was Brady. It was difficult to choose between them in their infamy, and at one point she could only say in explanation, 'That was not my voice at all, it must have been Brady'—the only time she sought to excuse herself at his expense.

There was no doubting her voice.

I do not propose to provide a transcript of the tape. I will only say that it started with what the judge described as 'fearsome screaming from the little girl'. The dreadful abuse must already have started. When the child pleaded, 'Please God, help me,' Hindley replied, 'Come on. Shut up.'—typical of her callous responses. The last anyone heard of Lesley Ann Downey was when she was being gagged. 'Put that in your mouth again, packed more solid,' she was instructed. The voice was the voice of Hindley.

The tape was the rock on which the defence finally foundered, for could one believe that after such treatment it would have been safe to let the child go?

Brady was convicted of all three murders, Hindley of two. She was acquitted on the Kilbride charge, but found guilty of receiving, comforting, harbouring, assisting and maintaining Brady, well knowing that he had murdered the boy. Brady was sentenced to three concurrent terms of life imprisonment, Hindley to two plus a concurrent seven years. For murder, of course, these were the only sentences that the law allowed.

'Could anybody be so wicked as that?' the judge asked. I confess that I would be hard put to think of anything much more evil than the story of these murders.

At the time of writing both murderers are still in prison. There has been some support for a campaign to release Hindley on the grounds that she has already served a long sentence, and that she is a changed person. I recognize the possibility of redemption, but it is interesting to note that there has been no similar campaign for the release of Brady. I do not wish to involve myself with this discussion—there are people better qualified than me, and with the latest information at their disposal, to make decisions about the timing of the release of convicted murderers. I want only to put the view that capital punishment may perhaps be the best way to deal with people as evil as these two particular killers.

I have spent a great part of my life in the criminal law, and I have defended more people than I have prosecuted. My work in this field, coupled with my special experience as Director of Public Prosecutions, qualifies me, I believe, to express an opinion on this controversial subject, and lest it be thought that all prosecutors are automatically in favour of severe punishment, I should add that I found very substantial differences of opinion about capital punishment within the Department. My own personal view was, and is, affected by the very serious increase in crimes of violence. Violence against the person is the most serious form of crime as far as society is concerned, and too many penologists seem to accept it with reprehensible complacency.

The cases for and against capital punishment have been fully argued in recent years, and I do not claim to have any original ideas on the subject. I can do no more than advance an opinion based on a lengthy experience of crime and criminals. The abolitionists say that there is no evidence that capital punishment deters, and I accept that the majority of murders are not committed by people who deliberately intend to kill. The death penalty would not deter a husband who on the spur of the moment picks up a hammer and belabours a nagging wife; but I do believe that its absence may encourage complete recklessness as to whether someone is killed on the part of a criminal who resorts to violence in the course of the commission of another offence, such as robbery. In my young days at the Bar there were many instances where a burglar was discovered on the job and said, 'It's a fair cop' or words to that effect, and waited for the police. It was very rare for someone who was committing a non-violent crime to carry a cosh, let alone a gun. This may well have been because his approach was not to use violence, for if he did and was caught he was at risk of corporal punishment or, if things went badly wrong, of the noose. Today, when there is no really effective sanction against the use of violence during the commission of an offence, the criminal—who is now much more likely to be armed—will endeavour to fight his way out, knowing that statistically there is an even chance of getting away without being detected. That is a risk that he dare not take if he is putting his own life at risk, and I believe that experience has shown that very long sentences are not an effective sanction against reckless violence.

We should, in my opinion, revert to the old system where the penalty for murder was death. What form execution should take is a matter of legitimate discussion. The number of executions would in any case be very small. Inevitably, many murder charges would be reduced to manslaughter by the courts. There would be the further safeguard that the Home Secretary would frequently recommend a reprieve, having usually ascertained the views of the trial judge and the Lord Chief Justice, and having had regard to medical and other opinion relating to the history of a convicted person. This admittedly is an onerous responsibility, and perhaps some other suitable authority should be set up to carry out what was the Home Secretary's function. In any case, where there seemed to be a redeeming feature, clemency should be exercised.

I was never very attracted to the Homicide Act that sought to distinguish between capital murder and non-capital murder. I do not think that it proved very satisfactory in practice. There were too many borderline cases, and it created as many problems as it solved. If a bank employee was killed during a bank raid, why was that less serious murder than the killing of a policeman endeavouring to catch the robber as he was running from the bank?

One thing that makes one hesitate is the possibility of a mistake occurring and an innocent person being executed—an irrevocable step that nothing can remedy. I have always felt this to be the strongest argument for abolition. Looking back, however, over the years, how many instances have there been where, despite all our safeguards, real doubt has arisen as to whether an innocent person has been hanged? The classic example, of course, is Timothy Evans, who would almost certainly not have been convicted, despite his own statements, had the jury known that Christie was a murderer. I have thought long and hard about this matter, and my conclusion is this: bearing in mind that nobody would be executed if there appeared to be redeeming features, the interest of society requires that we take what I believe to be the very remote risk of making a mistake.

It was apparently the view of Blackpool Corporation, which demanded the restoration of the death penalty and obtained wide support for their petition, which was presented to Parliament on the day the trial opened of five men accused, among other crimes, of the murder of a police superintendent.

Nine people were originally charged, but Mr Justice Kilner Brown agreed that four of these—who had played apparently lesser roles in the affair—should be tried separately. This then was the trial of whthe prosecution alleged were the five principals. They were, in alphabetical order: Dennis George Bond, Thomas Flannigan, Charles Henry Haynes, Frederick Joseph Sewell, and John Patrick Spry.

The case opened at Crown Court, Manchester on 1 February 1972, and lasted for thirty-four working days. All defendants were accused of the murder of Superintendent Richardson in Blackpool on the previous 23 August. They were additionally accused of the attempted murder of four other police officers, although one count was withdrawn. To these charges they all pleaded not guilty. A sixth count charged them with conspiracy to use firearms with intent to prevent lawful arrest, and all pleaded not guilty except Sewell and Spry. Finally, they were charged with robbery and using force for the purpose. To this charge only Flannigan pleaded not guilty. Sewell subsequently sought to plead guilty to manslaughter on the murder charge, but the prosecution refused to accept the plea—not surprisingly, since he was the one who fired the shot that killed the Superintendent.

The murder arose following the robbery from a well-known jeweller's shop of 684 rings, 117 watches, 38 bracelets, 18 necklets, 104 charms, brooches and pendants, 53 pairs of earrings and 71 pairs of cufflinks, valued at over £100,000. The circumstances of the robbery were broadly undisputed. Soon after opening time, just after 9.30 a.m., four masked men burst into the shop while a fifth man waited near by in a stolen car. At least two of the intruders were armed, one with a shotgun, another with a revolver, and a third carried an axe. Sewell, it appeared, was the man with the shotgun, Spry the man with the revolver, and Bond the man with the axe. Haynes was the man in the car, and although he did not admit his part, Flannigan was implicated by the others as the remaining man.

The two assistants were threatened by the shotgun and ordered to lie down in the Till Room. The manager meanwhile got into his office unnoticed and sounded the alarm. As the robbers made off they instructed the assistants not to move for five minutes.

A sub-officer in the local fire brigade happened to be passing when the men came out. He was told, 'If you move, I'll drop you,' then he was knocked unconscious. Four men were then seen to pile into the waiting car, Sewell in front with the driver. The police were already on their trail, and Sergeant Carl Walker pursued them in a panda car. The robbers had planned to transfer their loot to another stolen car, which they had left a few hundred yards away, but the police were too close for comfort, so they drove into a side alley where Haynes and Sewell changed positions. Sergeant Walker arrived and placed his car across the mouth of the alleyway. A gun was pointed at him, it is not clear by whom. Sewell—perhaps thinking that the way ahead was blocked—reversed at speed, hit the police car and managed to get the robbers away from Walker.

Sergeant Ian Hampson now took up the chase in his panda. Sewell pulled up suddenly, and the police car also came to a halt. Spry got out of the robbers' car, he said to remove the keys from the pursuing vehicle, but he stopped the Sergeant more effectively by shooting at him. A bullet went through Sergeant Hampson's arm, which had it been in a different direction might well have proved fatal.

Spry got back into the car, which drove off again. It was forced to pull up at a road junction, and all five men got out. Police Constable Jackson said that Sewell pointed a gun at him as he was getting out of a police car and shouted, 'Get out and you're dead,' words not unlike those used earlier to the fire-brigade officer.

There was some confusion about what happened next, but it was undisputed that Haynes made good his escape, and that Flannigan was caught and arrested. Bond and Spry were seeking to escape, with Sewell bringing up the rearguard. Sergeant Walker was once again in close pursuit, and Sewell fired three shots at him, according to police evidence. The officer's bravery was later the subject of a special tribute by the judge. He went after Sewell even after the first shot, continued towards him even after the second, but was struck down by the third bullet, which passed though his groin, leaving him helpless. Sewell was to say that he had meant only to frighten him in order to stop him, that he had fired into the ground, and that the wounding was the result of a ricochet.

Sewell then got into the driver's seat of a butcher's refrigerator van with Bond and Spry in the rear. Superintendent Richardson and Constable Jackson were in a police car close behind, with Inspector

Gray at the wheel. The police car bumped into the van as it drove off. Round the corner the van crashed into a wall near an alleyway. Bond and Spry were then chased by Inspector MacKay's car, and were eventually overpowered and arrested.

In trying to get away Sewell fired two bullets at the Superintendent, who was courageously pursuing him. One nicked the officer's sleeve. The other killed him.

Sewell, who later claimed that the shots were the result of an accidental discharge, was able to escape. He was not discovered until 7 October—over six weeks later—when he was arrested in London. The circumstances of the arrest at 6.45 a.m. are worth mentioning because a degree of violence was used which resulted in permanent damage to Sewell's right eye. An inspector admitted hitting Sewell on the eye, but the police claimed that force was necessary in the circumstances. The injuries to the arrested man gave rise to the questioning of police impartiality, and to whether reliance could be placed on what Sewell was alleged to have told the police at the time. Another police officer in evidence referred to Sewell as 'that thing'— perhaps understandably, but it was an unhelpful remark, just as the injuries were unhelpful to the prosecution.

A more serious difficulty for the prosecution in relation to four of the accused was that they were absent from the scene when Sewell shot Superintendent Richardson. Three men were actually in police custody at the time. The prosecution case was that all the accused were in Blackpool to rob a jeweller, and that they had agreed that at least two of them would carry loaded firearms and use them if necessary to escape and resist arrest. It followed that the murder was committed in pursuance of a common purpose to kill or do grievous bodily harm. Counsel for four of the accused naturally contended that there had been a termination of the conspiracy in their cases before the Superintendent met his death.

Flannigan's story was that he was in Blackpool to repossess a car, and that when a car with several passengers stopped at the place where he had been told to wait he got in, assuming it to be the car in question. He got out when the police rammed it, having by then realized from the evidence of all the swag that it had been used in connection with a robbery! The improbability of this explanation was underlined by the fact that he was implicated to some extent by the other robbers. It appeared actually that he was brought in as a last-minute substitute. 'He's mad', said Sewell, 'and we wanted somebody like him.'

As for Sewell, there was some evidence that he was pleased to be arrested and to get the matter off his chest. He did not personally complain about his injuries, and told Inspector Mounsey, the investigating officer, 'I'll help you all I can. I'll make a statement about it all—why I was there, everything about it. You can't put the clock back, but I've got to do the best for myself . . . I can't get out of this . . . In a way I was really glad you came.' The Inspector said that in all his years of experience he had never found anyone more willing to co-operate. Although he had killed a senior police officer in brutal and callous fashion, his attitude compared favourably to that of the two Moors murderers, who sought to blame anybody else but themselves.

Of course, Sewell's counsel very properly raised the issue of whether, following his injuries, he was in a fit state to make a sensible statement to the police. At the trial, referring to Sergeant Walker, he claimed that he never had any intention of hurting him, and that he did not point the gun at him. His story of the killing of Superintendent Richardson was that with the gun in his hand, he told the pursuing police officers to keep back. Richardson said something like, 'Don't be silly.' Sewell shouted, 'Get back' at the police as he ran away; he turned round shortly afterwards to see Richardson only six or seven yards away. 'I went to open the door of the van with my right hand on the door handle, and the gun was in my left hand. As I did so, Richardson dived . . . I had actually stopped by now . . . I went down backwards. His head hit the middle of my chest very hard, and he reached out with both hands and held my neck. His dive knocked me against the van and the back of my head hit the van. It was a very hard bump. I went down on my haunches and Richardson was on top of me. I went down on the floor. I bounced off the van first before I went down. I did not lose my feet, but went down backwards. Richardson was on top of me. We were on the floor and the gun went off. My right arm was back behind me. I did not intend the gun to go off. I was trying to get away. I was horrified when I realized it had gone off, and I tried to get it away from his body so that it was not pointing at him, and I moved my left hand up to my right shoulder and tried to get out from underneath him. I twisted round and my body went further round. He was on his knees. As I got up his hands went down on the ground. When the second shot went off I was twisted round and Richardson was there with his left arm holding me by my right shoulder. The first shot went through his body and the second nicked his sleeve.'

Sewell had admitted his part in the robbery and conspiring with Spry to carry guns and resist arrest. He had been willing also to confess to the manslaughter of the Superintendent, and had made it clear that he had killed him. I never cease to wonder at the British legal system which gives such a man and his co-accused so long and fair a trial. I do not believe that there is anywhere else in the world where they would be more considerately heard and fairly judged. In the event the jury, who were out for over four hours, found Sewell guilty of the murder, and Spry guilty of the manslaughter, of Superintendent Richardson; Spry was found guilty of the attempted murder of Sergeant Hampson, and Sewell of the attempted murder of Sergeant Walker. Sewell and Spry were, of course, convicted on the conspiracy charge to which they had pleaded guilty. All accused were found guilty in connection with the robbery. These were the only convictions. Apart from Sewell and Spry, none of the accused was found guilty of anything but robbery.

Sewell was given the mandatory life sentence for murder, and the judge recommended that he serve not less than thirty years; he was given twenty years' imprisonment for the attempted murder, fifteen for the conspiracy and fifteen for the robbery, all concurrent. Spry was given twenty-five years for the attempted murder, fifteen for the conspiracy and fifteen for the robbery, also concurrent. For the robbery, Bond was sent to prison for fifteen years, Flannigan for thirteen years, and Haynes for ten years.

Frederick Joseph Sewell was born in Brixton in November 1932, so was aged thirty-nine at the time of the murder, when he was working in the motor trade. Apart from two minor matters, his only serious criminal conviction previously had been at Nottinghamshire Assizes in November 1957, when he was found guilty of robbery with violence and conspiracy to rob. Bond, who had a very much worse criminal record, was among those involved in the same crime. The robbers rammed a car carrying wages, attacked the occupants with hammers and a pick-axe shaft, and made off with nearly £40,000.

It will be noticed that nearly fifteen years had gone by before the Blackpool robbery was undertaken. By then, however, Sewell and Spry at least had graduated from hammers to guns. If they had not carried guns it is possible that Superintendent Richardson would be alive today, and one wonders whether, if capital punishment had not been abolished, they would ever have taken guns to Blackpool with them.

Sewell himself paid Richardson the greatest compliment. 'Why kill him?' he was asked by Inspector Mounsey. 'He just kept on coming,' he replied, 'he wouldn't go back. He was too brave. He shouldn't have dived at me.'

'He was too brave.' One can only hope that this tribute from her husband's murderer may have given some comfort to the Superintendent's widow.

CHAPTER 11

The rule of fear

THE THIRD event that caused me to think long and hard about capital punishment was the abduction and murder of Mrs Alick McKay, wife of the Deputy Chairman of the *News of the World*. The kidnapping and imprisonment of the unfortunate lady, the mental torture to which her husband and family were subjected, and her disappearance from the face of the earth were as horrifying in their way as the Moors murders.

On 29 December 1969 Mr Alick McKay left his house in Wimbledon at 9.30 a.m. and was driven to work by a chauffeur in a Rolls-Royce belonging to the newspaper that employed him. His wife Muriel collected the elderly lady who cleaned the house and took her home again about 4.45 p.m., having earlier visited her dentist. It was the habit of the household to leave a chain on the front door following an attempted burglary some time before, so when the husband returned home at 7.45 p.m. he first rang the bell, and when there was no reply he tried the handle and found that the door was unlocked and that the chain was not in position. On entering the house he found his wife's handbag and a pair of her shoes by the stairs. The telephone was on the floor, and the whole place was in disorder.

Mrs McKay was not there. There were, however, strong indications of a struggle, and some wide tape and string had been left behind, suggesting that perhaps she had been tied up and prevented from shouting for help. There was also a billhook, strangely out of place in a suburban house. Very important, some pages of a previous day's newspaper, the *Sunday People*, had been spread out in the hall, and on one of these was found a palm-print.

Mr McKay of course contacted the police immediately, and gave permission for all telephone calls to his house to be recorded. Detective-Sergeant White was in the house five and half hours later when, at 1.15 a.m., a call was received which was traced to a telephone box in Epping. Both Mr McKay and the police officer thought the caller had a West Indian voice. 'This is Mafia Group 3,' was the message. 'We are from America. We have your wife. We tried to get Rupert Murdoch's wife. We couldn't get her so we took yours instead.' Mr Murdoch—the newspaper magnate who now owns *The Times*, *The Sunday Times* and *The Sun*, among other journals—was the chairman of the *News of the World*, and it was he who normally used the Rolls-Royce, the significance of which fact was later to become apparent. 'I haven't much time,' the sinister caller went on, 'don't waste it. You have a million by Wednesday night or we will kill her. Do you understand?'

The message came through in the early hours of Tuesday morning. The kidnappers were demanding a million pounds by the end of the following day. 'What do I have to do?' Mr McKay asked. 'All you have to do is wait for the contact. We will contact you on Wednesday,' was the reply. 'Just have the money. You will get your instructions.' 'But who are you?' Mr McKay persisted. 'The Mafia,' he was told again. 'Have the money or you won't have a wife.'

This was only the first of several telephone calls. The second came at five o'clock in the afternoon, informing Mr McKay that his wife had just posted a letter to him. 'For heaven's sake, for her sake, don't call the police,' he was urged. A letter was duly received the following day, Wednesday. It contained a pathetic message which I only reproduce because it says something about the sort of people who were keeping Mrs McKay captive: 'I am blindfold and cold, only blankets. Please do something to get me home. Please co-operate as I can't keep going.'

No firm instructions were given immediately, although telephone contact was continued over the following days, and the McKay family were cruelly left in suspense to speculate, and to worry about the fate of a woman they all loved who had been abducted shortly after Christmas and was spending New Year's Eve and the turn of the year goodness knows where and in what terrible conditions. It was not until 7 January—nine days, it will be noted, after the kidnapping —that a further significant approach was made in the form of a letter received by the Editor of the *News of the World*. It read:

> I am writing these lines to you because I can't get through to Alick McKay by phone for it is bugged by police. If you are his friend you will contact him discreetly, telling him his wife is safe and well. She is being treated by a doctor from abroad. How long this will continue depends on how much co-operation Alick McKay will give us. When he authorises police out of his home and he is free to talk, I shall

telephone him giving him instructions and proof of his wife's existence for a ransom of one million pounds to be collected on two occasions of a half million each time. If he co-operates, he shall see his wife. If he don't co-operate, I shall not be contacting him any more and his wife will be disposed of.

—(*For the sake of clarity I have slightly edited the document, including the misspellings.*)

The words 'disposed of' could hardly have had a more sinister ring. There was a reference in the letter also, linking it to a later telephone conversation of similar tenor, that Mr McKay should borrow the money from firms he knew if he could not raise it himself. One week later, telephone calls were made both to the Editor of the *News of the World*—who described the voice as being West Indian—and to Mr McKay, who was assured that his wife was alive and well. 'She's costing me a lot now,' the caller said.

It was not until 19 January, three weeks after Mrs McKay's disappearance, that a meeting was first mooted. 'We're looking for a place', the caller said, 'where you should meet us to bring the money.' He repeated his demand for a million pounds in two instalments. 'This is my order, and that is final. I've got nothing more to say.' Two days later, Mr Ian McKay—who was answering the telephone for his father, who was ill—took a call in which he was told that both his father and his sister would be receiving a letter from his mother which would contain instructions about delivering the first half of the ransom on 'the 1st February, 1970'. A letter was duly received—which might well have been written much earlier and kept by the kidnappers until they were ready to use it—and it was accompanied by specific instructions. The money was to be brought to a telephone booth at the junction of Church Street and the Cambridge Road in Enfield, north London.

> You will enter the telephone box and wait for us to telephone you to give you further instructions at 10 pm on the 1st of February . . . We shall be telephoning you if in case you wish an earlier day for our business transaction, providing you got the money, of course . . . Your wife Muriel is pleading with us that you cannot obtain one million pounds, but I am making no promises, but if you co-operate discreetly and we collect the first half million, our gang will hold a conference whether to satisfy with half million pounds. If we do agree, you will receive your wife within two days after business is settled.

Mr Ian McKay took a series of calls the following day. He was asked whether the letter had been received, and whether the ransom money had been raised. He in turn demanded proof that his mother was alive and well, but was told firmly that her letter was all the proof that would be provided. 'I'm not going to let her write anything again,' the caller said. 'Because you haven't got her,' Ian McKay said. 'I got her,' was the reply. 'Of course you haven't got her, she's dead and that's why.'

Mr McKay was fishing desperately for information about his mother, but I suspect that he was right in saying that she was already dead, whether he believed it or not. Why else would the kidnappers not have provided evidence more solid than a letter that could have been written days before? Some of the conversation between Ian McKay and the caller was almost bizarre. At one point he asked, 'How many kidnaps have you done then?' 'We have never murdered anyone, as yet,' was the reply, 'but there will always be a first time.' A little later he repeated his request for proof. 'You don't expect me to just put money in a telephone box and just expect two days later that you will be very nice and sort of send her back smiling,' he said, eliciting the fatuous comment, 'If we are doing business we deal with honesty as far as we are concerned.'

On 28 January a letter was received by Mr Alick McKay which I have again slightly edited for sense. It read:

I am sending you final letter for your wife's reprieve. She will be executed on the 2nd February 1970 unless you keep our business date on the 1st February without any error. We demand the full million pounds in two occasions. When you deliver the first half million, your wife will be saved and I personally shall allow her to speak to you on telephone. We will not allow you to tell us how to run our organisation. We are telling you what to do. You cannot eat the cake and have it too. This is our fourth blackmail. We have absorbed £3,500,000. We did not murder anyone because they were wise to pay up and their families were returned to them. You do the same and she will return safely. My next blackmail will be in Australia some time this year.'

Were the circumstances not so sinister, the letter might be the object of some hilarity, and it certainly gives some indication of the peculiar mind or minds with which the unfortunate McKay family were dealing. The writer continued:

Looking forward to settling our business on the 1st February at 10 pm as stated in last letter, in a very discreet and honest way, and you and your children will be very happy to join Muriel McKay, and our organisation also will be happy to continue our job elsewhere in Australia. We shall look forward to seeing your son when we visit Australia. You see, we don't make our customers happy, we like to keep them in suspense. In that way it is a gamble. That is why we don't accept you, Ian, telling us what to do. We give the order and you must obey.

It can be no easy matter to deal with a writer of this mentality. The family had no good evidence that Mrs McKay was still alive, and they were clutching at straws in the hope that police investigations would turn up something to help identify their tormentors and discover the place where Mrs McKay had been taken. This particular letter had been received only four days before the money was supposed to be handed over. A telephone call was made two days later, insisting that the Rolls-Royce be used to go to the telephone booth, presumably because it was easily recognizable. The arrangement was that Ian McKay was to make the delivery accompanied by no more than one other person. 'Just remember,' he was warned, 'any error will be fatal.' The caller said that he would check again on 1 February that all arrangements had been made for handing over the money as instructed.

We now come to the day in question. It was a Sunday, a day short of five weeks since Mrs McKay disappeared. Sure enough, at 8 p.m., a call was made to confirm the appointment two hours later. Ian McKay told the caller that he was getting ready. At about nine o'clock the Rolls-Royce left Wimbledon. It was driven by Detective-Inspector Minors, dressed as a chauffeur. The passenger was Detective-Sergeant Street, disguised to resemble Ian McKay. They took with them a suitcase.

Sergeant Street arrived at the call-box just after ten. The telephone rang almost immediately. A voice which the officer thought was West Indian directed him to another box farther north along the Cambridge Road, where he received a message, in the same voice, telling him that he would find a 'Piccadilly' cigarette packet on the floor. A message on the packet directed him farther along the main road to the High Cross junction leading to Dane End. This was already in Hertfordshire. 'You will there see two paper flowers', the message continued, 'and you will put the suitcase with the money where the paper flowers are.' Following that, he was to return to the original call-box at the corner of Church Street and await another message about the release of Mrs McKay.

The instructions were followed to the letter. The suitcase was deposited at about midnight, and the officers returned to Church

Street to await a call that never came. Other policemen, however, had been contacted by radio and were keeping observation at the Dane End junction—as they thought, unobtrusively and certainly not in police cars, but they were in fact under observation themselves, and no attempt was made to collect the suitcase. Eventually the police took it back. Two police officers reported seeing a dark Volvo saloon containing two male passengers in the area around midnight, and although they did not attach great significance to it at the time, one of them noticed that the rear nearside light was not working.

Nothing was heard from the kidnappers for two days. Then, on the Tuesday at about 11.15 a.m., Mr Ian McKay took a call that lasted nearly twenty minutes. 'Good morning, Ian,' it began. 'Is that Ian? . . . what a nice boy you are, aren't you? . . . This is a meeting now. First our business is being handled by the intellectuals, the heads. Now there is a meeting of the semi-intellectuals, to be passed on to the third party, the ruffians. This meeting is in consideration with your mum, what time she be executed, whether she should be executed and what time.' It was during this conversation that the caller, who claimed to be part of a large organization, said that he, his boss and 'all the boys' had watched Ian, as they supposed, arrive and deposit the suitcase, but that they had noticed motor-bikes and cars and suspected a police trap. 'Well, it's no good now,' he said. 'Mark you, I am very sorry for your mother and I don't like the idea of her being killed. . . It depends now on the meeting, this meeting I am going to now. Then I will be able to say whether we could pursue any matter or whether they are going to execute her. They have done so many jobs, but they've never executed anyone, because whatsoever the reason, they gave back the client; they get the money and then they return the client . . .'

A couple of hours later a second call was made to announce the decision of the meeting. The kidnappers had apparently relented, but were unwilling to deal further with Ian McKay. When he said truthfully that his father was under sedation, it was suggested that they deal alternatively with Ian's sister, Diane. Two further telephone calls were made two days later, and this time Mr Alick McKay was able to speak himself. He told the caller that there had been no attempt to trick him; that they had only had an hour's start before the police found out and followed them; and that if he had been less clever and not led them a wild-goose chase, the money would have been handed over to him before the police came on the scene. He also said that the money was in the bank because he dared not leave it lying around the house. This appeared to reassure the man. 'You've got to get the money,' he told Mr McKay. 'You will get a call any time now to tell you what you've got to do. It will be you and Diane. Both of you to come with it. You've got to put it in two suitcases this time. You'll be holding one and Diane will be holding one.' The kidnappers doubtless thought that by substituting his daughter for his son, Mr McKay would be more likely to co-operate in the second attempt to deliver the ransom money. He finally agreed that his daughter would drive him to the rendezvous, which was fixed for 4 p.m. on Friday, 6 February, at the original call-box on the corner of Church Street.

At three o'clock the car set off again from Wimbledon, this time with two suitcases. Detective-Inspector Minors was again passenger, only this time he was made up to look not unlike Alick McKay. In place of Detective-Sergeant Street was Woman Detective-Constable Armitage, in a blonde wig and wearing Diane's pink coat. A third person was in the boot of the car. Inspector Bland was no doubt thankful that he was crouched in a Rolls-Royce rather than a smaller vehicle.

They arrived on schedule, and Inspector Minors went into the booth, but he had to wait forty-five minutes for the call. He was directed to a telephone box in Bethnal Green Road, opposite the police station, and told that the caller would there want to speak to Diane. Just after six o'clock the caller rang and instructed Mr McKay and his daughter, as he thought, to take the tube to Epping and to await instructions at yet another call-box. The police officers drove in fact to the station at Theydon Bois and made the last part of the journey by train, carrying the two suitcases. They arrived at 7.15, and at 7.30 received another telephone call. 'You are being watched,' they were told. 'Now you will be taking a taxi. You and Diane go to Bishop's Stortford.' They were to find a place where used cars were displayed, and to leave the suitcases on the pavement next to the hedge opposite a particular car, the registration number of which they were given. 'Any error will be fatal to Muriel and Diane,' they were warned. 'You see, we deal with high-powered telescopic rifles. Anyone illegal that attempts to interfere, we shall let them have it.' The use of the word 'illegal' in this context has a certain irony about it.

The two police officers hired a taxi and picked up Inspector Bland, who was waiting for them by arrangement some distance away, having left the boot of the Rolls. He crouched on the floor of the taxi so as not to be seen, and when they reached their destination he crawled out on all fours and hid in the hedge. Two other officers had secreted themselves behind a low fence on the opposite side of the road. Officers Minors and Armitage deposited the suitcases as instructed, and returned in the taxi to Epping, where they waited in vain until one o'clock the next morning for the telephone call they had been promised.

At 9.5 p.m. a Volvo car, number XPO 994, with its rear side light inoperative, approached slowly, driven by a young man who stopped by the suitcases and leant out to inspect them. The car went off and returned, driven by the same person, half an hour later, and again ten minutes afterwards. On the latter occasion it stopped in an alleyway before going off again. At 10.47 it reappeared, driven by the same man but with a passenger in the front. It came almost to a halt where the suitcases were before again departing the scene, never to reappear.

Fate then took a hand in the form of two public-spirited pedestrians who spotted the suitcases. One kept watch while the other went to inform the local police, who arrived to collect them! Just what would otherwise have happened we shall never know, but the police of course now had the lead they needed. The Volvo car, the driver of which had been acting so suspiciously, and which fitted the description of a car seen at the scene of the first abortive attempt to deliver the suitcases, had been bought by a Mr Arthur Hosein and was registered in his wife's name. Mr Hosein, aged thirty-four, and his brother Nizamodeen (usually referred to as Nizam) aged twenty-two, were of Indian origin, but first came to this country from Trinidad. They lived on a fifteen-acre farm north of London, no great distance from Dane End and Bishop's Stortford.

The police arrived in force the following morning at Rooks Farm, with a warrant to search for stolen jewellery, a small quantity of which had disappeared from the house in Wimbledon along with Mrs McKay, but Inspector Minors told both brothers that he was also making another inquiry, indicating that Nizam had been identified as the driver of the Volvo and Arthur as his passenger on its last visit to the spot where the suitcases had been left. Exhaustive searches of the farmhouse and its grounds revealed plenty of incriminating material and evidence connecting the brothers with the kidnapping of Mrs McKay, but of the lady herself there was not a sign.

It is of course easier to prove a murder if there is a body, but death can be presumed. To quote an admirable example of Mr Justice Sebag Shaw (now Lord Justice), the judge who tried the Hoseins, if a person without a parachute falls out of a plane over mid-Atlantic and is never seen again, one would have little difficulty in saying that he is dead. In this dreadful matter, what other explanation could there be for the complete disappearance of a reasonably healthy and mentally stable woman in her early fifties? If the Hosein brothers were proved to be her kidnappers they would surely have revealed her whereabouts if

173

she were alive rather than face a possible conviction for murder. If they were proved to be the people who kept telling her family that she was alive and well, why were they unable to produce her? If they were proved to be the people who had threatened to kill her, should it not be presumed, in the absence of any feasible explanation, that they had actually done so? I do not wish to list the various gruesome theories about how the murder may have been carried out, but despite the difficulty of disposing of a body without trace, even on a farm, the presumption of death, in this case would appear inescapable.

The Hosein brothers were arrested, and it may be significant that no further letters or telephone calls were received from the kidnappers thereafter. The brothers stood trial at the Old Bailey between 14 September and 6 October, 1970, and the Attorney-General led for the prosecution. They were charged not only with the murder but with kidnapping, false imprisonment, blackmail and sending letters threatening to murder. As the judge pointed out on more than one occasion, the murder issue depended very much on the view the jury took about the very serious but lesser charges. He said that if it were not proved that they were parties to the kidnapping, the question of murder, so far as they were concerned, did not arise. An interesting feature of the case was that the brothers to some extent turned against each other, each contradicting in important respects what the other said, and it was stated that Nizam was frightened of Arthur and had been acting out of fear on his brother's instructions. It was a matter of record that they had come to blows in prison, after which they had been separated.

Nizam certainly had made the first move. Ten days before the disappearance of Mrs McKay he had gone to the Vehicle Registration Department at County Hall to get particulars about the owner of Rolls-Royce registration number ULP 18F. He gave a false name and false address. He was told that the car was owned by the *News of the World*. Not satisfied with this, he badgered the clerical officer who was dealing with his inquiry, in an attempt to discover exactly who at the newspaper normally used the car. In fact, as we know, this was Mr Rupert Murdoch, but the officer was unable to provide the information. The implication, from subsequent events, was that the Hoseins had noted the vehicle as belonging to somebody who was either a potential kidnap victim or wealthy enough to pay ransom. Nizam, who said his brother had driven him to County Hall, admitted making the inquiry, but claimed that he had done so on his brother's instructions and without any idea of why he had been asked to do so. He was dependent on his brother, under whose roof he was living, and he was also terrified of him. He never questioned, just obeyed. For his part, Arthur denied taking his brother there or asking him to get information. He knew nothing about it.

Nizam also behaved very suspiciously when he was visited in prison, five weeks after his arrest, by another brother. He was seen to hold up a note that read: 'Don't say anything to anyone, not even the solicitor, that I was by you on Monday night. Two farmers are saying that Arthur was down by them on that day at 6.30 p.m. I was *home*!' The word 'home' was underlined. Could this have meant that Nizam was claiming to have been at home on the Monday night when Mrs McKay disappeared, rather than at his brother's in Thornton Heath, which was a matter of only five or six miles from the McKay house?

There was a witness who claimed to have seen a Volvo saloon near Wimbledon Common around five o'clock on the afternoon when Mrs McKay disappeared. There were two men in it, one about thirty, a 'tanned Arab type'. Another saw two 'Indian gentlemen', or men of 'Asiatic origin', walking towards the McKay house on the other side of the road at 5.45 p.m. the same day. Among articles taken by the police from Rooks Farm were an empty red tin that had originally contained tape of the same type and width that was left behind in Wimbledon; paper flowers of the type that were found at Dane End; a note with the registration number of the car in Bishop's Stortford opposite which the suitcases were ordered to be left; and paper identical to that used by the kidnappers for at least some of their written communications. Indeed, there were indentations on a blank sheet of paper which corresponded exactly with two interpolations added to the letter sent to the Editor of the *News of the World*.

The billhook found at the McKay house was identified by a farmer who had done jobs for Arthur Hosein. When first shown it Arthur made the following comment: 'We used this to chop up a calf which had died. Nizam did the chopping, and we fed the calf to the dogs and threw the bones out with the rubbish.' The following day he explained that he had only meant that the billhook was similar to the one used on the calf. Nizam was not questioned about the billhook until a day later. According to the police, he began to tremble and said, 'Let me die'. No explanation was ever forthcoming for the billhook having been left behind by the kidnappers.

The kidnappers were clearly people of a certain intelligence, cunning and shrewd, but also stupid. The two can, and often do, go side by side. They obviously knew something about fingerprints, for despite the most thorough examination, not a single print was found in the house at Wimbledon, except for a palm-print on a page of newspaper in the hall. Whether or not they wore gloves most of the time they were in the McKay house, they took the most meticulous care not to leave their prints on any surface apart from the newspaper. This was in sharp contrast to their carelessness in leaving objects behind, and one wonders perhaps whether they were disturbed. I was always of the opinion that they may not have known that fingerprints could be left on paper. Why otherwise, if the Crown's fingerprint expert was correct, was Arthur Hosein's palm-print on a page of the *Sunday People* at Wimbledon and on one of the ransom letters; why was his fingerprint on the envelope containing the letter that Mrs McKay originally sent to her husband from captivity; and why was his thumbprint on the 'Piccadilly' cigarette packet left in the call-box?

It is only right to say that the expert evidence for the Crown on this issue was disputed by an expert called for the defence, but the Crown's expert expressed himself as 'positive' in two instances, and as having 'no doubt' in a third. Arthur Hosein's weak explanation was that if the ransom notes had been written on paper found at the farm it would not be surprising if his prints were on them, but anyone could have written them who had access to the farm. He told a weird and wonderful story to the effect that on three different occasions he had seen four men at the farm who had been invited there by Nizam. He described one of them as American, two as French—'sort of Maurice Chevalier type'—and one as British, whom he sought to identify as the well-known publisher Mr Robert Maxwell, who for a time was Member of Parliament for a near-by constituency! 'I knew that Nizam, who was anxious to stay in this country if he could, had found some people, amongst whom was a Member of Parliament, who were prepared to use their influence so as to get him a permit that he so dearly wanted, either being willing to help Nizam or, pretending that they could, were using him.' Using him to provide stationery, bearing his brother's fingerprints, on which to write ransom letters to Mr McKay? Small wonder that Nizam denied all knowledge of this improbable quartet. He said that Arthur had concocted the story while they were both on remand in prison, and that his refusal to go along with it was the occasion of their coming to blows.

The handwriting expert for the Crown, whose evidence was also disputed, believed that Arthur had probably written at least one of the ransom notes in a disguised hand, and some at least of the wording on the 'Piccadilly' cigarette packet. Arthur also misspelt words, to Inspector Minors's dictation, in the same way as the writer of the letter to the Editor of the *News of the World*.

It is interesting to note that Nizam admitted having been with

Arthur at Dane's End, and having planted two paper flowers in the ground, on the night of 1 February. He thought the suitcases were something to do with an eloping female. He said he was acting under his brother's instructions, but Arthur denied this whole story.

As regards the events of 6 February, Arthur admitted that he and his brother had been in Bethnal Green Road on legitimate business an hour before the call was made to the telephone box near the police station. He had then left Nizam with the car in Bishop's Stortford, taking a taxi the rest of the way home, so that Nizam could visit his girlfriend. Nizam collected him by arrangement from a public house near the farm at 10.20 p.m., and they had driven straight home. The younger brother said they did not leave Bethnal Green Road until six o'clock. Arthur stopped the car in Bishop's Stortford and told him to pick up two black suitcases opposite a particular car, the registration number of which Nizam wrote down. He was to collect the suitcases without looking inside, and take them to Arthur at the pub. He loitered for almost an hour, incidentally arousing the suspicions of a garage attendant who became worried about the safety of his cash-box and who eventually asked him to move on. He was obviously too early, so returned later, and this time he spotted the suitcases, but they were white not black. Fearing that they contained stolen goods, he decided not to pick them up, explaining to his brother that they were a different colour. He then drove Arthur to the scene, and they both saw that the suitcases were still there. 'Arthur never told me what it was all about.'

Arthur claimed that on the day of Mrs McKay's disappearance he was at home with Nizam until the early evening, when he went out on business, returning at half-past eight. The lie was given to this story by the people he was supposed to have visited. When told about Mrs McKay he said he did not read newspapers or watch the news on television. According to the police, he said, 'Where's Wimbledon?'

When asked where he was on the day of the kidnapping Nizam replied curiously, 'Where did Arthur say I was?' When asked whether he was at Wimbledon he said, 'I want to die. I mustn't speak. I can't. Let me see Arthur.' When the question was repeated he twice said, 'Ask Arthur'. The following day he said he thought he was with Arthur at the crucial time. 'We went to London in the Volvo, but not to Wimbledon.' He told a different story in court, alleging that he had remained at the farm all day until after eight o'clock, when he went to see his cousin in Norbury and his brother in Thornton Heath. Arthur, he said, had left the farm 'about feeding time', and did not return until about eight.

That both the brothers were involved up to their necks in this affair was surely beyond doubt, and indeed Nizam at one point told the police that he suspected his brother's involvement. The only serious question was the extent to which the younger brother had been acting as a free agent. The jury took the only view of the facts that they could reasonably have done on the evidence. After a retirement of just over four hours, they found both brothers guilty on all charges, but they unanimously asked for leniency towards Nizam. On the murder charge, of course, there was only one sentence prescribed by law—life imprisonment—but although the judge declared himself as not sure that Nizam was in any degree less culpable or less evil, he gave effect to the jury's recommendation by sentencing Arthur to a total of twenty-five years' imprisonment on the other charges, and Nizam fifteen years.

As an illustration of Arthur Hosein's character, it is interesting to note his outburst in court when asked by the Clerk, in accordance with tradition, whether he had anything to say why the court should not give judgment according to the law. 'I claim this privilege expressly this afternoon,' he said, 'that injustice has not only been done but also been seen and heard by the public gallery has not been done. The provocation by your Lordship, you have shown impartiality from the moment I have stood in that box and named Rupert Maxwell. I realize you are a Jew. I am not anti-Jew . . .'

The reader will note the conjunction of intelligence and stupidity, the misuse of 'impartiality' when 'partiality' was intended, the confusion of 'Rupert' for 'Robert'. After an interruption from the judge, he repeated his allegation of judicial prejudice to the obvious embarrassment of his counsel, who asked whether he might have a word with his client. 'I don't think he needs your assistance,' the judge said, 'but if he does, he will ask for it.' 'Again partiality exists, my Lord.' This time he had got the word right. 'Counsel wishes to advise me on certain things and you have denied me that advice. I think my word would be useless. Thank you, thank you, members of the jury. This is a gross injustice done.'

I doubt whether that opinion was shared by anyone in court. It was certainly not the view of the Criminal Division of the Court of Appeal, which refused the brothers' applications for leave to appeal. This was indeed a horrible murder, and it is difficult to find any redeeming feature in Arthur Hosein's favour. I prefer to quote the words of the judge: 'The kidnapping and the confinement of Mrs McKay was cold-blooded and it was abominable. She was snatched from the security and comfort of her home and for so long as she remained alive, she was reduced to terrified despair. . . . There could not be a worse case of blackmail. You put Mrs MacKay's family on the rack for weeks and months in the attempt to extort from them your monstrous demands.'

It is a case such as this that makes one pause when considering the problem of capital punishment, because no punishment can really fit that crime, but on the other hand it must be conceded that in principle there is a great danger in a person being executed when the victim's body has never been found.

The issue of punishment was raised in a different context more recently by former gangland boss Charles Richardson.

In May 1980, after serving fourteen years of a 25-year sentence, he absconded from prison, his application for parole having been rejected. It was almost nine months before he was recaptured. The breaking up of the Kray and Richardson gangs was one of the greatest achievements of the police during the time I was Director of Public Prosecutions. As we shall see, Richardson was responsible for torturing people who stood in his way. It is hard to imagine a more vicious and dangerous criminal, and I refute entirely his statement that he had been the victim of 'the myth and notoriety created by newspapers'. His crimes were only too real, but, as he claimed in a six-page letter to *The Times* following his escape, he had not himself committed murder, and yet had already served a longer term than many murderers.

Fourteen years' incarceration', he said, 'has taken its toll both in physical and mental terms and I and my family have become seriously concerned about this progressive mental deterioration.' I do not know who actually wrote the letter, but if indeed Richardson himself did so, it hardly attests to any decrease in his mental powers. Dreadful as his crimes were, however, one must take the point about the problems of long-term imprisonment, and at least recognize the possibility of a change of heart. He is not, he said, the man he was, but I would perhaps have been more influenced by his letter if in it he had expressed greater remorse for his wrongdoings.

I suppose too that Mary Bell—who was released from detention at almost the same time that Richardson escaped—is not the girl that she was. It may be interesting, before examining the Kray and Richardson cases, to look at hers, for it raises in an even more acute form the anxious question of what is the correct punishment to fit a peculiarly dastardly crime. Mary Flora Bell was only eleven years old when she was arrested and charged with the murders of four-year-old Martin George Brown and three-year-old Brian Howe in Newcastle upon Tyne. Her friend and namesake (although no relation) Norma Joyce Bell, aged thirteen, was charged with the same murders.

179

The sad and terrible story was unfolded in December 1968 at Newcastle Assizes before Mr Justice Cusack. On 25 May previously a schoolboy and two young friends had been searching for wood in some houses that were being demolished when they found young Martin's body. The cause of death was uncertain, but might well have been asphyxia. On 31 July young Brian's body was discovered on waste ground near a railway line. A pair of scissors had been placed on his left side. Death had probably been due to asphyxia caused by pressure on the nose and neck. An initial scratched on his stomach—either M, N or W—might well have been made with a razor blade. There were obvious similarities between the two deaths.

There were several matters linking one or both the accused girls to the two dead children, including four handwritten notes and some exercise books which contained certain references to the circumstances surrounding the two deaths. Mary admitted writing one particular note, but a handwriting expert thought she had written more, and he also took the view—which was disputed—that Norma had written some part of the notes. Fibres matching those from Mary's dress were found on both the little boys' clothing. When Mrs June Brown, Martin's mother, learned that her child had had an accident she went to the house where she was told she would find her son. Mary was on the spot, and conducted her to the scene by a complicated route.

Mary sought on one occasion to blame Norma. Two witnesses spoke of Mary saying, 'I know something that can get Norma put straight away.' Persuaded to elaborate, she claimed that Norma had seized Martin Brown by the throat. Norma told the police that Mary had confided to her, about Brian Howe, that 'I squeezed his neck and pushed up his lungs. That's how you kill them. Keep your nose dry and don't tell anybody.' Norma also alleged that Mary 'showed me a razor under a block and told me not to tell my Dad.' Norma led the police to the spot where a razor-blade was hidden.

'Norma's a liar. She always tries to get me into trouble,' Mary told the police, but we all along took the view that Mary was the protagonist. She was a strange girl, as witness the surprisingly adult comments she made to the police while being questioned. At one point she indicated that she wanted to go home, and when told she could not leave immediately, said, 'I'll phone some solicitors. They'll get me out. This is being brainwashed.' Later she asked, 'Is this place bugged?' When told she was to be charged with murder, she replied 'That's all right with me.'

Strangest of all, however, was her behaviour four days after the first death. According to Mrs Brown, Mary knocked on the door and

Two policemen on guard outside the Spaghetti House restaurant during the siege *(Chapter 8)*

David and Maureen Bingham *(Chapter 8)*

Myra Hindley *(Chapter 10)*
Ian Brady *(Chapter 10)*

Mrs Richardson   *(Chapter 10)*

Joseph Sewell *(Chapter 10)*

The Kray brothers *(Chapter 11)*

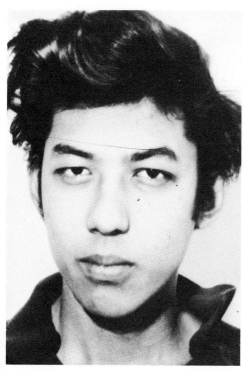

Nizamodeen Hosein *(Chapter 11)*   Arthur Hosein *(Chapter 11)*

Rooks Farm *(Chapter 11)*

The author in his office

Lady Skelhorn, with the family dogs

The author at the date of his appointment as Director of Public Prosecutions
(Chapter 5)

asked to see Martin. 'I'm sorry, pet,' the boy's mother said, 'Martin's dead.' 'Oh, I know he's dead,' said Mary. 'I want to see him lying in his coffin.'

Children of ten and above can be tried on a criminal charge. Here the jury acquitted both girls of murder, but Mary was found guilty of manslaughter on the ground of diminished responsibility. She was sentenced to detention for life, which in practice has meant her release after nearly eleven and a half years. She was a young child in 1968, and one hopes that she has been able to put these dreadful events behind her, and that she will be able to pursue a useful life as an adult. Why did she do it? I remember one theory that the two victims had curly, fair hair, whereas Mary—and indeed Norma—had straight, short, black hair. Could Mary have been jealous of the little boys' curls? Credence was given to this idea by the fact that someone had apparently started to cut off young Brian's hair after death.

Perhaps it was just a case of sadism, but Mary Bell had the excuse that she was only eleven. Charles Richardson had no such excuse.

After leaving school at the age of sixteen, Charles William Richardson set up in business on his own account, selling ice-cream at first, and later scrap metal. By the time of the events that were the subject of his trial at the Old Bailey, when he was aged thirty-two, he was said to be running a retail business, employing thirty people, as well as a wholesale fancy-goods company. He also had an interest in two mining ventures, one in South Africa in connection with which he had an office in fashionable Park Lane. He is entitled to credit for his success in legitimate business, but unfortunately one of his principal activities appears to have been to obtain goods, and particularly travel tickets, on credit, sell them and not pay for them.

Reprehensible as this was, the real gravamen of the case against him was that, in connection with this illegal behaviour, he controlled a gang of thugs whose practice over a number of years had been to enforce their master's will by violence and intimidation. They struck such fear into their victims that for at least three years no one dared complain to the police.

As many as nineteen people were originally believed to have belonged to the gang, including Lawrence Bradbury, alias John West, who in 1966 had been convicted in Johannesburg, South Africa, of murder, but at the 'torture trial' itself, as it came to be known, nine people faced charges. They included Richardson himself, described as a company director, and his brother. The proceedings took place at the Old Bailey, before Mr Justice Lawton, from 6 April to 8 June, 1967, and revealed in the words of Sebag Shaw, Q.C.

(who prosecuted), 'vicious and brutal violence systematically inflicted, deliberately and cold-bloodedly and with utter callousness and ruthlessness'.

This was no exaggeration, if the prosecution witnesses were to be believed. Jack Duval said he had twice been beaten up with golf clubs because he would not obey the gang. When he had asked why he was being subjected to this treatment, Edward Richardson, he said, ordered him, 'You do as Charlie tells you to do.' He also spoke about a victim named Blore who had had knives thrown at him by Charles Richardson.

Bernard Wajcenberg gave evidence that in 1963 Charles Richardson had summoned him to his office and claimed £5,000 from him which he was supposed to owe one of Richardson's companies. 'You will have to pay up,' Richardson threatened, 'or you know what will happen to you if you don't.' He alleged that Richardson had said, 'You have been making inquiries about me from a police officer,' and warned him that he would not get out of the office alive if he did not pay. Richardson had then grabbed him by the lapels, saying 'When I go berserk, you know what happens.' He had then been shown a cupboard containing knives, choppers and a shotgun. This experience had so unnerved him that he borrowed £3,000 and gave it to Richardson, although he said he did not owe him a penny.

Benjamin Coulston alleged that he had been abducted in the street, taken by car to one of Richardson's premises, beaten up and tortured for several hours. Lighted cigarettes had been stubbed out on his naked body, his toes had been struck with a metal object and an attempt had been made by one of the accused, Francis Fraser, to pull out his teeth with pliers. So serious was the assault that he had been admitted to hospital with a fractured skull, and so terrified was he that, although £30 was slipped under his pillow as hush money three or four days later, he had run away with twenty stitches still in his head.

It is not surprising, in the face of such intimidation, that few witnesses were willing to come forward, and the prosecution had necessarily to rely on criminals or those who had to live by their wits. Duval was serving a three-year prison sentence at the time of the trial. He and Wajcenberg, who had been in a German concentration camp, were both refugees from Eastern Europe. Coulston, who got into some confusion in the witness-box, was described by the judge as a 'petty, ineffectual criminal . . . almost illiterate'. The point about the Richardson gang was that they preyed on people of this type. There was no apparent reason, however, why the witnesses should have invented their evidence.

One of the most terrible tortures was known as 'the box', allegedly operated by the accused Roy Hall. This was an electric generator that was used to apply high-voltage shocks to the naked victims. It was often applied to the private parts, causing excruciating pain and severe burns. Two men treated in this way were said to have jumped high into the air from the chair in which they had been placed. An added refinement had been to splash their feet with water to render the shocks more effective.

All but one defendant, Alfred Berman, denied inflicting any injuries, but he not only gave evidence on his own behalf but also against Charles Richardson, Francis Fraser and Thomas Clark. Richardson described the evidence of Duval and Wajcenberg as fantastic lies. At one point he said, 'It sounds like something out of a James Bond book.' He alleged that they had made off with £32,000 belonging to a company with which he was associated. 'That is the reason they are saying these things.' As for Coulston, he had never known him, let alone seen him.

It had taken eighty-five minutes before the jury could be empanelled. Fifty persons had been challenged on behalf of the accused, and thirty-five asked to stand by for the Crown. The jury were out for nine hours and forty-six minutes before finding five of the accused guilty on some of the charges against them. Those convicted were the Richardson brothers, Thomas Clark, Francis Fraser and Roy Hall. Charles Richardson was convicted on four counts of causing grievous bodily harm with intent, two of assault occasioning actual bodily harm, one of robbery with violence and two of demanding money with menaces, for which offences he was sentenced to what in practice meant twenty-five years. As he turned to leave the dock he glared at the jury and said, 'Thank you—very much.'

Whether this was meant as a threat is doubtful, but the authorities did not immediately withdraw police surveillance from the members of the jury, indicating the view they took of the dangerous character of the Richardson gang. One particularly savage beating in which Edward Richardson was involved had been described by the judge as 'an outrage to the British public'. Addressing Charles Richardson— who all along protested his innocence—Mr Justice Lawton said, 'On the evidence I have heard in this case, I am satisfied that over a period of years you were the leader of a large, disciplined, well-led, well-organized gang, and that for purposes of your criminal desires, you terrorized those who crossed your path and you terrorized them in a way that was vicious, sadistic and a disgrace to society.' The judge added that he was ashamed to think that he lived in a society that 'contained men like you'.

Richardson, claiming that he is a changed man, believes that fourteen years is as long as anybody should spend in prison. He might in fact call Mr Justice Lawton in aid of this proposition, for the learned judge told him in 1967 that 'I have come to the conclusion that no penal system will cure you but time. The only thing that will cure you is the passing of the years.' I am prepared to accept as a possibility that Richardson may be a reformed character who will not revert to his old ways, but I vehemently reject any attempt to excuse or minimize his dreadful crimes. Indeed, I call in evidence the leader writer of *The Times*, who, on 9 June 1967 wrote: 'The "torture trial" which ended at the Old Bailey yesterday may come to be seen as a turning point in the fight against major crime.'

Just over eighteen months later the Old Bailey was again the scene for a case of equal, if not greater, importance in this same fight. This was the trial of the Kray gang. The great difference between the Krays and the Richardsons is that the Kray twins were murderers, and the taking of human life is the gravest crime in the criminal calendar. Charles Richardson rightly says that his gang did not kill anybody, and I suppose that an apologist for him might say that he only tortured other criminals and their associates, whereas the Krays' threats were in some instances directed at people other than criminals. Nevertheless there is not much to choose between the two gangs. Both were a law unto themselves, maintaining a rule of fear and dealing as they saw fit with anyone who opposed them or got in their way. There was another similarity in that two brothers were the principals involved in both gangs.

The Kray brothers were in fact three in number, but the twins, Reginald and Ronald, were far more seriously involved than Charles, who was seven years their senior. The twins were aged thirty-four at the time of their trial, which lasted from 7 January to 5 March 1969, and took place before Mr Justice Melford Stevenson. The three brothers and eight other defendants were accused in connection with two murders, those of George Cornell by shooting in 1966 and John McVitie by stabbing in 1967. Originally there were two separate indictments, but these were quashed and a voluntary bill preferred instead which charged Ronald Kray and John Barrie with Cornell's murder and Reginald Kray with being an accessory after the fact. The twins, Reginald and Ronald, together with brothers Anthony and Christopher Lambriannou, Ronald Bender and Anthony Barry—not to be confused with John Barrie—were charged with McVitie's murder, and Charles Kray, Albert Donaghue, Frederick Foreman and Cornelius Whitehead with being accessories after the fact.

It will be readily appreciated that it was no easier in the Kray case than in the Richardson one to find witnesses willing to come forward to testify against people with criminal records and a reputation for viciousness and violence. A barmaid, however, bravely gave evidence that Ronald Kray had shot Cornell in cold blood, and that another of the accused, John Barrie, had simultaneously fired a gun to divert attention. The Crown case was that the twins were drinking in a public house called The Lion, and that Ronald drove from there with John Barrie to The Blind Beggar near by, where Cornell was drinking in the bar. Following the murder, they returned to The Lion, which was deserted almost immediately by the twins and eight associates. Ronald and Barrie then apparently went into hiding, aided by Reginald Kray.

McVitie disappeared at the end of October 1967, and was never seen again. His body was not found, but the Crown sought to prove that he had been brutally killed with a knife by Reginald Kray, actively assisted by his twin and by others, after a gun failed to fire. It was alleged that McVitie had been lured to a basement flat in north London where the murder had taken place. One witness, who turned Queen's Evidence, stated that he had heard Reginald Kray tell Anthony Barry that he intended to kill McVitie that night. Barry's own evidence supported the story, for he admitted having been ordered to carry a gun to the basement flat, knowing that Reginald Kray intended to use it to commit murder, but he claimed to have acted under duress, being in fear for the safety of himself and his family if he failed to obey the instructions. The prosecution were also assisted by Donaghue's decision to plead guilty.

To some extent the Crown had to rely on the evidence of accomplices and people with criminal records, and it was not possible to say with certainty what the motives were for the murders, although presumably the victims had fallen foul of the 'firm'—as the Kray gang was known—and the murders were committed to assert, or reassert, the authority of the gang leaders. Whatever the reasons, the jury did not have any very great difficulty apparently in reaching their verdicts. They accepted that Barry had acted under duress, and acquitted him. The other accused were found guilty, and were sentenced to terms varying from life imprisonment, with a recommendation that they serve no less than thirty years (in the case of the twins), to two years' imprisonment (in the case of Donaghue).

I do not think that I and the Department ever did a better day's work than in helping to put the Richardsons and the Krays behind bars for a very long time, and our thanks are due to the police, who pursued their investigations in the face of considerable difficulties.

The services of Richardson and his cronies were available to debt-collectors, and they were prepared to torture to put pressure on debtors. The Kray firm demanded money with menaces from shop and club proprietors, and they were prepared to murder to achieve their ends. Had they not been put away, they would have brought the rule of Al Capone to parts of London.

CHAPTER 12

Nothing but the truth

I HAVE referred in this book to some of the cases in which I was involved, either as prosecutor or more usually as defender, while I was a practising barrister. In doing so I have of course chosen to write about matters that I hope will interest the majority of readers. The task of selection was very much more difficult when it came to my years as Director of Public Prosecutions, for I was involved in one degree or another with every major case that arose, and it would have been impossible as well as tediously repetitive to deal with them all. I have sought therefore to write about some of the most celebrated trials, and some cases that are largely representative of the others.

The law is not perfect—that in itself could be the subject of another book—but neither is it a bumbling ass. Whatever its shortcomings, our system is basically fair. Indeed, I would argue that if the scales of justice are tilted, they are tilted on the side of the criminal. I am convinced that in the vast majority of cases where there is a conviction, it is right; and where there is an acquittal, it is right on the basis that guilt has not been proved beyond reasonable doubt. The possibility of error always exists, however, which, as I have indicated was the strongest argument in my opinion for the abolition of capital punishment. A court of law is a very good way of testing the truth, but it can only have regard to the evidence before it, and if for some reason the evidence is unbalanced or incomplete a miscarriage of justice is always possible.

People have been known to admit to what they did not do, contrary to the usual practice of denying what they did do. If a man falsely confesses to a crime in circumstances where there is some corroborative evidence to support his story, is the system at fault if he is wrongly convicted? Truth is an elusive commodity. Unless we see something with our own eyes, we can never be certain about it, and two people who see the same thing will often differ in their description of it. Human fallibility must always be taken into account, and the idea that we ever hear 'the truth, the whole truth and nothing but the truth' is a legal fiction. How many of us always recognize the truth when we see it?

It is a far cry, however, from that position to assume that every criminal is innocent who claims he has been 'framed', and I am constantly surprised at the facility with which writers and politicians rush to judgment in an attempt to prove that justice has miscarried. Even where it has, in their anxiety to find fault they are often too eager to blame the system, approaching their task with the fervour of missionaries rather than with an impartial, judicial eye. In their favour, of course, is the fact that their reformist zeal makes it less likely that miscarriages of justice will fail to be remedied.

I should like to examine two cases where miscarriage of justice has been alleged, and in one case recently accepted—but in an attempt to discover how, if errors were made, they happened, and, if they were made, how they can be avoided in similar circumstances. I believe that a fair judgment about these matters will not support any general criticism of our system as a whole. The examples I have in mind are the so-called Luton murder case and the Confait case. The first, where the crucial issue was the truth or otherwise of an essential part of the evidence of a witness who turned Queen's Evidence, followed the murder in September 1969 of the sub-postmaster of Luton post-office. The second, where the primary issue was the value of confessions of three youths and the circumstances in which they had been obtained, arose from the murder in Catford in April 1972 of a transvestite male prostitute from the Seychelles.

The murder in Luton was a savage enough affair, and whereas no one can be other than gravely concerned if innocent people are convicted, it is also deplorable if guilty people get away with a crime of this nature. It appeared that a gang had gone to Luton to rob a post office. At the end of the day the postmaster shut up shop and went to his car. He was approached by three young men for his keys, one of whom was carrying a shotgun that somehow went off and killed the unfortunate man. What had started as an attempted robbery had ended in cold-blooded murder. Four men were originally charged—David Cooper, Michael McMahon, Patrick Murphy and the man whose evidence became so vital to the prosecution, Alfred Mathews. Eventually the charges against Mathews were dropped, and his evidence helped to convict the others.

Detective Chief Superintendent Kenneth Drury of Scotland Yard was in charge of the case from the police side, and he felt that he needed Mathews's evidence to secure a conviction. We were prepared to accept that there was sufficient corroboration of Mathews's evidence for it to be believed and acted upon, although he had given a false story to the police to begin with. We had no reason at the time to doubt the good faith of this senior police officer, and we formed our view after further consideration of the case that there appeared to be inadequate evidence on which to continue to charge Mathews with murder.

Of course, had the jury known that the officer would himself be convicted of a very serious crime, they would undoubtedly have looked at his evidence with far greater caution, and they might not have accepted it, in which case the trial might have had a different outcome. Had we in the Department known about Drury, the investigation would certainly have been conducted by another police officer. I was later responsible for prosecuting Drury on charges of corruption, for which he was sentenced to eight years' imprisonment, reduced on appeal to five. It does not follow, however, that Drury's evidence in the Luton case was false, and neither does it mean that because a police officer is proved to be corrupt in one matter, he is necessarily corrupt in all matters. There would be no obvious reason for him to seek to put innocent people in prison.

An accusation was made concerning an alleged payment by Mathews to Drury after the trial. The Post Office offered a reward of £5,000, and it was left to Drury, as the officer in charge, to distribute this sum as he saw fit among the people who had assisted the police with their case. The largest single sum, £2,000, was given to Mathews, who paid it into his bank, and on the same day withdrew £700 in cash which it was alleged had been handed to Drury. It is only right to say that Drury denied having received this money, and that Mathews denied having paid it to him, and in the last resort the allegation was not further pursued on appeal. It will be understood, however, that this allegation only arose after the trial, and was not an issue at the time we were called upon to decide whether there was adequate evidence, with Mathews turning Queen's Evidence, to proceed with the charges of murder against the three accused.

The convictions in the Luton case were probably due far more to the evidence of Mathews than to that of Drury, and it seems to me that the vital issue is whether on the essential parts of his evidence implicating the three accused Mathews was a reliable witness. He was fifty-three at the time of the murder. The others, Cooper, McMahon and Murphy, were in their twenties. Along with Mathews they attracted the curiosity of the police officer in charge of the murder investigation.

Whatever the position might have been in strict law, Mr Justice

Cusack advised the jury at the trial that it would be wise to treat Mathews as an accomplice, and he then proceeded to give the requisite warning about the need for corroboration and the danger of acting on Mathews's evidence unless there was corroboration. He also told the jury in respect of each accused what evidence there was which was capable of being regarded as corroboration but explaining that it was for them, not for him, to decide whether it should be regarded and treated by them as corroboration. Mathews's evidence was also subjected to rigorous cross-examination by the experienced counsel who appeared for the accused. Despite these warnings, the jury found the men guilty after a retirement of under three hours.

I admit in retrospect that there are aspects about the Luton case that cause me concern, mainly arising out of the questioning of the conviction of Murphy and of what is now known concerning Drury, but I do not believe that our system is proved to have been at fault because we did not know about these matters at the time. In my view it is very questionable how far one can possibly claim to be satisfied about the convicted men's innocence when a jury reached their verdict having seen and heard Mathews with everything about him being brought out by the prosecution, including his shocking criminal record and his untrue statements, and having been warned by the judge about the danger of accepting his evidence unless there were corroboration.

That was not the end of the story, however, for the case came before the Court of Appeal on no fewer than five occasions, and although the conviction of Murphy was quashed on the basis of fresh evidence—a witness of good character was found who testified that Murphy was in London and not in Luton on the fatal day—a number of distinguished and vastly experienced judges have refused each time to interfere in the cases of Cooper and McMahon. I certainly do not say that these two are in fact guilty, but I cannot say that I am necessarily convinced they are innocent. I do say, however, that at the trial the evidence against them appeared strong, and was fairly tested, although I must concede that the successful appeal by Murphy inevitably raises a question about the convictions of Cooper and McMahon, since all three men were originally convicted on substantially the same evidence. That is, of course, a matter for the Home Secretary, who three times referred the case back to the Court of Appeal (Criminal Division) for consideration, as he had power to do under the Criminal Appeal Act 1968. After that Court, constituted under different judges, had on each occasion refused to interfere with the convictions of Cooper and McMahon the Home Secretary himself eventually ordered their release from prison. However, according to a report in *The Times*, after saying that he shared the public unease which was felt concerning the matter, he later stated that his decision to quash the sentences did not imply that he was satisfied that these men were innocent: they were released by virtue of the royal prerogative of mercy, not a free pardon. He used his discretion concerning sentences, but he had no discretion over the validity of conviction. My concern in all this is to show that my Department did not err in practice or in principle in the way in which we dealt with the case.

Lord Devlin, in his book *The Judge*, and in the contribution that he made to *Wicked Beyond Belief*, edited by Ludovic Kennedy, has strongly criticized the decision of the Courts of Appeal, in that they either did not apply the right principles or did not apply them correctly. As one would expect from a judge of his eminence, the points that he put forward are to a very considerable extent convincing, but as I have already stressed, whether or not the courts applying the appropriate principles should, in the light of fresh evidence—notably the subsequent conviction of Drury and the alibi evidence for Murphy—have found that the convictions of Cooper and McMahon should be quashed as being unsafe and unsatisfactory, is not relevant to the questions that had to be considered by my Department at the time when it had originally to deal with the matter.

Our legal system contains many safeguards. In a murder case, evidence is considered by the police, by the Director of Public Prosecutions, by counsel instructed by him, by the accused's solicitors and counsel, by a magistrate or magistrates, by a judge and jury and often by the Courts of Appeal—in this particular case an extraordinary five times. This case also came to the attention of the Home Secretary and his advisers. It is no easy matter, therefore, for miscarriages of justice to occur, or if they occur, for them not to be remedied, and I do not know what more we can reasonably do to prevent them occurring. There is, of course, a special duty on the part of a prosecutor to look sceptically at certain classes of evidence—evidence based on confessions, evidence of identification and the evidence of 'supergrasses', for example—and in all such cases it is necessary to seek corroboration. In this case the trial judge, as I have indicated, warned the jury as to this, but did not suggest that there was none; on the contrary, he told the jury in respect of each accused what evidence there was which was *capable* of being regarded as corroboration, but explained that it was for them, not for him, to decide whether it should be so regarded and treated by them. We were entitled at the time to believe what we were told about the Luton murder by the senior investigating officer, and it was no part of our job to usurp the police function and make our own investigations, unless we had reason to doubt the police evidence. On the evidence presented to us, we concluded—in my view rightly—that there was sufficient corroboration to allow Mathews's story to be tested in a court of law, and the fresh evidence having been properly brought before the courts, it is not any part of the function of myself or of the Department to decide whether or not there has been a miscarriage of justice in relation to Messrs Cooper and McMahon.

The case generally known as the Confait case has, however, now been accepted—as a result of fresh evidence which has come to light—as one in which there was a miscarriage of justice arising from the convictions of three lads.

This has proved in a number of respects to be a most remarkable case. My interest in it as Director of Public Prosecutions was of course that my Department was responsible for the conduct of the prosecution, and I and one of the officers of the Department gave evidence at an Inquiry held some years later by a former High Court Judge, the Hon. Sir Henry Fisher.

During the night of 21/22 April 1972 a fire occurred at 27 Doggett Road. The fire brigade was summoned at 1.21 a.m., and arrived very quickly—by 1.23 a.m.—and the fire was extinguished by about 2 a.m. The two experts for the prosecution and the defence respectively were agreed that it was deliberately started in the basement in a cupboard under the stairs next to the bathroom and thence up the stairs (which it had practically consumed) leading to the ground floor, and then was also burning up the stairs to the first-floor landing. The dead body of a man named Maxwell Confait was found in a room on the first floor which he occupied as a lodger, and in which he had apparently been murdered by strangulation.

Confait was born in the Seychelles Islands, and at the time of his death was aged twenty-six. His childhood had been spent in the Seychelles and in Nairobi, Kenya, and in 1963 at the age of seventeen or eighteen he had come to live in England. From 1968 (or possibly earlier) Confait was a passive homosexual transvestite. He became a homosexual prostitute, and from 1970 onward had a number of convictions for importuning, and was a well-known figure in the area.

As a result of confessions alleged to have been made to the police by each of them, three lads named respectively Ronald Leighton (then aged fifteen), Colin Lattimore (then aged eighteen, but said at one time to have been classified as mentally sub-normal, with a mental age of eight) and Ahmet Salih (then aged fourteen) were charged with the murder of Confait, and with arson by setting fire to 27 Doggett Road. When the papers were referred to my Department by the Metropolitan Police, however, it was decided that the charge of murder against Salih should be dropped because the statement that he had made, while showing him to be present, did not establish that he participated in the killing, and there was no other admissible evidence against him on this charge. The charge of arson, however, remained operative.

The three lads were tried at the Central Criminal Court in November 1972, and after a trial lasting eighteen days Leighton was convicted of murder, Lattimore of manslaughter on the ground of diminished responsibility and all three on the charge of arson at 27 Doggett Road.

Applications for leave to appeal against their respective convictions and/or sentences were refused by the Court of Appeal (Criminal Division) in July 1973. Following representations by Mr Christopher Price, M.P., however, the cases were referred again to the Court of Appeal by the then Home Secretary in June 1975 under the provisions of the Criminal Appeal Act 1968, and that Court in October 1975 quashed all the respective convictions for murder, manslaughter and arson at 27 Doggett Road. This was on the ground that the evidence of the very experienced pathologists as to the time or possible time of Confait's death in relation to the time at which the fire started (it being the Crown's case that these were closely linked) rendered the confessions unreliable, and therefore the convictions unsafe and unsatisfactory. The Court said that further examination of the probabilities of the case to which it had made some allusions was unnecessary.

Following on this, on 28 November 1975 Sir Henry Fisher was appointed by the then Home Secretary and the Attorney-General in office at that date to hold an Inquiry into the circumstances leading to this trial. This Inquiry was postponed at Sir Henry's suggestion to enable very extensive further inquiries to be made by the police. These were eventually concluded, and the Inquiry commenced on 6 September 1976 and was held on forty-six days between that date and 2 December. Sir Henry heard oral evidence from 38 witnesses and also had before him written statements and other documentary evidence from 257 other persons. Interested parties, including the three boys concerned, were represented by counsel, who had the opportunity of examining and cross-examining witnesses and addressing Sir Henry.

After this full and exhaustive investigation Sir Henry Fisher's

Report dated 19 October 1977 was published in December 1977. It was a long and carefully reasoned report, and he set out in it a number of conclusions as to the facts which he had reached. He stressed, however, that his task was to examine the probabilities as to the facts in contrast with the burden which was on the prosecution at the trial to prove the case beyond reasonable doubt so that the jury was sure. By contrast also with what the Court of Appeal had to decide, which was whether that burden had been properly discharged. The Court concluded that it had not, and that the convictions were unsafe and unsatisfactory. His task, however, Sir Henry said, was 'to examine the probabilities of the case (which the Court of Appeal did not seek to do), and reach conclusions, with such certitude as I can after five years, as to what actually happened'. He said also that he had had a great deal of evidence and other material available to him which was not before the court of trial or before the Court of Appeal, and that he had been free to examine matters which could not be or were not investigated at the time.

The crucial questions were whether and if so which of the confessions which had admittedly been made were true or false, and whether any and if so which of the three boys was guilty of the offences with which they were charged. As to these questions, Sir Henry found on a balance of probabilities:

(1) Confait died not later than midnight 21/22 April, and probably died before 10.30 p.m. 21 April;

(2) he accepted the evidence that Lattimore was at the Salvation Army Torchbearer youth club from about 7.30 p.m. until about 11.30 p.m., and he found that he was not present at, and did not take part in, the killing of Confait;

(3) the confessions could not have been made as they were unless at least one of the three boys had been involved in the killing of Confait and in the arson at 27 Doggett Road.

He further found on the balance of probabilities that what occurred was

(a) that Lattimore's confession to having taken part in the arson was true, but that he was persuaded by Leighton and Salih to confess to having taken part in the killing, and

(b) that the confessions of Leighton and Salih to having taken part in the arson were true; that their answers and statements as to the killing were falsified to the extent necessary to incriminate Lattimore; but that both Leighton and Salih were involved in the killing.

On 4 August 1980 the present Attorney-General, the Rt Hon. Sir Michael Havers, Q.C., M.P., in the course of a long written answer to a question in the House of Commons by Mr Christopher Price, M.P., stated *inter alia*:

> On the evidence before Sir Henry death [of Confait] could have occurred at any time between 6.30 p.m. and midnight but it was improbable that it occurred after 10.30 p.m.
>
> In January 1980 new information came into the possession of the Director of Public Prosecutions [i.e., my successor] who ordered further investigation to be made in the case and subsequently instructed counsel to advise.
>
> Counsel's opinion was delivered on 23 July. I am satisfied that Confait died before midday on Friday 21 April.
>
> I am also satisfied that if the evidence now available had been before Sir Henry Fisher he would not have come to the conclusion that any of the three young men was responsible for the death of Confait or the arson at 27 Doggett Road.
>
> Counsel have advised, and the Director of Public Prosecutions and I agree, that there is insufficient evidence to prosecute any other person.

The Attorney-General concluded his answer by stating that the Home Secretary and he were agreed that no further inquiry was necessary. Following this, it was recently announced in the Press—on 19 June 1981—that the Home Office had offered a total of £65,000 in compensation, divided between the three young men.

I understand that the further investigation undertaken by the police following the receipt of fresh information by the Director of Public Prosecutions led to two men, one of whom was serving a sentence of ten years' imprisonment for causing grievous bodily harm, being interviewed by the police. Each claimed to have been present, and to have seen the other kill Confait, but not to have been involved himself. I have no doubt that the Attorney-General had more detailed evidence than this upon which to rely before giving his written answer to the House of Commons.

I note from a Press account of the matter that one of the men said to a Press representative that the other man strangled Confait through twisting a scarf round his neck while dancing with him. My recollection is that the Crown's case at the trial was that Confait was strangled by a ligature—thought to be an electric-light flex or a piece of wire—that this had left marks on his neck, and that these were seen by the eminent pathologist who performed the post-mortem, who presumably would have detected the difference in marks to any left by a twisted scarf.

I noted also that the Attorney had stated that he was satisfied that

Confait died before midday on Friday 21 April. I do not of course know the nature of the evidence by which he was satisfied as to this, but it will be appreciated that it is very much earlier than the possible earliest time given in the evidence at Sir Henry Fisher's Inquiry by the exceedingly eminent experts who furnished the evidence both there and at the previous hearing in the Court of Appeal on the basis of which the convictions were quashed. The estimate by them as to this must apparently have been entirely wrong.

It is fair to say that Sir Henry in his Report to some extent was critical of the police, though in a number of respects he found that the complaints made against them had not been established. It is also right that I should mention that in certain respects he was critical of my Department. In view, however, of the developments that have now taken place, resulting from fresh evidence having come to light —which was apparently not available either at the time of the prosecution or at the time of Sir Henry's Inquiry—I do not think that any useful purpose would be served by now dealing with these matters. Sir Henry's Report was of course published appreciably later than my retirement, but in so far as he suggested possible revision of procedures, both by the Department and by the police, I feel sure that they will have received careful consideration.

This was indeed a remarkable case. Since the Attorney-General had evidence which satisfied him of the matters to which he referred in his statement it was clearly right that all three lads should be completely exonerated in respect of the offences when their convictions had already been quashed by the Court.

CHAPTER 13

After fifty years

IT IS A matter of pride and pleasure to me that I have been able to maintain active contact with the Law, which has been my life and livelihood, since I retired as Director of Public Prosecutions. As I emphasized earlier, I had considerable doubts as to whether to accept that position when it was offered to me in 1964. That is, I think, understandable, apart from the other circumstances to which I have referred before, when one bears in mind that I had at that time for over thirty years been actively participating in the work of the courts, either as an advocate or in a judicial capacity, and suddenly to pull down the shutters was inevitably a great wrench. Although I thought that with the pressure, responsibility and interest of my duties as Director I would soon cease to miss my practice at the Bar and work within the courts, I never completely did so during my thirteen years in office. I decided to retire when I was still of an age at which the Lord Chancellor could, if he saw fit, recommend me to the Queen for appointment as a Recorder, and thus allow me again to participate at least to a limited extent in the work of the courts. However, a further —and I think the most important—reason why I retired was so that I could see more of my wife and home during such time together as might be left to us.

This book will be published just over fifty years after I was called to the Bar, and many changes have of course taken place during my half-century in the Law, both civil and criminal, and in procedure. Most, but not all of them, have I think on balance been improvements, but in one basic and important respect there has, I am glad to say, been no change. I am not, I hope, blind to the faults of our legal system, but I do testify to the meticulous care and thoroughness with which the legal process continues to be administered, notwithstanding the vastly increased volume of work with which the courts have to deal.

One of the most important changes in relation to the criminal law and procedure has been the abolition of all Courts of Assize and Quarter Sessions and the establishment in their place of an all-embracing Crown Court, sitting simultaneously at places throughout England and Wales, with jurisdiction in criminal matters. The judges of the Crown Court are drawn from High Court judges, Circuit judges or Recorders, and each of these may sit with not more than four Justices of the Peace and is required to sit with at least two magistrates in certain categories of case. When he does so sit, the magistrates are equally judges of the court and can outvote the legally qualified judge except on matters of law, which are his exclusive province. I have heard of this arising occasionally on appeals from conviction or sentence by the Magistrates Court, or when a person has been committed by magistrates to the Crown Court for sentence. However, I have never personally myself been in this awkward situation. The magistrates with whom I have sat have usually had the good sense to agree with me—or perhaps it is that I have had the sense to agree with them! I have always found them to provide most worthy, considerate and intelligent assistance.

I confess that I regret that it should have been deemed necessary to make such a radical change in order to deal with the greatly increased number of criminal trials on indictment resulting from the grave increase in serious crime all over the country. I believe that the holding of the historic Court of Assize in each county, and additionally in certain cities, some three times or more a year with the arrival of the High Court judge—the 'red judge'—with its attendant pomp and formality, helped to engender respect for law and order and esteem of the judiciary which alas is markedly disappearing as we become less and less a law-abiding country.

The abolition of Quarter Sessions has also altered considerably the position of Recorder. Prior to this abolition there was a court of Quarter Sessions for each county, and also in certain cities and boroughs to which the right to have their own Quarter Sessions had been granted by Royal Charter. The judges in the county Quarter Sessions were county magistrates presided over by a qualified chairman, and the judge at a Quarter Sessions for a city or borough was a Recorder appointed by the Sovereign from among members of the Bar. Now he is one of the Recorders of the Crown Court, of whom there are, I believe, substantially over three hundred, appointed principally from members of the Bar but also from solicitors.

In the days when a Recorder was appointed to a particular Quarter Sessions he had the advantage of getting to know the members of the Bar normally practising at those sessions. At some of them it was customary for there to be an adjournment in the afternoon when the Bar came in to have tea with the Recorder in his retiring room. I remember one such occasion when a lady barrister was appearing in a case before me, and she was among those who came to tea. She was a most promising advocate, and had she not eventually, I believe, given up practising, she would probably have been highly successful. In the early years of her marriage, however, she continued to appear in cases from time to time, such as the occasion in question. On coming into my room she inquired of me: 'Recorder, will you be sitting late this evening?' 'That is largely up to you,' I replied. 'I want to finish the case if I can, and you are in it.' 'Will you be sitting after six o'clock?' she persisted, and I asked whether she had some particularly important engagement at that time. Her reply was not what I could have expected. 'I have my baby in the robing room,' she said, 'and he (or it may have been she) has to be breast-fed at six o'clock.' I confess that this novel ground for an application to adjourn if necessary took me by surprise. However, I assured her that I would see to it that she was free at six, and fortunately we finished in time.

I have noticed as I have been sitting as a Recorder in the Crown Court, by contrast with the time when I attended Courts of Assize and sat at Quarter Sessions, a marked difference in the sort of attire that not only the accused but others such as jurymen now wear when attending courts. Some little time ago I was trying a case—not, I may say, in the height of a hot summer but in a comparatively cool autumn, when the accused appeared as is not uncommon nowadays, in an open-necked shirt beneath his jacket. It used to be thought to be important to endeavour to make a good impression by appearing in one's Sunday best. Of the nine men on the jury, four were without ties and two without jackets. (The three ladies on the jury were all neatly and, to my mind, appropriately dressed and seemed, as one might expect, to be more concerned about their appearance than were the men.) It is fair to say that this informality in the men's dress did not appear to detract from the care and attention with which the jury carried out their duties, but I noticed that the jury chose as their foreman the best-dressed man among them.

I refer to this trend not so much by way of criticism but because it reflects, I think, a significantly changing attitude in the respect felt for the Law and for the courts that administer it. There are some even among the practitioners who would favour the abandonment of the wearing of robes and wigs, which they refer to as fancy dress, by both the judges and the advocates. I do not share this view, and I am convinced that such a change would impair the calm dignity of the proceedings, the maintenance of which I regard as very important.

I recall getting support for my view from an unexpected quarter during a visit I paid with other judges and Recorders to a Borstal institution, where I talked to a young inmate. I must first explain for the benefit of non-lawyers that there are different types of legal wig. There is the full-bottom wig worn by judges and Queen's Counsel on special occasions, such as the service in Westminster Abbey to mark the opening of the legal year (and incidentally which High Court judges used to wear during the reading of the Royal Commission at the opening of an Assize). This they then changed for a smaller but distinctive judge's wig normally worn in court by them and by Circuit judges. Recorders, however, when sitting judicially wear the same ordinary barrister's wig that they use as advocates, which is noticeably different from the judge's wig.

I was talking to the Borstal youth about the offence with which he had been charged and the sentence he had received, and he was clearly aggrieved. 'My case wasn't before a proper judge,' he complained. 'What on earth do you mean?' I asked. 'He hadn't got a judge's wig on,' was the reply, 'he only had a small wig.' I was convinced that the youth would have been content with an even severer sentence had it been imposed by a 'proper judge'!

Most criminals bear no animosity towards the judge who has sentenced them, provided they feel that they have had a fair crack of the whip at their trial. I have been asked whether I receive abusive letters from those with whom I have had to deal, and as far as I am concerned I can only remember one instance, and I have been surprised when talking to judges with regard to this how comparatively few letters of this type are received. In my own case, the instance to which I refer arose following an appeal that I heard from an order by a magistrates court that a dog found to be dangerous be destroyed, and the abuse directed at me was not in any event from the defendant dog-owner. I am in fact a dog-lover, and would have been glad had the evidence permitted me to be able to allow the appeal. The dog was produced and brought up to me on the Bench and wagged its tail in friendly fashion. Unfortunately, the evidence proved that the dog had a most uncertain temperament and had on several occasions attacked and bitten people without any provocation. It plainly was a dangerous dog, and I had to dismiss the appeal.

The Press in reporting the case published a photograph of the dog in which he looked utterly harmless and attractive, and to my surprise I received a number of abusive letters, some actually from abroad, and one even expressing the hope that my wife might die in agony with me sitting by her bed.

But, as I say, that was an exceptional experience, and for the most

200

part I have nothing but kind memories of my fifty years in the Law. Now I am nearing the end of my career, although I hope to continue a little longer as a Recorder until I reach the statutory retiring age, which is not very far away. Looking back on a half-century, I greatly appreciate the privilege of having been actively associated with Law in one way or another. The Bar is a wonderful profession, and I have had the good fortune to make many most dear friends among those with whom I have been in chambers, those whom I have led and those whom I have known as opponents, and also among the judiciary. I have greatly enjoyed it all, and when the time comes I shall retire with regret but with sincere gratitude to all of them for the kindness and help they have so readily extended to me.

Index

A

Adams, Dr Bodkin, 47
Advisory Council on the Treatment of Offenders, 34, 43
Anderson, James, 144
Angry Brigade, 94–9, 131
Anningson, G. R. King, 43
Argyle, His Hon. Judge, 144
Armstrong, Janet, 54–9
Armstrong, John, 54–9
Atkinson, Sir Edward T., 67
Atkinson, Lord Justice, 18, 155

B

Back, Patrick, Q.C., 39
Baker & Company, 29–31
Barker, John, 95, 97, 98
Barrett, Captain, 39–40
Barrie, John, 184, 185
Barry, Anthony, 184, 185
Barry, Mr Justice, 37
Bell, Mary, 179–81
Bell, Norma, 179–81
Bender, Ronald, 184
Bennett, Sir Frederic, M.P., 115
Bennett, K. C., 7
Berman, Alfred, 183
Bingham, David James, 133–7
Bingham, Maureen Grace, 133–7
   passim

Birmingham IRA bombings, 86–94
Black, Sir Cyril, M.P., 139, 142
Blaker, His Hon. Nathaniel, Q.C., 41
Bodkin, Sir Archibald, 67
Bond, Dennis George, 161–5
Bott, Christopher, 95, 98
Bradbury, Lawrence (John West), 181
Brady, Ian, 151–9
Braithwaite, E. G., 80
Brandreth, C. D., 47
Bray, A. H., 55
Bridge, Lord, 90, 92, 93, 137
Broderick, His Hon. Judge, 38
Brown, Martin George, 179–80
Byrne, Mr Justice, 25, 42

C

Callaghan, Hugh, 86, 87, 89, 90, 92
Cassels, Mr Justice, 39, 47, 149
Casswell, J. D., Q.C., 10, 18, 36, 41
Charles, Mr Justice, 10
Christie, James Stuart, 95, 98
Christie, John Halliday, 161
Clark, Thomas, 183
Cockburn, Lord Chief Justice, 66
Collard, Dudley, 55
Commonwealth and Empire Law Conference, 48

Comyn, Mr Justice, 38, 78
Confait, Maxwell, 192–6
Cooper, David, 180–91
Cornell, George, 6, 184, 185
Coulston, Benjamin, 182, 183
Creek, Hilary, 95, 97, 98
Criminal Law Revision Committee, 48
Croom-Johnson, Mr Justice, 11, 119
Crowder, Petre, Q.C., 119
Cuffe, Sir Hamilton—*see* Desart, Lord
Cunningham, A. W., 80, 81, 82, 83
Curtis, P., 155
Curtis-Bennett, Sir Henry, K.C., 8
Cusack, Mr Justice, 180, 189–90

D
Davies, Franklyn, 128, 129, 130, 132
Davies, Captain Picton, 30–1
Dawkins, Iris, 12–16
Denning, Lord, P.C., 36, 43
Dennis, Felix, 144, 146
Devlin, Lord Justice, 37, 47, 116, 191
Devlin Committee, 116–17
Dick, Wesley, 130, 132
Dilhorne, Lord, P.C., 55, 103
Director of Public Prosecutions, office of, 63–76
Donaghue, Albert, 184, 185
Downey, Lesley Ann, 157–8
Drury, Detective Chief Super- intendent Kenneth, 188, 189, 190
Duval, Jack, 182, 183

E
Edinburgh, HRH the Duke of, 72–3
Edmunds, Humphrey, 41
Elwyn-Jones, Lord, P.C., 73, 155
Evans, Edward, 152–7
Evans, Timothy, 160–1

F
Fay, His Hon. Judge, Q.C., 39
Finestein, Israel, Q.C., 78
Fisher Report, 193–6
Fisher, Hon. Sir Henry (Mr Justice Fisher), 142, 193
Flannigan, Thomas, 161–5
Foot, Sir Dingle, P.C., Q.C., 41
Foreman, Frederick, 184
Fox-Andrews, Roy, K.C., 32
Fraser, Francis, 182, 183
Frisby, Roger, Q.C., 78

G
Goddard, Lord Chief Justice, 8–10, 36, 43, 46–7
Gorman, Mr Justice, 47
Greenfield, James, 95, 97, 98
Griffiths-Jones, Mervyn, 51, 53

H
Hain, Peter, 104, 108–17
Hall, Sir Edward Marshall, K.C., 19, 39
Hall, Roy, 183
Harris, Detective-Sergeant G., 76–8
Havers, Sir Michael, P.C., M.P., 107, 194–5
Hawke, Mr Justice, 29–30, 36, 43
Haynes, Charles Henry, 161–5
Heilpern, G., Q.C., 155
Henderson, J. S., K.C., 32, 41
Hetherington, Sir Thomas, Q.C., 74
Hijacking Act, 1971, 84
Hilbery, Mr Justice, 46, 47, 51, 52
Hill, Patrick Joseph, 86, 89, 90, 91
Hindley, Myra, 151–9
Hobson, Sir John, P.C., Q.C., 73
Homicide Act, 160
Hooson, H. E., Q.C., 155
Hosein, Arthur, 173–8
Hosein, Nizamodeen, 173–8
Howe, Brian, 179–81

Hughes, Robert, 38
Hunter, Robert Gerald, 86, 88, 89, 90, 91, 92
Hutchinson, Jeremy, 39

I

Inside Linda Lovelace (Lovelace), 148–50
Inskip, Hampden, Q.C., 41, 55
IRA, 85–94

J

James, Lord Justice, 98–9
James & Sons Ltd *v.* Smee, 47
Jones, Arthur Albert, 51–3
Jones, Mr Justice, 25
Judge, The (Devlin), 191
Judges' Rules, 90

K

Kelly, M. V., 80
Khaled, Leila, 73, 122–6
Kilbride, John, 155, 157
King-Hamilton, His Hon. Judge, Q.C., 114
Kinnock, Neil, M.P., 114
Kray, Charles, 184
Kray, Reginald, 184–6
Kray, Ronald, 184–6
Kuzmin, Lory, 134–7

L

Lady Chatterley's Lover (D. H. Lawrence), 140, 141
Lambriannou, Anthony, 184
Lambriannou, Christopher, 184
Lane, Lord Chief Justice, 142
Last Exit to Brooklyn (Selby), 138–42, 146, 150
Lattimore, Colin, 192–4
Law Officers of the Crown, The (Edwards), 64
Lawrence, Geoffrey, K.C.—*see*

Oaksey, Lord
Lawton, Lord Justice, 100, 102, 103, 104, 183, 184
Leary, Brian, 144, 149
Leighton, Ronald, 192–4
Lloyd-Jones, D. T., 155
Local Government Acts 1929, 1930, 18
Luton murder (1969), 188–92
Lynskey, Mr Justice, 42, 47

M

Macnaghten, Mr Justice, 18
Macnaghten Rules, 36, 37
Malone, Cavan, 49–51
Manningham-Buller, Sir Reginald, Q.C.—*see* Dilhorne, Lord
Mark, Sir Robert, 129
Mars-Jones, Mr Justice, 155
Mason, Mrs Margaret, 118–21
Mathew, J. C., 102
Mathew, John, 51
Mathew, Sir Theobald, 67, 73–4, 108
Mathews, Alfred, 188–92
Mathews, Sir Charles, 67
Maudling, Reginald, P.C., M.P., 82, 83
Maule, Sir John, Q.C., 65
McDade, James, 87, 88, 89, 90
McIlkenny, Noel, 86, 89, 90
McKay case, 166–79
McLean, Catherine, 95, 98
McMahon, Michael, 188–91
McVitie, John, 184, 185
Medico-Legal Society, 65
Mendleson, Anna, 95, 97, 98
Merrivale, Lord, 43
Molony, J. T., Q.C., 41, 55, 120, 121
Morris, Lord Justice (Morris of Borth-y-Gest), 35, 42
Morrison, R. P., Q.C., 43
Mortimer, John, Q.C., 139, 141, 144, 145, 147, 149

Munroe, Anthony, 130,132
Murphy, Patrick, 188–91
Murray, Michael, 86, 92

N
Nabarro, Sir Gerald, M.P., 117–21
Nash, Brenda, 52–3
Neville, Richard, 144
Newland, Sydney, 42
Newton, Andrew, 104, 106–7

O
Oaksey, Lord, 5, 30, 42
Obscene Publications Act, 1959,
    138–50 *passim*
Odgers, Dr Blake, 43
Oliver, Mr Justice, 25, 37
Oz case, 142–6

P
Parcq, Lord du, 6–7, 18
Parker, Lord Chief Justice, 47
Pascoe, Russell, 38–9
Perry, Michael, 77
Pilcher, Mr Justice, 12, 15, 24, 25
Pleas of the Crown (Hale), 103
Police Act, 1964, 68–9, 74
Poor Prisoners Defence Procedure,
    33
Pottinger, W. G., 80, 81, 83
Poulson, John, 79–83
Power, William, 86, 89, 90
Prevention of Terrorism
    (Temporary Provisions) Act,
    1974, 1976, 84
Price, Christopher, M.P., 193, 195
Private Eye, 107
Prosecution of Offences Act, 1908,
    65–6, 67
Prosecution of Offences
    Regulations, 1978, 67–8

R
R. *v.* Burt, 34–5
R. *v.* Kemp, 37–8
R. *v.* Sims, 35–6
R. *v.* Ridley, 15–16
R. *v.* Turnbull, 116
Rawlinson, Lord, Q.C., 12, 73, 96
Recorder, position of, 198–9
Richardson, Charles, 181–4
Richardson, Edward, 182, 183
Richardson, Supt. Gerald, 161–5
Rigg, His Hon. Judge, 149
Robertson, Geoffrey, 149
Robey, E. G., 19
Robson, Det. Inspector B., 76–8
Rogers, His Hon. Judge, 139, 141
Royal Commission on Standards of
    Conduct in Public Life, 82

S
Sachs, Lord Justice, 53, 115
Sales, W. H., 80
Salih, Ahmet, 192–4
Salmon, Cyril, 139
Salmon, Lord, 103, 139, 142
Salmon Report, 1976, 82
Scott, Norman, 104–8
Sewell, Frederick, 161–5
Sexual Offences Act, 1967, 68
Shaw, Lord Justice Sebag, 78, 181–2
Shawcross, Lord, 71
Sheehan, Michael, 86, 89, 92
Silkin, Samuel, P.C., Q.C., M.P., 73
Simpson, Dr Keith, 57
Skelhorn, Sir Norman, Q.C.:
    childhood, 3–4; elected to
    Western Circuit, 4; marshal to Mr
    Justice Swift, 5–7; first case, 7; and
    Dawkins case, 12–16; marriage,
    17; first big murder case, 19–23; in
    Trading with the Enemy
    Department, 32; Recorder of
    Bridgwater, 32–42; takes silk,

41–2; Recorder of Plymouth, 42–3; Recorder of Portsmouth, 43; and Armstrong case, 54–59; appointed Director of Public Prosecutions, 63–4; and Poulson case, 80–3; and terrorists, 84–99; Norman Scott case, 104–8; Hain case, 108–17; Nabarro case, 117–21; and Leila Khaled, 122–6; Spaghetti House siege, 127–33; Bingham case, 133–7; obscenity cases, 138–50; Moors murders case, 151–9; Sewell case, 161–5; McKay case, 166–79; Mary Bell, 179–81; 'Luton' and Confait cases, 188–96; final retrospect, 197–201
Skelhorn, Lady Rosamund, 17, 200
Slade, Mr Justice, 46, 47
Smalls, Derek, 100–4
Smith, Cyril, M.P., 107
Smith, David, 151–8
Smith, T. Dan, 80, 81, 82, 83
Spaghetti House siege, 127–33
Spokes, J., 118, 119
Spry, John, 161–5
Stable, Mr Justice, 140
Steel, David, P.C., M.P., 104, 115
Stephenson, Sir Augustus, 67
Stevenson, Mr Justice Melford, 184
Stock, His Hon. Judge, Q.C., 36
Straffen, John, 36–7
Swain, James, M.S., 17
Swift, Mr Justice, 5, 6–7

T
Talbot, Mr Justice, 18
Tatum, M. G., 39–40
Termine, Lillo, 130, 131, 133
Thesiger, Mr Justice, 38
Thorpe, Jeremy, 47, 48, 104, 107, 108
Times, The, 78, 95, 115, 125, 184
Trading with the Enemy Department, 32

Tucker, Lord, 7
Tunbridge, Graham, 80

W
Wajcenberg, Bernard, 182, 183
Walker, John, 86, 89, 90, 91
Walton, John, 42
Waterhouse, Mr Justice, 155
Wattam, Haydon, 23–4
Weir, Angela, 95, 98
Well of Loneliness, The (Radclyffe Hall), 140
Whitty, D. J., 38–9, 40
Wicked Beyond Belief (Kennedy), 191
Widgery, Lord Chief Justice, 116, 119
Willinck, Henry, K.C., 36
Wilshere, Myddelton, 3, 17–18
Wilshire, F. A., 3, 32
Woolf, Herman, 43–6
Wright, Malcolm, K.C., 41, 55
Wrightson, Paul, 47
Wrottesley, Mr Justice, 36